Rum Histories

New World Studies
Marlene L. Daut, Editor

Rum Histories

Drinking in Atlantic Literature and Culture

Jennifer Poulos Nesbitt

University of Virginia Press
Charlottesville and London

University of Virginia Press
© 2022 by the Rector and Visitors of the University of Virginia
All rights reserved
Printed in the United States of America on acid-free paper

First published 2022

9 8 7 6 5 4 3 2 1

Library of Congress Cataloging-in-Publication Data

Names: Nesbitt, Jennifer Poulos, author.
Title: Rum histories : drinking in Atlantic literature and culture / Jennifer Poulos Nesbitt.
Description: Charlottesville : University of Virginia Press, 2021. | Series: New world studies | Includes bibliographical references and index.
Identifiers: LCCN 2020058451 (print) | LCCN 2020058452 (ebook) | ISBN 9780813946580 (hardcover) | ISBN 9780813946597 (paperback) | ISBN 9780813946603 (ebook)
Subjects: LCSH: Caribbean literature (English)—20th century—History and criticism | Rum in literature. | Postcolonialism in literature. | Rum—Social aspects—Caribbean area. | English literature—20th century—History and criticism | American literature—20th century—History and criticism
Classification: LCC PR9205.05 .N47 2021 (print) | LCC PR9205.05 (ebook) | DDC 810.9/9729—dc23
LC record available at https://lccn.loc.gov/2020058451
LC ebook record available at https://lccn.loc.gov/2020058452

This book is freely available in an open access edition thanks to TOME (Toward an Open Monograph Ecosystem)—a collaboration of the Association of American Universities, the Association of University Presses, and the Association of Research Libraries—and the generous support of the Pennsylvania State University. Learn more at the TOME website, available at: openmonographs.org.

This book is licensed under the Creative Commons Attribution 4.0 International License (CC BY-NC), https://creativecommons.org/licenses/by-nc/4.0/legalcode.

https://doi.org/10.52156/m.5240

Cover art: "Interior of distillery. Slaves loading Rum Barrels. A scene in Antigua," William Clark, from "Ten Views in the Island of Antigua, in which are represented the process of sugar making, and the employment of the negroes . . . From drawings made by W. Clark, etc." 1786. C. 9, plate IX (London: Thomas Clay, 1823). (© The British Library Board [1786.c.9, plate IX])

*To Steve James Poulos (1933–2016) and
Laura Paige Rutherford (1970–2021)*

Like rum, family is good neat or blended.

What commodities are, and what commodities mean, would thereafter be forever different. And for that same reason, what persons are, and what being a person means, changed accordingly. In understanding the relationship between commodity and person, we unearth anew the history of ourselves.

—Sidney Mintz, *Sweetness and Power*

Contents

	Preface	xi
	Acknowledgments	xv
	Introduction	1
1.	Rum's (In)significance	35
2.	Frustrated Drunks: Masculine Identity and (Post)colonial Literary Ambition	57
3.	Drunken Sluts: Protesting Colonialism and Patriarchy	79
4.	Libations 1: Spirits of Change	101
5.	Libations 2: Reparative Models in Literary Criticism	118
6.	Is the Rum Gone? Imperial Nostalgia	145
	Notes	153
	Bibliography	179
	Index	199

Preface

THIS PROJECT began in instructional desperation and ends as an act of feminist reparation. It has been twenty years in the making, a time that has seen tremendous theoretical shifts in postcolonial studies and feminist studies, as well as the emergence of technologies that have intensified our awareness of global cultural immediacy. In 1998, however, I was simply interested in engaging my first-year composition students in a conversation about Jean Rhys's novel *Wide Sargasso Sea*. The novel's language was difficult, the characters perplexingly obtuse and self-defeating. How to salvage the situation? College students, I hazarded, are interested in drinking. Perhaps they would be interested in discussing the effects of alcohol consumption on relationships? The ensuing discussion bore fruit when all Rhys's references to rum lit up, creating a pattern I cannot now unsee. A paper at the First International Conference on Caribbean Literature (1998) followed, as did, much later, an article in *Tulsa Studies in Women's Literature* (2007, now part of chapter 3), plus twenty years of research in between completing my dissertation, achieving tenure, losing my father slowly to Alzheimer's, and raising two daughters. A global pandemic—exacerbated by extremists dedicated to maintaining white privilege—rages as I revise this manuscript, creating patterns we will not understand for some time.

What started as pedagogy became an opportunity for a feminist critique more attuned to intersectionality because I hoped the shift from more typical foci—characters or locations—to a commodity would get me out of my comfort zone by inhibiting the centering of white, mostly North Atlantic, mostly female privilege. The movement from character or location to thing also allows me to bring colonialism home, enmeshing it in sites cordoned off by habit, genre, or academic field. *Rum Histories* retains a strong current of better-reading-for-white-people. As I became more open to acknowledging the ways I have been "in, or thought about" Caribbean literature "because," as Edward Said says, I "*could be there,* or could think about it" (7, italics in the original) as I approached Caribbean literature from the vantage of modernist studies. I now see this work as the end of a beginning rather than an end in itself; *Rum Histories* has started to show me how far I have to go.

This book differs from other books about rum, which tend to divide between popular commodity histories or coffee-table compendiums: it is a study of the representation and reading of rum. I contend that rum figures a collective continued subjection to the legacies of European colonialism, despite the utopian promise of decolonization. Moreover, a resistance to reading rum at all, or at best a habit of unreflectively glossing its meanings, signifies an accompanying unwillingness to reflect on the complexities of colonialism's newer, overlapping forms: cultural imperialism, neocolonialism, globalization, and neoliberalism. This project meditates on the ways consumers and producers of the Anglo-Atlantic continue to dwell with the legacies of colonialism well beyond its putative endpoint due to the "physical and emotional attachments" created by the bonds of European dominance over Caribbean islands (Sheller 5). By reading rum's chains of signification, contradictory and multiple as they are, I chart the insidious patterning of everyday life by a collective colonial past and look for patterns that might help rethink how this past affects the future.

To claim rum as a kind of relay point for masses of cultural expectations and economic investments requires some intrepidity, given that this beverage is known primarily for its relationship with Coca-Cola or pineapple juice. Sometimes rum *is* just rum. It is precisely these anodyne expectations that fuel rum poetics. I have always been interested in the ways that small details can allow us to talk about complex phenomena and the point at which the gates go up to frustrate analysis and interpretation. Such formations encourage assumptions about drinking that, despite apparent paradox, comfortably coexist as interpretative frames. Both literature and alcohol are escapes from everyday life—a space apart from work, family, and politics—and resistance to analysis can be strong in both arenas. To the degree that this study is thus a buzzkill, I apologize in advance.

Finally, this study is about representation and interpretation, not science. Neuroscientists, biologists, and biochemists have advanced knowledge of the physiological effects of alcohol on the brain, and they have located a gene that predisposes some people to alcohol addiction. Their work explains, for example, that alcohol increases levels of norepinephrine, a neurotransmitter that governs impulsivity. How do we know that is what norepinephrine does, apart from the behavioral evidence, such as "hook-ups . . . after happy hour" or "streaking naked through a college campus" (Gowin 2010)? The interpretation of behavior is socially constructed: In a culture where nakedness is not taboo, would a drunken impulse involve streaking through a campus fully clothed? (So I do have a quarrel with science, but that is not the subject of this book.) In short, this study neither disputes scientific findings about the physiological effects of alcohol nor minimizes the devastation caused by excessive drinking. It does examine how texts and their variously sited readers value and evaluate drinking to describe, and to explain away, political and social effects that are fundamentally economic and racist rather than medical or moral.

Acknowledgments

I AM indebted to many people and organizations for supporting this project since its serendipitous inception during a spring 1998 composition class at Oxford College of Emory University. So, my first thanks go to those students, now nearly forty years of age, for their attention and inspiration. I hope I didn't forget too many people—it's been a long journey.

This work began when I was finishing my doctorate at Emory University, and, though it was a tumultuous time as we faced the inevitable dispersal of our cohort, I am grateful to my graduate student friends and colleagues there for their support. Among them are Su Fang Ng, Lovalerie King, Karen Bloom Gevirtz, Anya Silver, Kate McPherson, Laura Callanan, Karen Poremski, Leigh Tillman Partington, and Karen Brown-Wheeler.

An Institute for the Arts and Humanities Resident Scholar grant in the spring of 2011 helped to restart the writing on this project. I thank then-director Michael Bérubé and the fellows from that semester for their helpful feedback and support.

Penn State supported this project with two sabbatical leaves and numerous research grants; I am particularly grateful to my local administrative staff and leadership for their help over the years. In Penn State's University College, I have been honored to know exceptional scholars across our fourteen campuses, and the sense of community I have found among them is invaluable. I want to thank Kim Blockett and Gib Prettyman, my writing partners for parts of this project, for their excellent comments and even more excellent editing; Kelley Wagers offered commentary on the introduction that was especially useful. Janet Neigh and Jocelyn Stitt were invaluable, and Giselle and Shedley Duncan-Branche generously showed me around Port of Spain and the Angostura distillery.

Closer to home, my colleagues at Penn State York Mike Jarrett and Noel Sloboda, and the members of the Faculty Learning Community (Nicole Muscanell, Sonia Molloy, Joy Giguere, Suzanne Shaffer, Joel Burkholder, and Barb Eshbach) have supported the late stages of this project. Melissa Cook, Gloria Druck, and Sallie Francis kept me up and running and my head on straight during these years.

I am also grateful to the following organizations for permission to republish material that has previously appeared in other locations. Parts of chapter 1 were previously published in *Perennial Empires: Postcolonial, Transnational, and Literary Perspectives,* edited by Chantal Zabus and Silvia Nagy-Zekmi (Amherst, NY: Cambria, 2011), and reproduced by permission from the publisher. Central portions of chapters 2 and 4 were published, respectively, as "Rum Histories: Consumption and Decolonization in Sylvia Townsend Warner and Jean Rhys" in *Tulsa Studies in Women's Literature,* vol. 26, no. 2 (Fall 2007) and "Under the Influence: Signifying Rum" in *ARIEL,* vol. 39, no. 3 (July 2008).

I owe friends and colleagues many thanks for proofreading the manuscript and catching bloopers: Joe Downing, Ann Fetterman, Cecilia Heydl-Cortinez, Andy Landis, Sonia Molloy, Nicole Muscanell, Tom Nesbitt, Teddy Nesbitt, Marcy Nicholas, Judy Owen, and Suzanne Shaffer. Betsy Wentzel stepped in to proofread and copyedit a later version of the manuscript, and Enid Zafran was more than just a consummate professional indexer.

My family has lived with the ups and downs of this project from Atlanta, to Wilkes-Barre, to York. To them—Tom, Teddy, and Charlotte—I owe a debt of gratitude and a toast.

Rum Histories

Introduction

> Rum was indispensable in the fisheries and the fur trade, and as a naval ration. But its connection with the triangular trade was more direct still. Rum was an essential part of the cargo of the slave ship, particularly the colonial American slave ship. No slave trader could afford to dispense with a cargo of rum. It was profitable to spread a taste for liquor on the coast.
> —Eric Williams, *Capitalism and Slavery*

> In spite of my absentmindedness I mix cocktails very well and swizzle them better (our cocktails, in the West Indies, are drunk frothing, and the instrument with which one froths them is called a swizzle-stick) than anyone else in the house.
> —Jean Rhys, "Mixing Cocktails"

ERIC WILLIAMS, historian and later the first prime minister of Trinidad and Tobago, summarizes a familiar history: rum is a product of slave labor in the Caribbean, and its global reach as a commodity implicates producers, laborers, and consumers far from the plantations. Jean Rhys's young narrator, on a balcony overlooking the sea in Dominica, avers that thoughtlessness is no deterrent to good mixology. Williams offers bald economic facts; Rhys sketches habits and behaviors. In both cases the material and the social blur as Williams speaks of socializing consumers and Rhys of labor, already alienated.

These descriptions broach anxieties about ethics, consumption, and identity from opposite ends to bear on the peculiarities of rum as a product of slave trading and slave labor. Such anxieties are not new, yet rum is underexamined in literature, despite considerable interest in the commodities of empire—particularly sugar. Perhaps the aversion arises from a duality in discourse about drinking; while popular culture trumpets the evils and blessings of alcohol, individual cases of alcoholism remain sites of shame and silence. Or perhaps it is a confusion of terms: today the term *demon rum* has a specificity it lacked early in the last century, when the term *rum* referred generally to all liquors.[1] Demon rum is one of rum's many cartoonish cultural associations: drunken pirates, gangsters and gun molls carousing in Havana, and day-glow cocktails topped with fruit wedges.[2] Above all, it is the alcohol of the Caribbean. If rum lacks a certain seriousness, both mass market and scholarly publishers happily exploit its association with the exotic and the erotic to attract readers.[3] Seldom, then, is rum treated as more than a convenient stereotype, scapegoat, or guarantor of Caribbean verisimilitude.

Rum Histories makes of this problem a solution. Verisimilitude, after all, is necessarily selective: writers, consciously or not, choose what details will create "reality," and therefore interpreters may ask why something—in this case, rum—comes to be salient in conjuring a realistic effect and to consider the impact of this salience on the range of interpretation. Drawing on the rich literature on sugar as well as anthropological and literary studies of drinking, this study approaches textually what other revisions of postcolonial studies have done via genre, historiography, and cultural studies: consider the forces that retard the achievement of a postcoloniality that lives up to its ideals of equity. In the first place, this study's determined catholicity violates what Gary Wilder describes as a presumptive methodological nationalism that governed post-1945 decolonization protocols (3–5), a nationalism reflected in disciplinary subfields. The texts are Anglophone, which tilts the balance toward Paul Gilroy's idea of a Black Atlantic, encompassing works from the United States, Canada, England, and the West Indies.[4] In the epigraph to this chapter, Eric Williams's reference to fisheries, fur trading, and naval ships tells us that the products of plantation slavery were not solely coastal but traded deep into continental interiors. This Caribbean machine (or plantation) is "unfolding and bifurcating until it reaches all the seas and lands of the earth" (*Repeating Island* 3), in Antonio Benítez-Rojo's model, and the literary products of that process demonstrate this effect. This foundation in colonial trading provides the groundwork for a Global South Atlantic that tactically engages these routes for alternative uses. These uses are, as Kerry Bystrom and Joseph R. Slaughter contend, not universally resistant, but rather "an ideal or aspiration of solidarity and interconnection . . . that has come to pass (or not) precisely because of the structural and epistemological impediments" (4). In other words, when rum pops up in an unusual place—a pier in Hawaii or a train crossing Canada—how it gets there is not a mystery. What is mysterious is the little that is made of its presence as an impact of colonial legacies on current social formations. Rum poetics identifies these points of tacit mystification and reroutes them, pulling expected narratives off their plumb lines to create additional designs.

The introduction of terms like *Atlantic studies, Global South,* and *Archipelagic studies* have nearly rendered the term *postcolonial* obsolete. In my own field, modernist studies, scholars have introduced the concepts of geomodernism, planetary modernism, and interimperiality to reckon with the multiple temporal scales and spatial dimensions in which modernity and modernism are lived and produced.[5] These efforts to resist unified historical progression and prioritization of Anglo-European narratives have opened ground for this study, though my method registers the synchronous presence of the colonial past in postcolonial texts rather than focusing on duration. I retain *postcolonial* because it retains desires, though desires far from universally shared or identical in form, to put the period of colonization behind "us"—to be free of its demands. *Postcolonial* also allows the registration of shocks pertaining to a future in which historical privileges of Anglo-European dominance are no longer effectively reified to think and organize the world.

Rum is an interpretive lacuna available to manage those paradoxes. The study balances between a decolonizing Zeitgeist in which optimism met the realities of entrenched postimperial privilege, focusing attention largely on Anglophone literary works published between 1945 and 1973, a period ending with the establishment of the Caribbean Community (CARICOM). Chapters conclude with works that update rum poetics for a worldview attuned to networks of globalization and transnational connection. In broad terms, I argue that scenes featuring rum demonstrate the difficulties of "decolonizing the mind"—as Ngũgĩ wa Thiong'o famously puts it—when identity is so thoroughly imbricated in dynamics of consumption and production inherited, largely unchanged, from colonial-era models.[6]

Rum Histories emphasizes reading and provides careful and close descriptions of textual operations around rum. In this sense, historical particulars matter less than general historical knowledge and mythologies of rum that create the cultural context in which readers encounter literature. However, not all readers are created equal; prior scholarship points out the complex interactions between early postcolonial writers, their mentors and colleagues, and the institutional gatekeepers of publishing and literary reputation. These relationships have shaped our ideas of postcolonial literature as a category and replicated the misogyny of literary institutions.[7] There is thus a distinction, as Carrie Noland writes, "between the alienation one feels toward language (or the Symbolic) in general and the alienation one feels toward the language of the colonizer in particular" (*Voices of Negritude* 20), and *Rum Histories* registers both the implicit presence of powerful white readers whose interpretive privileges form the cultural context for a publishable text and the anxieties of such readers in the face of their own colonization. "Language in general" estranges itself to become "the language of the colonizer" (who you are not/no longer/never really privileged to be), substituting proximity to for difference from the "colonized Other."

Rum's position in Anglo-Caribbean sugar production—its material history—makes it a viable tool for charting confrontations with the potential of postcoloniality to change who we know ourselves to be. Produced from the waste of sugarcane processing, rum is simultaneously an intensification, by-product, and waste product of sugar, the white gold of the glory days of colonization and plantation slavery. Rum survives as a Caribbean brand while sugar has lost its regional affect. Rum captures the remarkable speed and intensity of individuated ideological negotiations around residual colonial dominance, globalization, and emergent cultural and economic power zones affiliated with what has become known as the Global South. Central to this intensity is a perception that the legacies of colonialism remain so deeply entrenched in the positioning of subjects who are supposed to be postcolonial—beyond all that, no longer beholden to it—and an accompanying realization of the value or cost of this legacy. In literature of the "post-" colonial period, interactions with rum suggest that current conditions and identities are simultaneously attenuations and accumulations of colonial pasts that have not been superseded. At the same time, rum has been superseded by other drugs (most often, marijuana and heroin) now deemed external threats to Western civilization. Susceptibility to drunkenness signals backwardness, entrapment in the past, as a reason for a lack of personal or national progress. And, as I attempt to indicate in later chapters, rum can be a point of speculation for futures that exceed the "post-," "neo-," or "de-" colonial formations, leading, as Ian Baucom theorizes, to a future we might look back on as a transition between United States dominance and "?" (*Specters* 27).

To investigate these negotiations, I propose a rum poetics that capitalizes on the dual meaning of rum as "strange," its materiality as a product of imperialism, and its participation in shared understandings of alcohol use. Drawing a critical insight from Bill Brown's seminal essay "Thing Theory," this study resists the critical tendency to skim over rum/*rum* and rather invests it with "thingness": it "stop[s] working for us" and its "flow within the circuits of production and distribution, consumption and exhibition, has been arrested, however momentarily" (B. Brown 4).[8] I will belabor the point, working over sensory experiences that question the autonomous postcolonial self.[9] In articulating the ideological work necessary to create the interpretative aporia in which rum frequently lies, rum poetics surprises, confounds, and discomfits. Scenes involving rum display a collective intoxication by colonial ideologies as well as the anxieties and panics engendered by a collective failure to move into a desired postcolonial state, in both senses of the word. Critical discourse around rum/*rum* reenacts these anxieties through the relative absence of critical discourse around rum, compared to the prolific discourse on sugar. The language of reparation, which draws equally from Eve Kosofsky Sedgwick and the discourse around reparations for slavery and colonial occupation, speaks to the disciplinary subfields across which this study travels. Edouard Glissant's theorization of *relation* from *Poetics of Relation* is entirely relevant here, in that he invokes shared submission to an unknown future as essential to his poetics, but I want to leave some space between Sedgwick and Glissant to mark my positionality as I approach Caribbean literature from a white feminist modernist origin point. Rum poetics focuses on the selective blindness of privilege and an ethics of *repair* that, understanding the impossibility of absolute redress for the crimes of the past, starts with recognizing accountability. My optimistic intent is, as Sedgwick argues, to mark in texts "ethically crucial possibilities . . . that the past . . . could have happened differently from the way it actually did" and to give "the reader . . . room to realize that the future may be different" (146). But not everyone loves a surprise: this study meditates on the anxiety, even panic, induced by the merest suspicion of what a genuinely postcolonial future could mean for those whose identities abide in unacknowledged privilege.

Rum, then, is rum: it acquires a stubborn alterity that resists easy glosses even as it enables them. As a noun, *rum* means "an alcoholic spirit distilled from molasses and other sugarcane products, prepared chiefly in the Caribbean and South America"; as an adjective, it means "odd, strange. Also, bad, spurious, suspect."[10] The bland scientific description of fermented sugarcane, together with the geographical reference, marks and masks rum's historical association with Caribbean slavery. The noun's definition implies, with some truth, that rum is now just a product; only its primary location of production conjures any association with the labor extracted from enslaved people. These are distant connections, no longer relevant to producers or consumers. The adjective, by contrast, suggests that something odd is going on. *Rum Histories* zooms in on the strangeness, attempting a reparative view from the level of the text.

Rum Histories: How Did We Get Here?

The current range of signification for rum depends on a set of associations inherited from the history of plantation slavery in the Caribbean. These associations were largely in place by 1800 and consolidated by the time of emancipation. Later, as British Caribbean colonies negotiate independence, or greater independence, from the Crown after World War II, the symbolic implications of rum remain in place to characterize sociopolitical conditions in emerging Caribbean states.[11] First, the West Indies—the Caribbean in general—has been associated with excessive drinking long before tourism promotional materials. Alcohol was a pervasive feature of life in the West Indies, although this situation was not unusual at a time when water safety was not guaranteed. Europeans and Africans in the West Indies drank rum for medicinal or nutritional benefit as well as for the other well-established reasons: tradition, celebration/ritual, and solace. However, according to Frederick Smith's excellent study *Caribbean Rum* (2005), early accounts from travelers and planters establish the drinking patterns among planters, poor whites, and slaves to be excessive according to European norms. These accounts may be biased by ignorance of African drinking customs (F. Smith 109) or of the ways European drinking patterns shifted to accommodate conditions in the West Indies; however, they create a pattern that persisted as stereotypes of louche, drunk planters (fig. 1) and dangerously intoxicated slaves.[12]

Rum also played an integral role in the Black Atlantic economy; it deserves its iconic status as a lubricant for the plantation system. Traders exchanged casks of rum for human beings, thus commodifying people in the interests of imperial trade. As Jay Coughtry explains in *The Notorious Triangle* (1981), Rhode Island rum-men traded rum for slaves in Africa, and then slaves for molasses in the West Indies. "Frequently," he states, "molasses served as a partial payment for the slaves, thereby making the circle of Caribbean involvement complete. Viewed from this perspective, the slave trade was simply the most profitable method of selling rum, Rhode Island's most important export" (21). African trading partners were neither passive consumers nor unlimited markets for rum, and slave traders monitored demand and preferences when supplying ships.[13] West Africans could profit from reselling rum they received

Figure 1. "A Spanish Planter of Porto Rico, luxuriating in his hammock," lithography after Ralph Sennett (?), from *A Voyage in the West Indies,* John Augustine Waller, 1820. (John Carter Brown Library, Archive of Early American Images, Brown University)

in partial payment for slaves or as wages (81), and African traders saw rum as a high-status drink that amplified their standing in the community (83). Coastal traders also discriminated between varieties of alcohol, negotiating for rum—particularly Rhode Island rum—instead of other alcohols (Ambler 81–82). Thus, as Ian Williams states, "rum soon became a double enslaver, both depending on the toil of slaves to make and being the main trade item to buy slaves in West Africa" (90). The importance of rum to the slave trade appears in its centrality to boycotts during the British abolition movement (Midgeley 35–40); any number of abolition poems capitalize on the fact that sugar and rum could contain the blood of enslaved people.[14] The Royal Navy, which policed and enabled the slave trade, supplemented the naval diet with a daily rum ration, introduced in 1731 and discontinued in 1970.[15]

Rum also is central to the operation of a plantation's internal economy. Before emancipation, planters supplemented the slave diet with rum and, after emancipation, wages were often partially paid in rum (see F. Smith 103–4, 175–76). Rum served as preparation for or a reward for arduous tasks, and it was used to accustom people to enslavement (103–4).[16] After emancipation, plantation owners manipulated the price and availability of rum to shift indentured South Asian workers away from marijuana because they "were as interested in creating a captive consumer class as they were in enhancing the labor of those already working under indenture" (Angrosino 102).[17] Even when the rum trade declined, the association of rum with the economic prosperity of the West Indies remained.[18]

Rum circulates through local plantation finances and global trade routes lubricated by overlapping cultural taboos and shared uses of alcohol among enslaved people, overseers, planters, traders, sailors, and regular folk. In the twentieth century, this combination of the ludic and the vicious provides a moral and cultural correlative for problems that are primarily historical and economic. As decolonization began, the systemic weakness and dependence of individual islands, which arose from long-term extraction of natural and human resources, rendered the transition to independence difficult. British control over the West Indian economy in the mid-twentieth century was still tight, and English firms planned to retain their assets through any transition to independence. Although sugar no longer produced the extraordinary revenues it had in the eighteenth century, it was still a lucrative trade item, particularly during wartime, when access to foreign sugar supplies was limited by hostilities and the Ministry of Food purchased the entire crop (Stahl 27). West Indian sugar imports to England were subsidized by the British government, giving it a price preference over foreign sugar.[19] In her 1951 study *The Metropolitan Organization of British Colonial Trade*, Kathleen M. Stahl reports that the sugar industry of which rum is a subsidiary was still headquartered in England (32). She notes, "A high proportion of the century-old firms engaged in colonial trade are family businesses. . . . They show a general tenacity in maintaining their offices either on, or as near as possible to, their original sites in the City" (7). This economic interest merged into political influence with Parliament, as the executive of the West India Committee "is still to a large extent composed of members of the leading firms controlling sugar production in the West

Indies" (15). Thus, those with strong economic self-interest maintained an official political role in West Indian policymaking; the West Indies is the only colonial area under this type of administrative control.[20]

As a product already imbued with degradation and shame, rum conveniently focuses affects surrounding the difficulties attending the transition from colony to independent state, and there are connections between discourses surrounding alcoholism in the region and the emergence from direct rule. Historian Jan Rogoziński has reported that, as negotiations for decolonization proceeded in the 1960s and 1970s, British officials "were convinced that the smaller colonies were too poor to survive as viable states" and thus planned to introduce self-government gradually (267). Even earlier, Perham had pointed to the uniqueness of each colony as a warning against "some generalised 'colonial' plan" (51). While she noted that some West Indian islands "have less of the handicaps in the race for self-government than others," the general backwardness of the colonies in terms of education, resources, and institutions undermines their ability to support and supply an independent democratic government (52). The British also favored a federated government that would combine the resources of the many islands. Federation efforts failed because Jamaica and Trinidad, which were developing local resources (bauxite and oil, respectively), "feared that their economies would be drained by the poorer islands of the eastern Caribbean" (Rogoziński 269).[21] Despite these logical explanations for potential weakness in new West Indian states, the failure of West Indian islands to achieve self-government was also seen as a national or regional tragic flaw. According to John Darwin, fractious negotiations led the British government to conclude that "the British West Indies were a monument to colonial failure: poverty-stricken, politically backward, economically as well as politically fragmented, with a golden past and a leaden future" (217).

Key to these pessimistic expectations, which might also be styled self-fulfilling prophecies or wishful thinking, are the trajectories of Haiti and Cuba, island polities that escape colonial control. According to Laurent Dubois, the Haitian revolt of 1791 achieved a remarkable feat: "The expansion of citizenship beyond racial barriers despite the massive political and economic investment in the slave system at the time" (3). Eventually, it led to Haitian independence in 1804. Although Haiti inspires anticolonial resistance as a "romance of revolutionary overcoming" (Dalleo 15), its struggles—often, but not solely, a product of Western manipulation and racism—serve as an object lesson for the importance of economic independence to liberation.[22] In the twentieth century, Cuba provides another failed state narrative despite achieving independence in 1959 and becoming, as foreign policy specialist Walter Russell Mead admits, a "powerful voice" resisting US foreign policy in the region and the world (29). Yet even where a Caribbean state earns praise, it still, in choosing Communism over capitalism, gets independence wrong.

As the United States emerges as the dominant force in the Caribbean Basin, popular media and government policy characterize the region as an uncooperative, unproductive thorn in the side of a progressive postwar world (barring its existence as a tropical paradise). The United States had been heavily invested in the West Indies during World War II, maintaining a series of bases under an agreement with England.[23] Robert Freeman Smith, in a Twayne general overview of US relations and policy in the Caribbean, reports that after World War I US interest waned, and policy took on the form of "ambiguity and confusion."[24] President Franklin Roosevelt was "perplexed" by the failure of New Deal programs to bring stability and growth to Puerto Rico, which he attributed to faulty leadership and overpopulation (R. F. Smith 35). Texts about US-Caribbean relations chronicle a familiar oscillation between negligence and officious interference. George Black, writing in 1988, explains that the problem with US policy toward the Caribbean is "a kind of recurrent historical amnesia": "When there was no crisis, or when the crisis did not directly involve the United States, it was as if the country in question had simply ceased to exist" (80). Other sources have characterized the attitude of the United States as "reactive and cautious" (Soderlund 157), and many note that Cold War concerns, which reached peak intensity with the Cuban Revolution of 1959, often skewed the commitment to democratization in the region (Sunshine 231). President Reagan's Caribbean Basin Initiative, designed to promote free trade and discourage radical experiments like those of the New Jewel Party in Grenada, "will create some beneficiaries, but these are more likely to be U.S. corporations than Caribbean people" (Deere et al. 182).

The prominent image of Caribbean states remains one of instability, extremism, privation, and profligacy. Supriya Nair remarks that "most postcolonies are newsworthy to the Western media only when some natural or political disaster strikes," yet the Caribbean is marketed as a locale characterized by "decadent hedonism" ("Expressive Countercultures" 72). Violence, for example, is one of two common denominators found in a survey of media coverage of events in the Caribbean during the 1990s (Soderlund 162). This pattern is consistent with earlier depictions in popular films of the 1970s and 1980s (Black 123, 141), in which

"Central America and the Caribbean were now just places where people went bananas" (123). Richard Nixon, following a vice-presidential trip to Haiti under Duvalier, called the nation "a picture in poverty and pregnancy" (qtd. in R. F. Smith 52). The United States tends to approach the Caribbean Basin with the idea that it must monitor, and occasionally act, to preserve strategic interests, but that what happens to these island polities should not really be a US problem.

These attitudes evince an inverse civilizing mission: having invested time and money to gift the islands with enlightenment and conceded readiness for self-determination, former imperial governments expect gratitude and repayment—and peace and quiet. Saidiya Hartman's discussion of the rhetoric of debt surrounding emancipation in the United States analogizes to the West Indies: "The transition from slavery to freedom introduced the free agent to the circuits of exchange through this construction of already accrued debt, an abstinent present, and a mortgaged future. In short, to be free was to be a debtor—that is, obliged and duty-bound to others" (131). Hartman figures the individual burden as both behavioral, requiring postures of gratitude and worthiness, and financial, because freedom has a cost. Each person and each sociopolitical unit are now "obliged" and "duty-bound" to behave worthily of investments that are constructed as already made by metropolitan governments and do not account for the wealth generated by extracting it from people (enslaved labor) and the island environment. Never mind that, as Deere and her colleagues explain, postwar international lending entities "have reinforced traditional patterns of subordination in the relationship of Caribbean economies to metropolitan centers" arising from the days of plantation slavery and indenture (7). Further, Hartman's middle adjective, "abstinent," provides the moral sting: the first and last adjectives are contractual and financial, but "abstinent" implies a code of behavior. In such language, Hartman signals how the register of morality imposes narratives of profligacy, incompetence, corruption, and indulgence on polities emerging from colonization.[25] This logic leads to decreased empathy for Caribbean locations when natural disasters exacerbate extant financial and infrastructure problems, as when Hurricane Maria devastated Puerto Rico and the president quickly transferred blame to the island (Glanz and Robles).

In Hartman's word "abstinent," denotational meaning spreads into more generalized beliefs about behavior and attitude. Thus, drinking—and, more particularly, rum drinking—whether excessive or routine, gets mapped onto and naturalizes a range of dysfunction with roots in broader effects of colonization. These attitudes are linked in discourses about drinking in Caribbean societies and applied by external observers. In 1957, M. H. Beaubrun spoke on the radio and later published in the *Caribbean Medical Journal* a call to understand alcoholism as a "social" problem with immense costs for Trinidad (137). He grants the utility of alcohol in generating sociability and relaxation, but he decries the cost of overindulgence: "Trinidad's bill for alcoholism is round about six million dollars" (138) in lost productivity and medical expenses. Beaubrun subscribes to the idea that alcoholism is "an *incurable* illness" (138), but he attempts to excite communal awareness by noting that the social costs are not private or individual; they affect the country, sapping it of resources and threatening future productivity. In a study of Barbados, Graham Dann writes: "In the context of a developing country some may find it disturbing that approximately 1 in 5 drinkers spent at least 10% or more of their discretionary income on alcohol. In a few extreme cases there were individuals spending the equivalent of their entire earnings on drink" (29). Janet Stoute and Kenneth Ifill also comment on the costs of the rum shop and male drinking for the development of the society of Barbados in the postcolonial era: "Expenditure on alcohol severely reduces a source of potential investment. Knowledge of the extent of the phenomenon may also seriously reduce the inflow of capital from overseas, thereby affecting local employment and consequent possibility of development" (165).

A more recent World Bank study comments that "the poor in developing countries perceive alcohol use—particularly among men—as detrimental to their well-being and their efforts to build human and social capital" (Pyne et al. 1). Taken out of the immediate context of individual effects, these remarks feed into racialized temperance narratives. In their introduction to *The Serpent in the Cup: Temperance in American Literature,* David S. Reynolds and Debra J. Rosenthal emphasize the connection between abolition and temperance movements in the United States in the nineteenth century, noting that the enslavement of the personal will under slavery was mapped onto the enslavement of the will to the bottle (5).[26] Nineteenth- and twentieth-century temperance efforts focused on the degradation wrought by alcohol and thus "helped magnify the evils of the slave trade" (F. Smith 97).[27] Denise Herd, who has written extensively on alcohol use in Black communities, notes that "temperance workers drew vivid parallels between enslavement to a master and bondage to alcohol" ("Ambiguity" 155); simultaneously, she states elsewhere, images of the "drunken black brute" encouraged restrictions on the sale and consumption of liquor to Black people during enslavement, after emancipation, and throughout Prohibition ("Paradox of Temperance" 367). These discourses were carried through the Caribbean, as Brian Moore and Michele A. Johnson report in their study of late nineteenth-century Jamaican temperance campaigns. In Jamaica, they write, these campaigns are "to some degree racialized" and were largely rejected because the promoters sought to enforce an "imported moral code" (156).

In discussions of alcoholism and temperance in the Caribbean, problems of personal will and responsibility intersect with perceived problems of cultural will and responsibility that lead to failed or weak modern polities. This confluence enables an economy of reading, meaning both a shorthand and a set of protocols, that flows across discourses that engage the Caribbean. Histories of extraction and exploitation, while acknowledged, lose purchase on analyses of present conditions in favor of racialized, moralistic stereotypes. The history of rum in the Caribbean is part of two economic phenomena, plantation monoculture (single-crop agriculture) and slavery, that created economic and political vulnerability as British direct rule mutated into other forms and ceded influence to other state actors—notably, the United States—after World War II. Superficially, the claim that West Indian states are dysfunctional (a judgment subject to perception as well) because people there drink too much appears ridiculous, but representing drinking habits captures affective responses to the unresolved contradictions of decolonization, marking a pivot where historical or economic explanations become moral or cultural, and vice versa. Rum's multifaceted semiotic associations give rise, paradoxically, to a convenient evacuation of specific reference, creating a vacuum in which power operates. The next sections trace the nodes of reference that flexibly attach and detach from rum in order to deflect acknowledgment of the burdens colonialism leaves with contemporary subjects and states.

Foundations of Rum Poetics 1:
Drunkenness, Disease Models, and Moral Stigma

The specifics of rum's history as a Caribbean product merge with a more general history of drinking customs. These customs, especially as they apply to drinking judged excessive, are inflected by class, race, and gender, and they are largely shared across the areas dealt with in this study. Cross-culturally, these ideas are baked in. To unseat this dominant narrative, this section lays out the common evaluation models for excessive alcohol use and then counters them with anthropological cross-cultural studies of drinking behavior. Dominant public health and popular understandings of drinking encourage and reinforce moral stigma generally. When academics and policymakers discuss drinking, they discuss drinking as a problem to be deplored—even condemned. In other words, "drinking" means excessive drinking or alcoholism rather than normative cultural behavior. The construction of alcohol consumption as a problem currently rests on the disease model of alcoholism, with its attendant focus on drinking as a social problem. This model of alcoholism, widely known and accepted in popular contexts, surmounts the moral "disease of the will" model that prevailed from the nineteenth century through the Prohibition period.[28] While the stigma on problem drinking retains its force, the emphasis in discourse surrounding treatment has shifted from moralizing to therapeutic. In this scenario, excessive alcohol use remains individuated to the person—addiction—or to specific social contexts (e.g., fraternities). Although there is a general awareness of larger cultural context, the focus remains on fixing a localized abnormality: drinking perceived as excessive and dangerous.

The prevalence of this model inhibits understanding drinking in broader cultural terms.[29] In the late 1990s, the Social Issues Research Centre reported that "dysfunctional drinking" rather than normative drinking habits continued to dominate the research and public-policy agenda (SIRC). Stigmatizing drinking limits the range of analysis and distorts the role of alcohol in culture in several ways: first, the presumption that all drinking is potentially excessive and damaging begs the question of definition;[30] second, we overlook the broader context in which judgments about what constitutes inappropriate alcohol use are made; and, third, the personalization of stigma deflects attention from the institutional and economic investments in perpetuating this discourse.[31]

The strong tendency to stigmatize alcohol consumption perceived as excessive has enabled corporations and governments to distribute alcohol deliberately to gain power over indigenous and/or colonized subjects, expropriate their resources, and then stigmatize them, as individuals and groups, as feckless, unproductive, morally lax others. Anthropologists who have examined the introduction of rum specifically include Marcia Langton, whose discussion of the stereotype of the "drunken Aborigine" in Australia asks "who profits" from the purveyance of alcohol to aboriginal groups (199). She concludes that "some" social scientists need "to consider the role of the Western imagination, and their own imaginings, in some of their notions about contemporary Aboriginal society as dysfunctional" (205). June Nash chronicles the relationship between the promotion of binge-drinking rituals in Chiapas and "anesthetizing Indians to the injustice in which they were held captive" (628). Michael Wagner investigates the ethnic segmentation of the retail trade in postemancipation British Guiana to discover that the "colonial elite" promoted the control of the rum trade by Portuguese immigrants to suppress the Creole population: with the Portuguese as a "buffer group" (415), "the resultant 'new society' was as near a reconstitution of the old slave society as was feasible" (407). In these analyses, anthropologists agree that constructing drinking behaviors as pathological often enable exploitative material relations grounding the production, distribution, and consumption of alcohol. Thus, the ability to position drinking as excessive or inappropriate has enormous power to deflect attention from economic and political injustice through vocabularies of personal or cultural shame.

The idea—or, one might say, ideology—of drinking pathologies traverses North American, English, and Anglophone Caribbean interpretive strategies because these areas broadly share drinking norms around gender, though they divide along race. In each region, social drinking rises in general acceptability after World War II, yet, whether regular, heavy, or alcoholic, drinking is naturalized among men; women's drinking always requires an explanation.[32] Strictures against women's social drinking slowly relax, but the cautionary figure of the "drunken slut" persists as a control on female behavior. Alcohol research expands in the postwar years, but its goals largely reflect this naturalized gender divide in alcohol consumption: research on women's experience lags behind studies of men. Differences among ethnic and racial groups are rarely studied before the 1980s,[33] and research into alcohol use and abuse in the Caribbean Basin is also sparse.[34] In the Caribbean as in the United States, drinking by men in groups outside the home remains an important—sometimes lamented—part of male socialization, identity formation, and community. Female presence in public drinking places like bars and pubs is also more accepted, but the rum shops of the Caribbean remain a male preserve, and Caribbean women tend to abstain at higher rates than women to their north.[35]

Two conclusions can be noted here: first, stereotypes about gender, race, class, and ethnicity strongly affect the assessment of alcohol use. Second, all these cultures value drinking as it encourages sociability and community while strongly stigmatizing consumption perceived to threaten economic and communal health—that is, alcoholism.[36] Similarities across cultures of the Atlantic create the impression that drinking habits and behaviors are essential, mandated by physiology rather than culturally constructed. In other words, we know what *drunk* means.

Alcohol promotes disinhibition, which traditionally leads to two simultaneous and paradoxical judgments: drunken people are both more themselves (*in vino veritas*) and less so—drunk people do not appear in control of their actions and words. Alcohol use raises questions of will, (self-)control, and truth that resonate at individual and societal levels. Does intoxication represent an abominable failure of will, a congenital disposition to dysfunction, or a genial insouciance, an unpretending conviviality? The answers to these questions depend on who is doing the judging, about whom, where, and when—yet the notion that drunkenness could be learned behavior, a form of social performance, or a cultural construction, remains uncommon in mainstream thinking despite fifty years of anthropological research indicating otherwise.

In *Drunken Comportment* (1969), Craig MacAndrew and Robert B. Edgerton lay out a theory that behavior under the influence of alcohol is contingent and learned rather than innate and physiological. MacAndrew and Edgerton make two major claims—still largely accepted—that undermine "conventional wisdom" about the effects of alcohol on human behavior.[37] First, their cross-cultural review of anthropological studies demonstrates that alcohol impairs sensorimotor skills, but psychological response varies considerably based on context. The presumptive "disinhibiting effect" (36) of alcohol on behavior is, they claim, contingent.[38] The attribution of "all other sorts of drunken 'incompetencies'" to alcohol, and "thus similarly unintentional and similarly beyond the drinker's voluntary control," results from social training rather than physiological fact (170). Second, across cultures, "drunkenness . . . takes on the flavor of *'time out'* from many of the otherwise imperative demands of everyday life" (90). What people do under the influence of alcohol is a) not under their control and b) does not count. (Unless it does, of course.) Paradoxically, the presence of alcohol labels a situation as out of bounds for critical analysis and interpretation. In situations involving alcohol, MacAndrew and Edgerton stress that "not only can the drinker explain away his drunken misbehavior to himself . . . those around him too can decide, or can be made to see, that his drunken transgressions ought not—or at least, *need* not—be taken in full seriousness" (169). Alcohol functions under erasure, its meanings somehow apparent and impervious to analysis.

The provisional nature of the phrase "or at least, *need* not" calls for an analysis of power and agency as they impinge on the evaluation of drinking behaviors in specific contexts. "When looking at the drink question," writes James Nicholls in *The Politics of Alcohol,* "we are rarely looking at simple moral panics but we are almost invariably looking at ways in which concerns over drink also reveal other, less explicit, social values, assumptions, and beliefs" (254–55). Nor is alcoholic "time-out" simply a matter of the amalgam of items we might call "culture": Anthony Marcus argues, extending and altering MacAndrew and Edgerton, that intensive regimens of state regulation for all sectors of alcohol production, distribution, and consumption shape the availability and location of alcohol's "time-out." Paradoxically, the freedom from social control signified by alcohol consumption is highly scripted, heavily supervised, and carefully managed, not only by conventional beliefs but also by state regulation. The times one feels most free from social control could be, in fact, moments when one is most clearly governed by systemic, institutional forces. The notion of "time-out" also implies its syntactic reverse: "out of time." In the sense that alcohol marks a zone of freedom from familial and institutional demands, it is also available—as a signifier—to depress or repress historical implications of the past in the present.

Rum poetics bridges this gap, progressing toward libations as a figure for readings that recognize the past in accounting for present relations. Libations consecrate communal purpose, often by reference to ancestors (recently or anciently deceased) or gods. As an interpretive strategy, libations flood alcoholic time-out with shared history. The effect of establishing recognition of the other(s) makes of a gap a link where material and social relations could transform while acknowledging how consistently, and for what reasons, such opportunities may be lost or ignored.

Foundations of Rum Poetics 2:
Rum as a Commodity in Anglo-Atlantic Consumer Culture

The figure of libations replaces a more superficial consumption model prevalent even when authors overtly canvas exploitation and violence as part of rum's brand. As a commodity, rum is part of "a general imaginary of the Caribbean totality" as defined by Mimi Sheller (7) and "a cultural symbol" tightly wed to the Caribbean even though rum is produced in any number of locations.[39] Perusing tour guides of the time provides adequate proof of rum's specific association with regional culture. *Holiday*'s 1973 guide is typical in stating, "In the Caribbean the drink is rum. Period.... You are bound to feel out of step unless you join the rum bibbers at least part of the time" (31). Fodor's 1960 *Guide to the Caribbean, Bahamas, and Bermuda* evokes the taboos with the imperative: "Demon Rum.... is the national drink of the Caribbean" (70). Yet

Sheller's claim of a "totality" of Caribbean-affiliated products (from zombies to bananas) that creates a "general imaginary" is important because she captures how dissemination or substitution can weaken the politics of a poetics centered on a specific commodity: If any number of products can symbolize "the Caribbean," how is the specific significance of rum secured and justified?

Similarly, a spate of commodity sagas about rum create a continuum of equivalent consumers that suppresses ethical concerns. While not silent on the score of slavery, these sagas end optimistically by celebrating the commodity's ability to connect a diverse, global world—past and present. The conclusion to Charles Coulombe's *Rum: The Epic History of the Drink That Conquered the World* (2004) is a case in point: "So the next time you hold a glass of rum or a rum cocktail in your hand, think of all who came before you, who made it possible for you to lift the beverage to your lips. Planters and slaves, pirates and sailors, World War I Tommies and voodoo priestesses, rum-runners and African kings, missionary priests and Yankee traders all played their part, hate them or love them, in bringing this nectar to you. And as you drink, know that you yourself are joining their company" (262).

Coulombe draws on celebratory drinking rituals—the toast—to acknowledge past injustice, but he positions the contemporary consumer as a knowing, yet innocent, beneficiary of a historical parade of individual consumers. In separating individual consumers from the systems that govern their relationship to consumer goods, Coulombe illustrates a convention of commodity sagas in which individuality and subjectivity are held in tension. Bruce Robbins narrates the phenomenon as follows: "What a wondrous system this is, you are told, that has brought to your doorstep or breakfast table all these things you never would have known existed, yet things without which you would not, you suddenly realize, be yourself" (456).[40] Your individuality is a product of a system, but this system must be equally good for everyone because it has produced "you," the singular, individual self. In Coulombe's hands, history is an alcoholic time-out. He simultaneously flattens rum consumers into a transhistorical consumer community while the chronological order in which he lists consuming subjects prevents a direct confrontation between contemporary consumers and the "planters and slaves" (Coulombe 262) who are their ancestors. This passage accomplishes linguistically what Coulombe's book, which cuts off its account in 1945, disallows in content: a recognition of present material conditions that make, as Robbins indicates, "you" (the consumer) "yourself." Anthony Maingot may inadvertently update this phenomenon when he concludes a discussion of twenty-first-century globalization in the rum industry, not with the promised outline of marketing solutions for Caribbean producers, but with advice to connoisseurs navigating the new rum marketplace (259–60). The shift to "discerning individuals" (260) prioritizes consumer identity over ethical and strategic questions about labor, production, and distribution.

The knowing obliviousness of consumers has long been associated with trading in the Caribbean. William Cowper, in his well-known poem "Pity for Poor Africans" (1788), expresses the equation concisely:

> I own I am shock'd at the purchase of slaves,
> And fear those who buy them and sell them are knaves;
> What I hear of their hardships, their tortures, and groans
> Is almost enough to draw pity from stones.
>
> I pity them greatly, but I must be mum,
> For how could we do without sugar and rum?
> Especially sugar, so needful we see?
> What? give up our desserts, our coffee, and tea! (2.1–8)

Cowper's poem exposes a psychology of acquiescence in which communal worldview negates the relational aspect of consuming products made by enslaved people. Cowper makes visible the intuitive calculations that divorce everyday practice from systemic oppression, concretizing Arjun Appadurai's principle that "in . . . small scale exchanges of things in ordinary life, this fact [politics] is not visible, for exchange has the routine and conventionalized look of all customary behavior" (57). The speaker, "shock'd" by the notion of human beings as commodities, cannot change his or her purchasing habits *just* because laborers are tortured. The imperative "must be mum" and communal norms of an English "we" notably fail to specify the authority to which the speaker reluctantly bows. Economic conditions cycle into cultural norms, producing a rhetorical question: "How could we do without . . . ?" Because "we" cannot. While this "we" has some connection to national security against the claims of "the French, Dutch, and Danes" (1.9), Cowper's speaker is a corporate person, mouthing as personal the desires of shadowy institutional forces. The apparent powerlessness of individual consumers in the face of an overwhelming political-economic system is rather a contractual agreement to notice and deplore, perhaps, while continuing to enjoy and purchase.

Marx and Engels declared a commodity "a very queer thing" (31) because it negates the human component in production, and *rum* might be said to inherently embody that queerness in its double signification as a product (alcoholic beverage) and an attribute (strange, odd). Under the pressure of observation and analysis, rum evolves from a neutral object of exchange into a site of fraught, contested signification, capable of producing what Priti Ramamurthy calls a "dizzying relay" of information (737) that, in Bill Brown's terms, "disclose[s]" information "about *us*" (5). Those who study alcohol consumption as a cultural phenomenon contend that "drink is one of the most noticeable, emotional and important ways in which people express and discuss their identities and cultures" (T. Wilson 7). Much is invested, psychologically and economically, in these cultural ways, and there is a strong disinclination to confront them as powerful constructions. The ability to *express* and *discuss* is accompanied by an equally strong impulse to silence and repress. Wilson's statement is reversible: "Drink is one of the most noticeable, emotional and important ways in which" *cultures express their people.*

Foundations of Rum Poetics 3: Drunken Comportment in Literary Study

These questions are intimate and literal. As Mervyn Nicholson notes, "Food is not simply a thing or object. It is, properly, a mediating power" (2). Rum, like other ingestibles, confronts the self with the possibility that what one perceives as agency, physical autonomy, and even principled resistance may be an effect of external forces rather than internal motivation. Alcohols, as intoxicants, figure this dilemma as disinhibition, a loss of physical and social control. Yet the overcoding of alcohol has led, in literary study, to a speaking silence on the significance of drinking; there is plenty of work on addiction but much less attention to other possibilities. Marty Roth claims that in texts "there is a constant hum of alcoholic reference that should dominate all other indicators of meaning and yet can be apprehended only as cultural white noise" (xviii). In other words, the stigma of alcoholism and the risks of problem deflation tend to produce elliptical, euphemistic conversations about drinking habits in literary scholarship.

Authors with excessive drinking habits may be elevated to legend or sensitively protected to preserve their reputations for genius. Thomas Gilmore chronicles the "invisibility" of drinking in literary criticism because of social taboos and a desire to ignore its effect on a writer's work (4–6). Even so, both he and Tom Dardis claim alcohol was ruinous to the production of great writers.[41] For women writers as well, excessive drinking eventually destroys art: for example, Renate Günther chronicles "alcohol as an agent of female transgression" that becomes "an instrument of destruction" in the work of Marguerite Duras, and in Duras herself (201).[42] These taboos and hesitations pervade classrooms as well. As Krista Ratcliffe describes, students and teachers may collude in "classroom denial" that reinforces the idea that alcoholism and addiction are not "appropriate" for discussion (107). Ratcliffe's discussion, which centers on Louise Erdrich's *Love Medicine* (1984), may also suggest that we invoke taboos more quickly when the characters in question are women and/or from stigmatized racial or ethnic groups.

Nancy Topping Bazin unintentionally captures this double standard in one of the only articles published that considers depictions of alcoholism in postcolonial novels. In her concluding paragraph, she states, "To fail to notice and analyze the impact of alcoholism on the characters in literature by third world writers is to fail to understand fully the exact nature of the pain they are describing. . . . their condemnation of economic, political, and social injustices should not blind us to how clearly many of them also reveal through their characters the destructive impact of alcoholism on human lives" (132). Within the article, Bazin clearly connects alcohol use to sexism and racism, but in her conclusion she separates "the destructive impact of alcoholism" from "economic, political, and social injustices." Bazin, reasonably concerned about "problem deflation" as another troubling aspect of stereotyping cultures as pathological, focuses on symptom and diagnosis rather than the intersection of cultural codes in everyday objects. More important, Bazin's reading calls for a check on interpretive lenses for distortions that encourage biases and silences around drunken comportment.

Roth's rendering of alcohol's signifying range as "white noise" is happily suggestive for this project because it points to the whiteness that makes a lot of the noise both in the texts and in the critical discourse around them. While *Rum Histories* moves toward what Edouard Glissant calls "cross-cultural poetics" that acknowledges "the irreducible density of the other" (*Caribbean Discourse* 133) through shared interactions with rum, many of the readings are accounts of white privilege confronting its ephemerality and, in two words, freaking out—physically and verbally. I have also charted this phenomenon when the privilege accorded a body is partially or incompletely anchored in a racial binary structured as North/South. Roth's characterization of that "white noise" as a "hum" also unites the linguistic and the somatic, emphasizing the relationship between embodiment and agency at the inflection point of language. This practice builds on the ethical component of Brown's thing theory, following Noland's claims about the racialized body in *Agency and Embodiment* (2009). Responses "closer to the involuntary, autonomous body" may offer "access to an interiority that culture cannot entirely control": "If the racialized subject must take part in the meaning-making systems of an alienating culture, at least this subject can struggle to reexperience what those systems physically require" (205). I seek to make visible in white subjects crises of embodiment that register the proximity of colonizing and colonized subjects as subjects: this strategy illuminates whiteness as a constructed advantage reliant on the persistence of colonial ideology despite the myth that postcoloniality releases white subjects from this ethical conundrum. As in Noland's analysis of Fanon's racialized body, these moments do not necessarily produce empathetic or progressive results, but they provide sites for rereading that may.[43]

But before that, we need to address another kind of white noise that obscures the role of rum in the analysis of postcoloniality: sugar.

Candy's Dandy, but Liquor's Quicker (Sugar . . . and Rum)

Although historians and literary critics have attended to the significance of sugar in literature and culture, rum has not merited similarly dense investigation. Sidney Mintz opened sugar to cultural studies in *Sweetness and Power: The Place of Sugar in Modern History* (1985), chronicling the factors that expanded the market and taste for sugar. Even so, he marvels at the fungibility of these explanations: "There is no way to avoid the term [power]—or one like it—when the objective is to clarify under what conditions the population of an entire country changes its behavior radically without the compulsion of open force and violence" (166). Four years later, Stuart Hall would provide the pithiest and prickliest dictum on the ethical dimensions of sugar: "I am the sugar at the bottom of the English cup of tea" (48). He claims to speak "symbolically" (48), but he also speaks literally, historically, of blood sugar: abolitionists reported that sugar and rum could contain body parts and fluids from enslaved laborers injured or killed during production. Hall extends the remark to the tea itself, reminding his listeners that the quintessential English image, the cuppa, is not native, but a bricolage of colonial commodities in which things and people are indistinguishable as tradable consumables.[44]

Studies of sugar as symbol and commodity explore the pressure points identified by Mintz and Hall: virtue/vice, agency/control, pure/polluted, whiteness/race. This study of rum invokes these binaries as well, drawing on and extending these studies by pushing their insights into the post-1945 eras of decolonization and postcolonialism to show that rum captures the intensification, or distillation, of colonization's legacies even as historical ties to slavery attenuate. Many of the extant studies of sugar in literature focus on pre–twentieth century contexts. Two studies by Keith Sandiford and one by Timothy Morton choose their end points to coincide, roughly, with emancipation. Tobias Döring and Carl Plasa each compare colonial texts to contemporary responses by Anglophone Caribbean writers, charting resistance to the tropes developed to promote colonization and slavery in the Caribbean. Antonio Benítez-Rojo and Vera Kutzinski focus on Hispanophone Cuban literature and Cuban nationalism in the nineteenth and twentieth centuries. The turn to a Global South has prompted new work tracing the influence of sugar in twentieth-century art, including the *novela de la caña,* or sugarcane novel (Mahler "South-South Organizing"), memoir (Gernalzick), and multimedia art by Rita Indiana Hernández (Horn). This scholarship articulates examples of, or the potential to, cooperate across national and regional boundaries through shared experience of sugar's multinational production. Mahler and Gernalzick excavate the cultural context for analyzing novels that address sugar, and Horn attends to semiotic operations as they reflect cultural conditions.

While rum poetics draws on these perspectives, it can describe slippage or switching points more thoroughly because intoxication unhinges dualities from their poles. For example, many scholars stress a dialectic of control and resistance, either within the text itself or, in the case of comparative studies, intertextually. Morton, for example, describes an "anxious play between sweetness and power" in which discourses of guilt and virtue collide at the intersection of sugar production and sugar's figurative potential (175). In *The Cultural Politics of Sugar* (2000), Sandiford draws on the term *negotium* to argue that sugar—"natural object, prized commodity and metaphysical idea" (175)—allowed early white Creoles to accommodate a metropolitan audience, on which it relied for support and protection, to "the epistemologies of colonization and its particular productive underpinnings in sugar," diffusing resistance to slavery as an economic base for a new civil society (16). In Sandiford's later study, which contrasts obeah and sugar, he argues for "an Atlantic imaginary that is processual, multiracially informed, and fluid" (*Theorizing* 11); however, in practice, Sandiford locates sugar with "secular powers" and against obeah as part of slave resistance (52).

This dichotomy produces dissonances when rum appears because neither scholar can account for its material difference from sugar even as they recognize a difference. In *Theorizing a Colonial Caribbean-Atlantic Imaginary* (2011), Sandiford analyzes the preservation of Three-Fingered Jack's dismembered body in rum as a "collusive irony of immersion" that both subjects Jack to colonial power and enables memory of his heroism. In Sandiford's account: "What is categorically established here is a convergence of flows generated from sugar, obeah and marronage. Three-Fingered Jack flees to the mountains. . . . There he is free to arm himself in the power of his fetish, obeah. He is later captured and returned to the secular power, sugar. His members are drenched in fluids of disparate meanings to each order, rum and blood" (52).

Sandiford contends a "flow" occurs because this scene signifies differently "to each order." By "order," Sandiford means audiences, one which supports slavery (order) and sees rum as signifying of "the master's power," or sugar, in Sandiford's constellation (*Theorizing* 51), and one seeking inspiration for resistance and recognizing rum's importance as part of blood oaths. But there is no actual sugar on the scene, and it is not sugar that enables the divergent audience interpretations. The flow is rum, and while Sandiford states the difference between sugar and rum—"as an alcoholic beverage" (51)—the analysis registers indifference to this distinction by assuming that sugar is rum and vice versa. Morton confronts this dilemma in an analysis of Robert Southey's third sonnet on the slave trade, undermining as he enacts his argument about "the language of surplus" around sugar (6). After a three-page analysis of the phrase "the blood-sweeten'd beverage," in which the beverage in question appears to be tea, Morton produces the following sentence: "It is as if the flow of blood, of rum and tea, all pooled in the same space, generating recoil and revulsion (and possibly, revolution)" (201–2). Is this fragment an editorial lapse (twice over), accidentally left over from a supplementary analysis of rum that Morton eliminated? This sentence implies that Morton has been talking about rum *all along* but has assumed he need not state that fact, yet it is not the sugar that produces the effects in this case.

Kutzinski, Döring, and Plasa take comparative approaches to resistance, juxtaposing works that forward colonizing efforts with those that resist. Kutzinski focuses on gender politics and developing national identity in Cuba, identifying the figure of the mulatta as a site at which discourses of sugar and national identity anxiously converge. The mulatta, Kutzinski argues, is consistently imaged as a form of sugar, whether to reinforce colonial power or to support "the paternalist political fiction of a national multiculture" (13). Kutzinski's analysis of sexist sugar imagery recognizes that some modern depictions of the mulatta's sexuality as "sugar" do not advance far from the endemic sexual violence central to enslavement; instead, these representations grant women the freedom to be sexually available to all men (instead of to only white men) rather than equal citizenship (37). In the Anglophone context, Plasa and Döring each consider "the ways in which black writing of sugar revises the white archive out of which it grows" (Plasa 3), and Plasa echoes Kutzinski's concern that in this literature "the black woman [is marginalized] in favor of a focus on the predicament of her male counterpart" (97).

Both Plasa and Döring, like Morton, invent a poetics; these capture linguistic effects used to shape audience (or audiences's) response. Döring uses the phrase "sugar-cane poetics" to name an aesthetic that attempts to "domesticate" the Caribbean landscape using Georgic forms, signifying exotic landscapes and exploitative labor practices into submission (55). Like both Sheller and Sandiford, Döring is interested in the transportation of these effects to audiences in "discontinuous spaces, located on different continents, linked only by maritime transfers" (52). Plasa introduces the terms "Muscovado poetics" (8) and "muscovado textuality," which he intends will capture a "tension between refinement and residue" (72), a concept that resonates with Sandiford's *negotium* but takes a dimmer view of colonial-era texts that sugarcoat slavery. Plasa notes the distinct semiotic potential of *rum* in texts about sugar, calling attention to the use of *ruminate* in Andrew Burn's 1792 abolitionist text (47), but his analysis is inconsistent. In a discussion of masculinity in Austin Clarke's 2002 novel *The Polished Hoe,* Plasa fails to distinguish rum as a source of masculine identification (rum-shop culture) and its role in authorizing sexual assault against women in the cane fields (161), foreclosing an intersectional critique of rum. Likewise, Benítez-Rojo lauds poet Nicolás Guillén for depicting a "neo-African beauty" (340) whose sexuality has a "revolutionary quality" (341), but he overlooks—as Kutzinski does not—the depiction of women as consumable in "one gulp,/like a glass of rum" (Guillén, qtd. in Benítez-Rojo, "Nicolás Guillén" 343). Kutzinski's insights into the gendering of sugar pave a path toward similar potentials in rum, which, as an alcoholic beverage, is highly coded through gender.

More recent scholarship on sugar, and sugar and literature, relies on the modernization of the sugar industry to examine new forms of international political efficacy, and in this context limited references to rum are associated with past industrial formations. Popular manifestations of this phenomena are Brian McKenna's 2005 documentary *Big Sugar* and a 2013 *National Geographic* article "Sugar Love," by Rich Cohen. Both of these works connect the origins of the sugar industry in slavery to modern conditions. For McKenna, the exploitation of Haitian cane-cutters on American-owned plantations in the Dominican Republic is enslavement; Cohen attributes obesity rates among African Americans in Clarkson, Mississippi, in part to economic inequities rooted in enslavement. Historical conditions for sugar production have changed, but the effects on health and life options for Black and brown people remain devastating and relevant. The exploitative nature of sugar production has not been superseded through historical changes in conditions of production and consumption. New scholarship shares this view. In claiming cane sugar as "a material index . . . of the descriptive and critical potential of the concept of the Global South," Nadja Gernalzick considers how "the complex phenomenology of the global sugar economy" can anchor potentially transformative alliances among people working in the industry across regions, national borders, and oceans (108–9). Maja Horn narrates the history of sugar production in Hispaniola to articulate how Rita Indiana Hernández's *Sugar/Azúcar* project resists commitments to "postcolonial futures . . . formulated without these regions and peoples in mind" (272). Like both Horn and Gernalzick, Anne Garland Mahler examines "the possibilities and limits of a transnational, translinguistic, and transracial political community" ("South-South Organizing" 9); her example is the sugarcane novel, a subgenre of the novel of the land (*novela de la tierra*) specific to twentieth-century interwar Latin America. Mahler, examining a literary form that is simultaneously modern and historical, concludes that the genre identifies the forces that prevented, at that political moment, "a pan-Caribbean political collectivity" (20). In each case, the efficacy of sugar as a category of analysis depends on modernized conditions of production or the continued relevance of sugar as a global commodity.

Rum, when it is mentioned in discussions of sugar, remains a cipher for a superseded colonial past. Most frequently, rum is replaced by drugs as a dangerous foreign product, but rum can produce this opposition in other ways as well.[45] Neither Horn nor Gernalzick mention rum, but Mahler briefly explains that for a middle-class protagonist, drinking rum leads to alcoholism, which she reads as a figure for "a choice to turn away from political consciousness" rather than consolidate his identification with the workers. This reading seems logical, but from the perspective of rum poetics, the leap from rum to alcoholism plus regressive politics requires further analysis. Mahler seems to recognize this possibility in that she both quotes the novel's English translation ("everything is rum") and then repeats the phrase in her own prose, but she does not explicate further because the original Spanish *ron* does not carry the connotations of *rum* ("South-South Organizing" 19). One might argue, however, that the linguistic inflexibility of *ron* makes a statement like "todo es ron" even more interesting in the context of an analysis of Communist organizing (23n96). This repetition without explication is a shorthand, a reference so economical as to be obscure and obvious at the same time. This strategy joins the elision/substitution practice noted among earlier scholars of sugar as a phenomenon in literary-critical writing about rum, an issue I address specifically in the penultimate chapter of this study.

Rum is often rum when it appears in literature and other discourses engaging the Caribbean. As a method for unpacking this strangeness, rum poetics hews closer to Plasa's muscovado textuality and Morton's poetics of spice than to Döring's sugarcane poetics in that it concerns, as Morton states, "the political . . . within the minutest particulars of the poetic" (7), but it retains an emphasis on the circulation of texts that both Döring and Sandiford trace. Thus, rum poetics retains priorities identified by scholars of sugar, but it also recognizes that rum retains cultural associations with vice, libations, pollution, and the Caribbean that, for sugar, have either been lost or transmuted. "I was on a sugar high" registers differently, in terms of both shame and exculpation, than "I was drunk." People do not travel to the Caribbean expecting to eat sugar as part of regional culture. In dominant Western discourse, negative views of sugar concern obesity and diet, which does not obviate geographically specific scholarship on sugar any more than the existence of multinational alcohol conglomerates obviates rum's status as a Caribbean symbol. Rum poetics pursues, at the textual rather than the generic level, David Scott's recognition that "the colonial past may never let go" (220) and, in fact, may bind its subjects more tightly just as they announce their freedom from its demands. On the other hand, rum poetics identifies opportunities, mostly missed, for reparation and relationality. While these questions about subjectivity, agency, and embodiment echo abolitionists' attempts to promote ethical consumption, this approach articulates how rum circulates semiotically in new sociopolitical conditions emerging as European empires recede.

Rum Poetics: Economical Readings

Rum has a set of standard associations, many of which feed into a generalized, popular Caribbean imaginary and inhibit critical investigations of rum. To conclude, then, I want to consider how this popular imaginary appears and to suggest its resonance in critical discourse. Baz Dreisinger's essay "On a Tropical Rum Trail" appeared in the *New York Times* travel section in 2014, topped by a nearly 11 x 11 photo that fronts the print version of the article (fig. 2).

Pictured is a young Black woman relaxing in a hammock, glass in hand, solitary against a backdrop of crystal-blue water. The caption reads, "At Jake's hotel in Treasure Beach, Jamaica, a worker relaxes" (Dreisinger). This photograph draws on two visual traditions of depicting the Caribbean: first, those of planters reclining while enslaved workers labor and serve (see fig. 1) and, second, images of plantations and beaches from which photographers and artists erase labor (Strachan 84–85; Kutzinski 52). It also eliminates the presence of rum, the subject of Dreisinger's story. The visual rhetoric endows "a worker" with the pleasures of plantation

Figure 2. From "On a Tropical Rum Trail" by Baz Dreisinger, *New York Times*, February 23, 2014. Originally captioned "At Jake's hotel in Treasure Beach, Jamaica, a worker relaxes." (Photo/Piotr Redlinski)

slavery and Caribbean tourism. Her employment conditions are so comfortably paced and placed that her work is the vacation this travel piece promotes. Juxtaposed with the story's subtitle—"Touring three Caribbean islands, sip by sip, and taking in tales of blood, sweat, and sugarcane"— the article visually and textually renders rum's history a "tale" to be heard ("taking in") but not owned ("taking on"), a mode of consumption that Ian Baucom describes as "a melancholy but cosmopolitan romanticism" that allows viewers to "move on" after passively witnessing the scene (*Specters* 296). Capping this effect is the beer the worker drinks. This image, the centerpiece of an article on rum, does not venture to show a worker enjoying the fruits of her labor, erasing the accumulation of history that might link sophisticated rum-tasting tourists, tourist industry workers, and enslaved people. An artful reversal of images of pristine beaches occupied by a solitary sunbather, this image implies that when she is there, the tourist is not, and when the tourist is there, she is not.

This kind of disappearing act translates into images of rum in literary texts that mark erased, declined, or untraced connections. Critics, as seen above in the sugar literature, also decline to see what rum can disclose even when they mention it. In *Specters of the Atlantic* (2005), Baucom traces "a financializing, decorporealizing logic of equivalence" that he first identifies in a naval minute book detailing financial compensation given to "workmen of the empire" for lost body parts (6). He contrasts this accounting habit to the absence of similar compensation to enslaved people, bought and sold in a separate financial register. This contrast opens his study of the "specter of slavery" (7) and founds a revision of historical periodization. To demonstrate his point, Baucom balances the minute book against the logbook of the slave ship *Ranger* and provides the following summary of the evidence:

> For the crew, if we can reconstruct a portrait of their lives from these scant details, five months of boredom . . . one hundred fifty days of restlessness broken up by the intermittent raid on the ship's rum supply, the stray talk of mutiny, the intimidating of the human cargo mounting up below the decks. For the captain the greater stress of finding work to keep his men occupied, diverting them from rebellion, holding the crew in line and his ship in place as he builds his cargo with frustrating slowness, one or two slaves at a time, and works the calculus of profit and risk; too long at the coast and the talk of mutiny may convert itself into a real rebellion. . . . For the slaves? . . . For them, nothing unusual, nothing to make their terror, their captivity, their sorrow particularly

interesting, memorable, worth writing about. Nothing momentous. Just the typical. (14)

While Baucom professes outrage, he is not surprised. But consider how the tone moves from dismissiveness for the crew to empathy for the captain to outrage for enslaved men, women, and children. "Restlessness" and "boredom" among the crew, Baucom implies, is stressful, but not as stressful as for the overworked captain. The crew's actions Baucom assumes are largely aimless, as rebelliousness is only "stray talk" rather than legitimate complaint. By contrast, this summary attributes organized competence to the administrative leader. The logbook, however, tells a slightly different story. What Baucom translates as "intermittent raids on the ship's rum supply" is labelled "embezzling" in the ship's log (12)—a financial crime directed at corporate assets vital to the financialization on which Baucom bases his argument. It is possible to use rum to push the interpretation of the log toward one that credits the crew with greater strategic knowledge about their role in the slave trade than Baucom allows. I hope I can make this point without overestimating the probability that the crew actively frustrates trade in solidarity with the enslaved, or by denying the crimes—far beyond "intimidating"—crews *and captains* commonly committed against their so-called cargo. The attacks on rum, used to trade for slaves, may not be entirely hedonistic. In this reading, Baucom relies on rum to economize.

On Overreading

My disagreement with Baucom's reading here does not keep me from agreeing with other parts of his argument, and it might seem petty to call him out for an incident that covers four pages of a roughly four-hundred-page monograph. Yet it is precisely a transhistorical generalization about the morals of working-class alcohol use that allows rum to countersign stereotype, an interpretive practice that reinforces the murky divisions between some kinds of waged labor and enslaved labor as well as pitting lower-class white men and captured Africans against each other *necessarily and completely*—and with a minimum of semiotic effort.

This study grew in the shadows of the transformative theorizations of modernity and modernism enabled by the advance of postcolonial theory. However, to zoom in, as Susan Stanford Friedman recommends at the end of *Planetary Modernisms* (2015, 312), *Rum Histories* offers an angle of vision rather than a corrective lens. It is not my purpose to berate scholars who do not share my specific interest in rum, but this study interests itself in the dissemination of rum (and *rum*) in the texture of discourse and everyday life; I therefore dwell in some unlikely places, pulling normative discursive emphases askew. As readings toggle between the significance and insignificance of rum, often looking both ways at once, I replace economical shorthand with lavish spending that, given the paucity of prior information, may appear excessive—overreading, in fact. Following David Kazanjian, I suggest that charges of overreading can be a disingenuous form of institutional gatekeeping and propose instead to characterize the project of rum poetics as "speculative" (80). Delving into short scenes in larger works, yoking brief references to broader contexts, and examining scholarship as part of a network of signifying practices flatten hierarchies that insulate literary scholarship from its objects to illuminate a literal and metaphorical economy of reading rum. What does it mean to pull rum to the center and insist on its gravity? What can this practice reveal about the workings of texts that need rum to operate seamlessly as part of the scenery? What work is required to be accountable to and for rum's presence, to recognize consistently the histories that bring rum to be present, and to imagine how it might augur "post-" colonial futures?

Rum Histories: Where They Go

Thus far I have laid out the major historical, cultural, and economic structures that feed into the contemporary signification range of rum in literature, positing that these inflows make rum an economical image for capturing, condensing, and disseminating the anxieties of living with the systemic legacies of colonialism as a "post-" colonial subject in relation to other "post-" colonial subjects. Chapter 1 retraces some of this ground, but with a shift in the balance from context to textual representation. I describe the signification of rum in a panoply of texts, from canonical literature to historical surveys. The connections rum forges between novels set in Western Canada, Hawaii, upstate New England, Jamaica, and Dominica, as well as between literary texts and historical or secondary texts, demonstrate the semiotic currents rum carries across literary territories—some far removed from sites of production—and illuminating the consumption of Caribbean stereotypes even when the Caribbean is not a main subject or setting.

Chapters 2–5 divide along several axes to examine the interplay between individualized and systemic explanations for alcohol use as a form of investment in legacies of colonialism. Chapters 2 and 3 lean toward personal and interpersonal relationships and the potential for reparative readings of "the other," and readings focus heavily on gendered alcohol use in an intersectional context. These chapters continue to develop hitherto unrealized connections between texts scholars would define as products of the Caribbean or the Caribbean diaspora and texts defined as American (chapter 2) or British (chapter 3) because these cultures, as I have indicated earlier, largely share *gendered* norms for alcohol use. This similarity provides a useful point of departure from which to explore intersectional ramifications for relational and reparative thinking. Chapter 2, featuring V. S. Naipaul's *Miguel Street* and Hunter S. Thompson's *The Rum Diary* (written 1959, published 1998), articulates masculine ambition in the context of drinking as homosocial bonding, creating a tension between drinking as communality and the desire for cosmopolitan exceptionalism. Chapter 3 examines historical novels by Sylvia Townsend Warner (*The Flint Anchor*) and Jean Rhys (*Wide Sargasso Sea*) to chart an alternative semiotic economy of alcohol exchange among servants, women, and enslaved people that, in showing how the past could be different, recuperates a narrative space in which to envision a different future. These two chapters focus on texts produced during the height of decolonization, when the idea of being postcolonial had dates attached to it—one day there is a colony, the next a nation-state—and this official separation of the colonial past from the postcolonial present usefully illustrates the anxieties produced when real-time experience does not match official histories. The latter parts of these two chapters track the evolution of these paradoxes in more contemporary work, where tropes associated with rum migrate and intensify as they are redeployed to engage globalization and potentially resistant forms aligned with a Global South.

From regional and international comparisons, chapters 4 and 5 turn to focus exclusively on works produced by authors from the Caribbean and the Caribbean diaspora. I propose the figure of libations as a site where joint political purpose could lubricate movements toward a postcolonial world, but this potential is retarded by pathological readings of rum drinking. In chapter 4, novels about political action describe the process by which political activity is reframed as drunken chaos, either missing or rejecting joint recognition of the imprint of colonial legacies on present international, intercultural, or interpersonal relationships. Chapter 5 revisits this constellation metacritically, as a problem of reading in literary studies. By reengaging the phenomenon I trace in scholarship about sugar, I analyze the ways literary critics invoke rum as a critical aporia, present but unaccounted for, even when the text appears to call for rum as a site for critique. The undigested presence of rum in these critical arguments highlights what I have called an economical, rather than a critical, use of rum.

Despite the Caribbean settings of these novels, however, the authors in chapters 4 and 5 represent the reach of Caribbean representation in the Anglo-Atlantic. Only Earl Lovelace and Diana McCauley among these authors consistently reside in the Caribbean—a statement that has no bearing on their literary scope in any case. Michelle Cliff and Paule Marshall both lived in the United States, and their work is as likely—perhaps more likely—to appear in American literature courses as it is on Caribbean literature syllabi. George Lamming, like Naipaul, represents a literary field that becomes Black British writing. Sylvia Wynter's only novel, *The Hills of Hebron*, is set in Jamaica, but she was born in Cuba, spent significant time in England before obtaining an academic post in Jamaica and is arguably better known now as a philosopher and theorist based in California. As in prior chapters, the concluding section addresses a more contemporary text in which obscuring politics in a haze of rum reveals the difficulties of forging an inclusive "postcolonial" relationality as a result.

In the concluding chapter, I turn to the reification of rum poetics in mass media, balancing an examination of 2016 Trump/*rum* memes featuring Captain Jack Sparrow with an analysis of the film *Pirates of the Caribbean: Curse of the Black Pearl* and its catchphrase "Why is the rum gone?" I return to the notion that rum poetics can trace intensifications and condensations in the paradoxes of postcoloniality as the past transmutes into a future that does not yet look different enough, despite the siren calls of imperial nostalgia.

Rum captures conditions of postcolonial subjectivity because it models the structuring of agency by forces that are external and prior (histories of economic and political arrangements) and internal and current (incorporated as values and customs that appear coextensive with identity). Perhaps you are what you drink (or not). How external conditions are internalized as norms and expectations may be a mystery of digestion, but it is a disturbing realization, as it suggests we may act on desires we perceive as, but that are not, in fact, our own. When rum is rum, it may dissolve logic and crystallize reason, speak truth and lie to power, coerce and forge unions, encourage and quell resistance. The results of the postcolonial "hangover" are not entirely predictable. New readings may establish tenuous points of coalition among divided subjects, states, and cultures. These coalitions rely on telling rum (hi)stories together rather than apart, allowing the strange and surprising, the danger and the difficulty, to be a risk worth taking.

1 Rum's (In)significance

> First things first. The lurid title is misleading. Although the book contains a fair amount about sodomy, it has little, too little, about the lash, and, alas, nothing at all about the kill-devil rum.
> —Marcus Rediker, review of Hans Turley's
> *Rum, Sodomy, and the Lash*

ALAS, MARCUS REDIKER is correct. Hans Turley's *Rum, Sodomy, and the Lash* contains so little about rum that neither *rum, alcohol,* nor *drunkenness* rates a listing in the index. Nowhere is it written that titles must pedantically reflect the contents of a book, but that coy "alas" captures a melancholy knowingness about rum: so much promise, so much disappointment. In the background, the economy of rum purrs along. I have taken Rediker's opening flourish too seriously, of course. What if, however, a serious consideration of such offhand references were de rigueur? This chapter outlines the semiotic operations of rum that make it likely to be taken at face value rather than invested with extended analysis—the subject here is the significance of insignificance, and the insignificance of significance. Taking a cue from anthropology's concept of alcohol as time-out, I link alcoholic time-outs to interpretive time-outs that position Caribbean people and lands as out of time—out of history, out of politics, out of narrative—independent of discursive context. The sections of this chapter operate concentrically, starting from classic associations of rum with alcoholic disinhibition and eroticized violence and moving outward toward reflexive meditations on rum and national identity and, finally, rum and access to literary institutions that enable self-representation.

Rum Rules: Desire and Depravity

As described in the introduction, alcohol consumption signals disinhibition, and rum, because it is associated with the total control of human beings subjected to enslavement, has the uncanny effect of vilifying and permitting dehumanizing, often sexualized, violence. Rum helps to reclassify the rape and sexual coercion intrinsic to slavery as consensual, licensing the voyeur's—the reader's—gaze. Historical accuracy about the practices of slave owners allows pornography, and, to state the obvious, this violence is represented as dominantly heterosexual, and it is committed by white men against Black women. This point is worth emphasizing, for, as Michelle Stephens, Vera Kutzinski, and Belinda Edmondson (among others) have argued, decolonization does not have the necessary effect of empowering women as either national or literary citizens. These effects travel on rum's trading routes and across time, accumulating and condensing in the future.

Hal Underhill's lurid historical novel *Jamaica White* (1968) uses rum and marijuana as perverse libations to elevate sexual abuse to mystical eroticism. Protagonist James Arthur—newly arrived from England to take up a bookkeeping position on a plantation—declines to share the pleasures of town with overseer Broderick, establishing Arthur as the novel's moral center, but the narrative follows Broderick to his appointment with "three black women ranging in age from twelve to twenty" for a night of sex and drugs. The scene establishes the immorality of the Caribbean world in which Arthur finds himself, but it is presented as alcoholic time-out. Ganja and rum reposition the rape of a twelve-year-old girl into consensual, mind-blowing sexual "initiation." The girl experiences "mindless erotic joy," but the details of Broderick "poking at her as she moaned" and her pubic area "stinging" with rum as an anaesthetic suggest that the pleasures may be the perpetrator's rather than the girl's. The two older women endorse this process, offering to Broderick and his observers plausible deniability of responsibility for systemic sexual abuse and coercion (37).

Rum is part of the scenery, a supplementary indicator of the depravity intrinsic to a society built on enslavement. In Underhill's novel, it saturates a system of exploitation, running through the litany of ways rum kept plantations running: compensation for enslaved people, confirmation of jointly concluded business, and relief from the boredom and anxiety of plantation responsibilities (18, 11, 21). The scene described above passes under the guise of historical accuracy, but it has a phantasmal relationship with the 1960s as well, as the marijuana ties the scene anachronistically to hippie stereotypes. Both the historical and anachronistic references mask the fact that Broderick's recreation is work time for these women. In advancing this scene as, arguably, one of pleasure for all, Underhill proposes that exploitative relations are equitable, mutual experiences of pleasure; he perpetuates the misrecognition of submission to colonial power as equitable exchange.

Underhill, writing as decolonization was underway, exhibits a repugnance and fascination with England's Caribbean history that delivers rum, as it were, straight. Novels published later in the century invoke rum more self-consciously, as part of a set of tropes that enables domination and erases the suffering and abuse of enslaved people. In the 1992 novel *Indigo; or, Mapping the Waters,* by Marina Warner, the acknowledgment and dismissal of rum histories operates through the counterpointed plots of half-sisters descended from the inhabitants and colonizers of a fictional Caribbean island Liamauga (renamed Enfant-Béate, or Blessed Child). *Indigo,* itself one of many reinterpretations of *The Tempest,* features Miranda, who descends from both colonizer and enslaved populations of the island, and Xanthe, whose nickname, Goldie, signals her economic (wealth) and racial (blonde hair/whiteness) advantage. The birth of Xanthe disinherits Miranda, substituting neocolonialism for a new postcolonial world. Recapitulating colonial history as family history, Xanthe invests in heritage tourism to revive Liamauga's economy and stages a celebration of "the 350th anniversary of the landing of the pioneer planter Sir Christopher Everard, their ancestor" (264). Xanthe invokes the promises of Caribbean tourism and geniality in her invitation to Miranda: "Sun'n'sea! Rum'n'cokes! Rum'n'*tokes!*" (269, italics in the original). Xanthe's litany slips between neoimperial slogan and alcoholic time-out to loosen any substantive acknowledgment of the past. Miranda counters, internally, by restoring the horrors of the past to these tropes: "The slaves, the slaves. The sugar, the Indians who were there, . . . Feeny and Feeny's parents and grandparents. . . . The plantations. The leg irons and the floggings. Sugar. Sugar" (267). In her thoughts, Miranda tracks back to sugar, the dominant cash crop of plantation slavery, as the basis for the economic conditions of the present and she restores enslaved laborers and indigenous people to the narrative.

Miranda commits to the presence of this accumulated history as part of a working future in small-scale economic development in the metropolitan center. She marries Shaka Ifetabe, a restaurant owner whose "gleaming oiled cane rows" (366) make his body a living landscape of the past. Ifetabe has repurposed a Lyon's Corner Shop, emblematic of the English love of tea with sugar, to promote Afro-Caribbean foodways: "We serve, ah, Creole food, peas and beans and pepperpot just the way my grandmother used to make it—of course!—good music, and three hundred and ten varieties of rum" (371). Ifetabe counters Goldie's totalizing expansionism with local "variety," resisting the chain model of commodification inherent in Lyon's. But Miranda's localized happy ending does not model romantic overcoming, even when Xanthe dies attempting to save her investment from an island coup. Xanthe's properties survive and reconnect to the interests of a global, cosmopolitan elite: a specialty oyster Xanthe developed is "flying . . . out by the barrel in great shipments all over the area, of course, and further too," and the new government is establishing a Technical College with "hotel skills . . . still on the syllabus" (360–61).[1] *Indigo* recognizes that a postcolonial future is already here as "a *condition* . . . of having to live under [globalization's] rule (and rules) and survive" (López 7, italics in the original), yet just as ferociously the novel represents Scott's insight that "the colonial past may never let go" and indeed redoubles its profits at the sites of its defeat.

The Underhill and Warner examples chart a traditional metropole/periphery relationship between England, the heart of the British Empire, and its antipodal possessions, but the corrosive power of the slave economy circulates beyond these poles. Although rum is not a primary product of US slavery, it penetrates the American scene, North and South, to trope the immoral oppression of enslaved and indigenous women. In Toni Morrison's *A Mercy* (2008), the presence of rum in a Maryland tavern announces the intrinsic depravity of a society built on enslavement, indicting all engaged in trading slave-produced commodities. Morrison establishes the general case when Jacob Vaark, fresh from the objectionable negotiations with a Catholic slaveholder, "listen[s] to the talk around him, which was mostly sugar, which was to say, rum" (29). A soupçon of *rum*'s adjectival meaning animates Morrison's otherwise standard rehearsal of the trade relations Eric Williams describes in the epigraph to the introduction of this book. The emphatic placement of rum doubles as Vaark's commentary and Morrison's alert to ironies to come. The talk shifts to sugar plantations in the Barbados, and a local trader activates the tropes of hypersexualized sexual exploitation exemplified in *Jamaica White* with "a hilarious description of the size of the women's breasts in Barbados" in comparison with those of the local prostitutes (30). Vaark dismisses both stereotype and financial boasting as exaggerated, but the trader's response—"Rum rules, no matter who does the trading" (31)—draws on rum as currency and culture. This alliterative phrase settles on Vaark's earlier remark to suggest the strangeness of the rules and distantly chimes with America's "peculiar institution." Vaark's distaste for slaveholding does not stop him from deciding to "look into" the rum trade; if such profits are possible, moral discomfort with slavery is an inconvenience.

By following Vaark home to New England, Morrison proliferates the responsibility for slavery by demonstrating its reach and its role in exploiting indigenous populations. She travels Williams's trade routes. The story of Vaark's Native American servant Lina draws on temperance narratives (demon rum) and "drunken Indian" stereotypes to create sympathy for Lina lacking internal to the text. Lina is a typical abused spouse, who first excuses her husband's behavior as a fluke: "Only rum the first time because a man of his learning and position in the town would never dishonor himself so if sober" (104). Time-out! Lina's incantatory repetition of the excuse "rum I told myself it was rum" draws attention to the word *rum,* foreshadowing her recognition that spousal abuse is not, in fact, a product of drunkenness despite cultural narratives promoting that explanation. "There is no rum the second time nor the next," she thinks (104). Paradoxically, as James Nadelhaft concludes, standard temperance narratives bring attention to domestic violence without recognizing "a society which tolerated, perhaps even encouraged women's physical suffering" (38). Stereotypes of the drunk Indian redouble her victimization by blaming Lina and rendering the abuse invisible: "Because her eyes are closing she stumbles and people believe she is in liquor like so many natives and tell her so" (Morrison 104).[2] Morrison's concatenation of stereotypes exploits common knowledge and makes it strange, linking multiple locations and vectors of oppression (gender, indigeneity, enslavement, prostitution) through the circulation of rum in her narrative.

The circulation of rum to other locations, where it has explanatory power in locations that are not Caribbean, reflects globalized flows of culture and commerce. In Christopher Moore's 2003 comic novel *Fluke,* set among whale researchers in Hawaii, the character Kona, an ersatz Rastafarian, contextualizes the alcoholic rage of Tako Man, a Malaysian black-coral diver, as a legacy of slavery: "Rum. . . . Too much hostility in that buzz. Rum come from da cane, and cane come from slavin' the people, and dat oppression all distilled in de bottle and come out a man mean as cat shit on a day" (99). In fact, Kona's analysis is an accurate representation of, first, some outcomes of an accumulated history of oppression, and, second, the politics of Rastafarianism. It echoes arguments offered by scholars like Benítez-Rojo (*Repeating Island*) and Elizabeth DeLoughrey (*Routes and Roots* 7–9) about the proliferation of the plantation model and the interconnection of Caribbean and Pacific Island cultures, and it resonates with David Dabydeen's similar narration of a causal chain from enslavement to structural violence in "Introduction to *Slave Song.*"[3] In the mouth of a surfboard Marxist apparently guilty of cultural appropriation, the remarks land flat and pat. Moore trails the idea that plantation economics survive and persist in distant and superficially unrelated locations like Hawaii, but the emergence of the argument in quotation marks, as it were, allows its dismissal as a fluke. Yet the narrative proposes the relationships, and, reoriented in archipelagic scholarship, it is possible to connect these distant contexts.

To end a consideration of rum's association with bad behavior, I return to pirates, who take their stereotypical fondness for rum on adventures around the world through the urtext of twentieth-century piracy, Robert Louis Stevenson's *Treasure Island* (1883). Pirates, often depicted as "lawless" troops of sea-faring bandits, symbolize resistance to growing marine policing of the seas in the name of global trade, but pirates were often privateers, operating freelance in conjunction with the military for "political and patriotic purposes" (Yolen xiv). Pirates represent the most extreme version of excessive drinking as "a central feature of maritime communities" and "typical of Caribbean port towns" (F. Smith 138), creating a treasure trove of legendary exploits—some thrilling, many horrific. This notion of inappropriate consumption in hyperrealized alcoholic time-outs inflects the activities of the crew of the *Ranger* to point out the proximity of pirates to other maritime laborers and the economic rationale behind moral codes.

Treasure Island consolidates pirate stereotypes, including a rapacious quest for treasure, profligate spending, drunken violence, a tendency to treachery, a lamentable inattention to duty at critical times—and a devotion to binging on rum. Stevenson wrote "Dead Men's Chest," with its refrain "Yo-ho-ho, and a bottle of rum," for the novel. (*Pirates of the Caribbean*, preciously, includes the anachronism of Elizabeth Swann teaching this song to Jack Sparrow well before it was written.) The refrain appears in the opening pages of the novel, followed by the appearance of a suspicious "captain" demanding rum (11). Despite Doctor Livesey's admonition that "the name of rum for you is death" (16), the captain remains committed to his addiction: "I lived on rum, I tell you. It's been meat and drink, and man and wife, to me; and if I'm not to have my rum now I'm a poor old hulk on a lee shore" (18–19). Most famously in *Treasure Island*, the pirates left in charge of the *Hispaniola*, "plainly the worse for drink," allow young Jim to loosen the ship from its anchor (161). Still brawling, neither the shipboard watch nor their companions ashore singing "Dead Man's Chest" realize disaster until Jim's success is assured. There is nothing strange about the appearance of rum in *Treasure Island*. If rum renders a seasoned crew vulnerable to a mere boy, the lesson is clear. Circling back to Rediker's lament at the lack of rum in *Rum, Sodomy, and the Lash,* we must reckon with rum's romantic appeal to pleasurable chaos that is simultaneously antithetical, and essential, to the motivation of colonial subjects.

Rum and National Destiny

It may be hard to credit the notion that rum supports a progressive national imaginary, but both England and the United States include rum as part of a national progress narrative, downplaying its roots in slavery and jettisoning it in the transition to decolonization. The discourse around rum's role shifts as the United States becomes the dominant power in the region, eventually centering on the metaphor "rum and Coca-Cola." Representatives of Caribbean cultures take an ironic view of this practice, as the deployment of rum in national narratives positions the Caribbean as chaotic and primitive.

H. Warner Allen's 1934 jingoistic booklet *Rum* captures the twin elements that characterize nationalist discourses of rum: rum's role in the development of the nation and the civilizing effects rum can have, in the proper hands. Allen associates rum with "the true spirit of adventure" because it "calls up heroic memories of the iron seamen who on their lawful and unlawful occasions built up the British empire overseas" (3). He points to the military's daily ration of rum as a source of power, but he slides over the evidence that rum initially "was a drink for the slaves" produced as part of England's slave economy (8). Instead, he offers an anecdote to show rum is part of Britain's antislavery activities: "Rum and slaves have been connected . . . by a far more humane memory" of Allen's father reviving dying slaves found in an Arab dhow (19). This kind and civilized treatment reflects the moderating and uplifting qualities of English or British rums (Allan shifts his adjective over the course of the booklet) in comparison to alcohols associated with other nations. He excoriates the "cheap Gin of the most noxious quality" made by the Dutch (15) and describes American rum as "a base spirit which had no honest claim to the name" (18–19). He disputes the US claim, promulgated by Charles William Taussig in *Rum, Romance, and Revolution* (1928), that rum is an American alcohol (Allen 19). By contrast, "real Rum" (19) is a "most warm and comforting spirit" that supports the physical and mental health of Britons, whether they face the humidity and heat of the tropics (4) or the "cold and rain" of England (30). Whether straight, or mixed with such elements as hot milk, tea, or the ingredients of punch, rum creates conviviality and solidarity among genteel Englishmen (not women).[4] Allen's nostalgic portrait renders rum an engine of imperial

England's civilizing mission, as Englishmen model appropriate drunken comportment for the rest of the world.

This rhetoric emerges in force at the end of the twentieth century, when the Royal Navy announced the end of the rum ration (or "tot"), a three-hundred-year-old tradition, as of August 1, 1970. The navy first proposed this change in 1958, at the height of decolonization and two years after the Suez Crisis; in 1970 decolonization was largely an achieved fact, although it took a variety of forms. Those protesting the policy objected that "teetotal cost-benefit analysis did not win and would not have won Trafalgar" ("Mean-Spirited and Modern" 9) or connected the tot to "duty,/To country and the throne" (qtd. in Gingell 1)—nostalgia, in a word. On the other hand, the secretary of the navy argued that the ration was inappropriate for the navy's current mission: daily drinking on duty endangers "efficiency" when operating "complex and often delicate machinery" (Gingell 1). Admiral of the Fleet Lord Hill-Norton called the ration "an anachronism," and Admiral Sir Frank Twiss stated that "rum, with its aura of the days of sail, does not help our 'image'" (qtd. in R. Moore 71, 72). The debate pits modernization and technology against tradition, with the naval leadership on the side of progress. An attachment to the rum ration demonstrates a nostalgia for British imperial strength long gone. The cessation positions the navy, and the nation, as postcolonial because the modernized navy is no longer in thrall to systems and habits of bygone eras.

Similarly, the United States claims rum as central to its nation-building narrative, but shifts into a nostalgic mode to signal its status as a world power and advanced society. Rum is an important part of Revolutionary War iconography: it is relatively common knowledge that Paul Revere stopped in Medford for "two drafts of rum" before heading off to do his duties with lanterns (qtd. in Burns 27). Rorabaugh reports that drinking heavily could be associated with an anticolonial stance: "A man who drank alone could feel not only free but independent and self-sufficient" (166). Further, during Revolutionary times, "rum was the currency of the age" (64). Like Eric Williams, Rorabaugh emphasizes rum's fungibility as a commodity and centrality to the growing economy of the thirteen colonies, with the result that the Navigation Acts made rum a byword for anti-British protest. This argument is borne out in titles like Charles William Taussig's *Rum, Romance, and Rebellion* (1928) and Ian Williams's *Rum: A Social and Sociable History of the Real Spirit of 1776* (2005).[5] Taussig insists "without doubt" that *rum* is an American word, implying that rum is an American liquor (4)—the line that later causes Allen fits. While

Taussig addresses rum's essential role in slavery and slave trading, he, like Allen, notes that its "sweet aromatic redolence . . . , a mystic charm, a soft soothing fragrance that beguiles one into forgetting its more sinister and vicious history" (Taussig 3–4). In the post–Civil War United States, there is a desire to move past a practice contrary to American principles.

Despite these early associations with freedom and independence, rum declines as an American spirit in the nineteenth century. Abolitionists, as seen in the introduction, excoriated rum for perpetuating slavery, and this negative association merged with temperance movements to create "demon rum." Economic forces converged with moral ones to make rum less attractive as a symbol for the new nation. American rum distillers suffered when European nations choked off trade with the new nation. In these new conditions, rum was now identified with colonialism, and locally produced forms of alcohol become symbolic of the American spirit (Rorabaugh 66–67). Further, there were concerns that an inebriated populace made for a dysfunctional national culture. Concerns about the threat that rum, and alcohol generally, posed to American democracy are chronicled in Matthew Osborn's *Rum Maniacs* (2014), a study of "intemperance as a dire threat to the nation's physical and moral health and a pressing danger to fragile republican institutions" (2). Progress requires a sober citizenry. In closing his study, Taussig reconciles the importance of rum to the creation of the United States by stressing its developmental importance: "The Rum Epoch was but a manifestation of erring humanity, and, though we still make similar mistakes, it is encouraging to realize that we are slowly shaking ourselves free from our smug self-satisfied past" (252). In the mythos of an endlessly progressing, perfectible American nation, commentators situate rum's positive associations and negative consequences in the past.

The narratives promulgated for the United States and England exist in tension with an acknowledgment that rum is an alcohol sourced in the Caribbean and historically produced by enslaved Africans and, later, Indian and Chinese immigrants. Caribbean commentators thus view the association of rum with Caribbean cultures with a more jaundiced eye, recognizing the mixed messages and motives that govern the manipulation of rum as a symbol. Around 1940, the Trinidad humor magazine *Picong* published "With Me Rum in Me Head" by Jean De Boissière, in which the author argues that middle-class nationalists have missed an obvious source on which to base claims of a unique Trinidadian culture: the rum shop. Paired with the anonymous "Cocktail Politics" that follows, *Picong* undermines the feminized Anglocentrism of political elites who seek legitimacy by mimicking their former overlords. De Boissière argues that instead of considering rum shop patronage "a degrading habit," Trinidad should exploit it as "a native Trinidad culture" that will "let the rest of the world follow our culture instead of us pretending to other people's cultures" (18). De Boissière invokes cultural independence and equality, much as Taussig and Allen do, by attributing the distaste for rum shops to class prejudice and mimicry. De Boissière closes by eliding *rum* with *culture:* your boss, he says, "wants to get you as cock-eyed as he can so as to seal your mouth the next time you happen to run into him in the club when he has been overcome by the culture" (18). Set with the imperialist accounts of rum from the prewar era, De Boissière's essay intimates the intransitive nature of colonialist rhetoric for a postcolonial age; to put it another way, the patterns Keith Sandiford (*negotium*) or Tobias Döring (sugarcane poetics) identify as promulgating colonialism to metropolitan audiences do not invert to promote Trinidadian nationalism abroad. The dignity of peasant experience and the cooperative communality of the rum shop does not signal modernity and competence on an international stage.

Twenty years later, Trinidadian V. S. Naipaul would cast a similarly skeptical eye on rum as a Caribbean symbol. At the beginning of *The Middle Passage: The Caribbean Revisited* (1962), a passing reference to rum effectively contrasts metropolitan, modern England with the recycled culture of Trinidad: "In the baby's basket one saw the things of England, a few minutes ago commonplace, now the marks and souvenirs of the traveller: a bottle of Lucozade, the plastic baby bottle (in the West Indies it would have been a small rum bottle), the tin of baby powder" (2). These emigrants, returning to the West Indies after a sojourn in England, carry the markers of modern childcare: products designed especially for baby. In the West Indies, necessity is the mother of invention. Because he understands the significance of the difference, Naipaul authenticates himself as a cultural insider and a translator to legitimate the forthcoming travelogue. But there is a whiff of Hogarth's *Gin Lane* in Naipaul's description: What kind of mother repurposes such a morally incongruous item as a rum bottle to nurture an infant? Practically, Naipaul marks the exigencies of subsistence, but he also marks the technological distance between London, the world of plastic bottles and Lucozade, and the West Indies, littered with rum bottles.[6] The ensuing travelogue, a chronicle of mismanagement, poverty, ignorance, and disorder, fulfills the expectations created by his parenthetical remark. Naipaul documents colonialism and slavery as the root of this dysfunction, but the moral smear on West Indian culture remains.

The emergence of the "rum and Coca-Cola" metaphor to describe twentieth-century relations between the Caribbean Islands and the United States, although rooted in satire, has become a shorthand phrase that mystifies the exploitative character of US foreign policy in the region. The phrase originates as the title of Lord Invader's 1943 calypso "Rum and Coca-Cola," a satire on Trinidad's relationship with the United States during World War II. The well-known story of Morey Amsterdam stealing, and profiting hugely, from the song during the war illustrates the ironies Lord Invader marked in his calypso.[7] The song critiques, as Nicole Waligora-Davis explains, "the coupled power and privilege marshalled in the Yankee dollar" as it affected the economy—particularly the sexual economy—of Trinidad because G. I. wages were incommensurate with local pay rates (201). Waligora-Davis argues that the calypso's original satire of US power is depoliticized, transferred to US popular culture, and redeployed as a national anthem that legitimates US "superiority" and influence in the Caribbean region (203). Waligora-Davis's argument tracks with observations forthcoming about the phrase *rum and Coca-Cola* in that she shows the role of deracination from historical context in depoliticizing a frame of reference; once deracinated, the item (here, a calypso) can be made to serve a very different set of national interests. This process also works within the song: the Andrews Sisters version avoids direct references to prostitution by transforming the women into "beach vendors selling rum and Coca-Cola to presumably thirsty US-American men" (Waligora-Davis 202), a shift that replaces sexual exploitation with mutually beneficial libations. Thus, the sanitized Andrews Sisters version of "Rum and Coca-Cola" leads into the ways the phrase migrates into other discourses about Caribbean relations with the United States, condensing a range of stereotypes about sex, race, and money into three economical words.

Although the song "Rum and Coca-Cola" refers to a specific historical moment in Trinidad, the phrase *rum and Coca-Cola* now refers to the United States and "the Caribbean" rather than any specific island or historical moment. As Charles Coulombe remarks, it "can be seen as a potent symbol of a changing world order—the marriage of rum, lubricant of the old colonial empires, and Coca-Cola, icon of modern American global capitalism" (97–98). Rum, which the United States had claimed as an iconic product, is now exclusively Caribbean, juxtaposed to the "modern" soda. The conjunction *and* implies equality, and Coulombe's use of the term *marriage* exposes a host of additional inequities that may be built into the semiotics of this phrase. "Rum and Coca-Cola" survives its immediate frame to become a deceptive economical shorthand for US-Caribbean relations. References can be ironic, but superficial, as in Ralph de Boissière's novel *Rum and Coca-Cola* (1956), which chronicles the impact of and resistance to America's presence without making rum specifically relevant in either plot or imagery. More insidious is Robert Freeman Smith's use of the phrase in his Twayne history of US-Caribbean relations, subtitled *Mixing Rum and Coca-Cola* (1994). Smith promotes racism as he promotes democracy when he speaks of local rums and their relationship to Coca-Cola: "The light rum of Bacardí makes a most palatable Cuba Libre . . . , but the dark and heavy Appleton rum from . . . Jamaica produces a drink resembling old-fashioned cough medicine. . . . Some cultural elements blend and harmonize—others clash" (91). Smith's promotion of Cuban rum as "light" affiliates skin color with an affinity to democracy in contrast to a "clash" with "dark and heavy" Jamaica. Likewise, Walter Russell Mead deploys the phrase to question the wisdom of Cuban resistance to American economic models: "The revolutionary wine has been drunk; and the revolutionary hangover has set in. After 35 years of heroic struggle, the tourists are back. . . . Cuba stormed the barricades of Heaven; now it pours rum and Coca-Cola for foreign tourists, working for the Yankee dollar" (30).[8] Cuba's resistance to free markets has, nonetheless, led to a fitting national end for all Caribbean islands: a tourist economy with no claim to the status of historical actor. Mead evinces a kind of schadenfreude in Cuba's economic disappointment. Much better, he implies, to have prostituted to the "Yankee dollar" to begin with.

Phyllis Shand Allfrey's "Antique Romance"

The inevitability of a future dominated by the United States—specifically a white United States that rehabilitates white colonial dominance in modern ways—plays a pivotal role in the way Phyllis Shand Allfrey depicts rum in *The Orchid House* (1953). Her novel, like Jean Rhys's *Wide Sargasso Sea*, explores these issues at a historical distance. Allfrey sets her novel after World War I rather than World War II to critique England's declining investment in its Caribbean possessions as a betrayal of the beneficent white population. In this text, habitual rum drinking by Black people is a sign of cultural primitivism, while among white men, addiction is a historical and personal coping mechanism for the contraction of Europe's imperial mandate. *The Orchid House* unites the lost generation novel with the "antique romance" of imperial nostalgia (Naipaul, "Dog's Chance") to lament an imperial future that should have been.[9]

There are two generations of addicted Young Masters depicted in *The Orchid House,* and their attenuated futures indict decolonization plans that transfer productive white control to a disorganized Black mob. Neither the Young Master (son of the Old Master) nor Andrew (representing the next generation) can equal the exercise of noblesse oblige modeled by the Old Master in an atmosphere of weakened commitment from the metropolitan government to the white bodies and institutions that govern the colonies. The Young Master returns from World War I shell-shocked, unfit for his hereditary duties, and the narration implies that the British government has not adequately conserved and protected his body during an imperial war for an imperial future. The narrator states the Young Master flew "a very old-fashioned aeroplane" that "of course . . . crashed" (149–50). If these "diabolical machines" (179) signify the dangers of twentieth-century progress, they are also outdated—a paradox that captures anxieties about the future of the colonies as colony-metropole relations are revamped. While the Master's family complains about English colonial policy, they are not receptive to an expansion of political action in the majority-Black population. Demonstrators demanding self-government and better wages under the guise of union organizing are perceived as ungrateful, disorganized, and disingenuous. The assault on white Creole power from the metropolis and the local population destroys the body of the Young Master, whose traumatic experiences in World War I lead to drug addiction. Metropolitan policy (the war) damages his body and mind, which subsequently drains financial health from the family to feed his addiction to opium-laced cigarettes, which are supplied by Mr. Lilipoulala from Haiti.[10] The spectral presence of the Haitian Revolution—perceived by whites as chaotic racialized violence that could spread from island to island—links current political movements in Dominica to long-standing fears of slave revolts.[11]

Andrew, suffering from tuberculosis, portends the melancholy future of white male rule in the colony. He represents the next generation of patriarchs and suitable husbands for the Young Master's three daughters, each of whom admits being in love with him at one time or another. He also represents social decline as a racial decline because he generates his income in ways proximate to those of Black men. "Andrew laughed heartily at the recollection of how he cheated the stupid old drunk violinist," the narrator reports. "Just as the boatmen and guides laughed when they cheated the well-to-do tourists; but his laughter sounded hollow and came from the back of his chest" (54). He self-medicates with "weak rum punch" (72), which is considered a problem because it damages his prospects.

Drinking among Black characters, on the other hand, is culturally endemic and impervious to change. In contrast to Andrew's tuberculosis, a problem to be solved with medication beyond rum, Lally's use of rum to palliate a cancerous tumor passes as normal for the white folk. The cook, Christophine, is an alcoholic, a fact the family tolerates with humor.[12] Lally reports early in the novel that she found Christophine "lying under the dresser, dead drunk" (7), but the Master's daughter Joan romanticizes Christophine's drinking, telling her, "You still smell so beautifully of rum" (102). Servants are also humiliated for associating the family with pervasive local drinking cultures. Buffon must apologize for leaving a donkey, which the grandchildren ride, outside a rum shop: "I never tie-up that donkey outside a rumshop again, jamais, jamais" (142). Attempts to curtail alcoholism or excessive drinking are ridiculed: "Baptiste had gone out to the kitchen, perhaps to read his mother the article on *Rum-our Ruin*. Now and again he used to try to reform her: but she took it very kindly. It generally ended by his having a shot of rum himself—just one" (89). Even the invocation of temperance literature places Baptiste on a delayed historical path compared to his white counterparts; Joan aspired to promote temperance as a child, but she has moved on to labor organizing. Rum drinking, its various consequences and its motivations—from blackouts to inadequate medical care—appears habitual, attributed to racial cultural norms rather than to historical or material conditions.

The juxtaposition of rum and race undermines Afro-Caribbean political action by activating stereotypes of drunken people of color and justifies the escape of white Creoles into "post-" colonial modernity figured spatially, as the United States, rather than temporally. Joan's organizing advice to local activists is for naught because their resolution disintegrates into requests "for drink: Baptiste satisfied them with rum and water" (151). As Haiti's revolutionary spirit is reduced to a dangerous drug, local activism disguises a desire for rum, undermining the seriousness of labor organizing and socialist thought that characterizes the interwar period. Allfrey's novel manipulates a trope used to discredit political action among working classes as drunken chaos in a specific geographical context. This trope has already been noted as shaping interpretations within and external to texts; in chapter 6, this trope is given more expansive analysis as one that retards a relational reading of political novels from or about Caribbean islands.

The Orchid House resolves the tension between an expiring white future and an emergent Black future by substituting geography for time. At the conclusion, a modern airplane flies the Young Master and Andrew to advanced medical treatment in the United States. The United States will restore their white bodies to full functionality so that they are neither dependent on an outmoded economy—represented by "weak rum"—nor polluted by insinuating natives. This is white flight in its most literal form. Lally is left behind with her tumor—and to medicate with her bottle of rum.

When Titles Are Rum: Postcolonial Literary Worlds?

The balance of this chapter has focused on rum as a product, an alcoholic beverage associated with slavery, that, when present, permits a strategic assignation of time-out to the interactions that occur under its influence. Rum's typical signifying range overlaps strongly with that of alcohol, and its roots in slavery both titillate and shame. Some of the examples, like Morrison's *A Mercy*, invite a metacritical approach to *rum* by introducing its adjectival meaning into instances that appear to signify as nouns, but most of these examples rely on an ideologically smooth operation to efface inconsistencies. Rum poetics disrupts these operations to examine their effectiveness in positioning, and repositioning, Caribbean locations and subjects as untimely, out of time, or superseded by historical progress. What happens when entire texts function, as it were, under the sign of rum? A claim that a text thus positions itself against interpretation seems ludicrous. Paulette Jiles's anonymous heroine argues that sitting in the club car drinking rum and Karma-Kola is a political act of deliberate waste operating in transnational solidarity with "Third World" protests against structural debt. Similarly, the protagonist of Barry Unsworth's *Sugar and Rum* (1988), novelist Clive Benson, might argue that his entire story is a series of encounters with Liverpudlians who resist interpreting the Thatcherite present as *in any way* a product of Britain's slave-owning, sugar-producing past. Uniquely woke as these heroes appear to be, their plots illustrate economies of privilege that reform and reconfigure to accommodate resistance, dragging down reparative impulses in the plots.

Jiles's experimental detective novel, *Sitting in the Club Car Drinking Rum and Karma-Kola: A Manual of Etiquette for Ladies Crossing Canada by Train* (1986), posits an alliance between feminist and anticapitalist/ postcolonial activism. If the heroine anticipates forms of transnational coalition that could energize global social justice movements, the modes and scope of exploitation are incommensurate. The heroine's generalized equivalences between her personal experience of sexism *in* the United States and neocolonial exploitation *by* the United States make for what the narrator calls an "engaging and oddly believable" story (9) that undoes itself from within. The novel begins in the realm of a media economy, as the protagonist works for a media company that defines "a good story" on the basis of the subject who tells it: the heroine's idea is rejected because "*researchers aren't supposed to have good story ideas*" (49–50, italics in the original). Her outrage reverberates to include other groups underemployed and disadvantaged by global capitalism, from "Thousands of women in offices!" (50), to "single mothers who crash their fists" on ATMs, to citizens of Central America whose dollars she will "liberate" from abstractly envisioned "American money" (11).[13] The anthropomorphization of money subjects identity to economic value, making the protagonist's plan "to run up debts of Third World proportions" (50) an act of political alliance and political exploitation. In the heroine, Jiles reactivates a long-standing trope in feminism—that of the feminist who capitalizes on the suffering of racialized others to forward her own cause. It is possible to draw these lines of equivalence, as Gayatri Spivak makes clear, without meaningful investment in the agency of these others. Thus, while Susan Brown links Jiles's experimentation with narrative to a critique of "the power of the texts, the stories, and the conventions which are allied to economic imperialism" (399), the devil is in the details.

The title of the novel points to those details as it cites the location (club car), activities (drinking rum and Karma-Kola), and subject position (lady) that mark the limit, or perhaps "etiquette," governing her resistance. A drink at the club car bar is a break for the protagonist and her analytical romantic interest/pursuer, from the existential reflections on narrative and performance that characterize the novel. The Jamaican bartender registers the reemergence of noir clichés: "*Another train romance*" (77, italics in the original). His internal ruminations mock the heroine's participation in transnational resistance to globalization:

> The bartender wonders who the story really belongs to—to himself, the marginal observer who is so dignified and deferential that nobody even notices his deference; to the porters, who make up the beds; to the women on the train who support the work of loving and of conversations without even knowing they're doing it; or the white men who seem to be locked in privilege—or if a story is property at all and can be owned? The bartender is reticent and Jamaican, and so nobody has inquired enough to know that his mind is a sailboat made of magical disturbances, like all minds; and it is sailing sideways through the moving universe under a Genoa jib and full main. But the Americans want him to be The Butler again in their endless game of Clue. (77)

The heroine fails to notice the bartender except as a prop, but the bartender underlines the heroine's geographical blind spot, which allows her to act globally without thinking locally. Her desire to figure as a feminist femme fatale fatigues him as much as the generalized "Americans" casting him as the inevitably guilty party. He extends her critique of privileged storytellers, theorizing stories as "property" derived from systemic forces that locate some subjects as labor supporting someone else's plot and others, like "the white men" and "Americans" and even the heroine subjected to the feminine "work of loving and of conversations." By putting a *noir* in *noire*, the novel registers both the justice and the limitations of the heroine's analysis.[14]

Thus "Rum" in the novel's title riffs on the "rum and Coca-Cola" metaphor for globalization, highlighting the heroine's interest in the multinational dynamics of corporate exploitation. However, analysis of the novel as postcolonial critique overlooks the presence of a Jamaican immigrant on the train. Susan Brown gestures toward, but does not digest, this connection when she appends a sentence on rum to her discussion of Gita Mehta's *Karma-Cola* (1979), to which Jiles alludes in her title. Although Brown rightly understands Jiles's allusion to Mehta as "a reminder of north-south relations" and a generic link to Mehta's "witty postcolonial satire" (398), she leaves unstated the implications of rum: "And with the simple addition of a dash of spirits to make one of eastern Canada's favourite drinks, Jiles also works in rum, historically one of the key cargoes in Canadian colonial trade routes" (398). This verb choice—"works in"—only vaguely characterizes the relationship of rum to the novel's major themes, reducing rum to a flourish or a dash. Brown's critique reifies the generalizing practices that allow the heroine of the novel to identify with imagined Hondurans but not the man mixing her drinks. Rum poetics, attending to the presence of rum, inserts the bartender's "magical disturbances" into the novel and its critiques, "sailing sideways" to the protagonist's anticapitalist, antglobalization plot that nevertheless leaves some conventions untouched.

As Jiles points to stories unnoticed and unimagined, Unsworth examines the role of literary culture in suppressing or constraining these stories.[15] The novel delineates the joint between general cultural resistance to the stories of the "lamentably alien" (Said 207) and the concrete manifestation of this resistance in publishing networks. The novel follows Clive Benson, a respected author suffering temporarily from writer's block, who ekes out a living as a literary consultant to a group of writers he dubs "Benson's Fictioneers" (*Sugar and Rum* 9). The possessive in the title is both anxious and patronizing: anxious because writer's block has made Benson vulnerable to slipping out of the category of author, and patronizing because he believes only one of the writers to be publishable. The writers represent various oppressed groups and devalued literary genres: Miss Jennifer Colomb is a spinster who writes anachronistic historical romance; Hogan is a middle manager obsessed with confessional autobiography; a working-class "retired builder" exceeds publishable length with a six-hundred-page opus; and Anthea is an angry young female poet. The final Fictioneer, the only one whose work Benson admires, is Elroy Palmer, a young Black man with dreadlocks who writes science fiction. As clients, the Fictioneers acknowledge Benson's authority, but they also ignore and circumvent him. They submit work, but they do not pay regularly. They allow his critiques but challenge his judgment by creating alternative audiences. For example, Benson cannot identify "a very complicated pun" in one of Anthea's poems, but Hogan gives a fluent and immediate explication of this "feminist poem" (85). As they acknowledge each other's stories, the Fictioneers develop from flat to rounded: Hogan's "face [loses] some of that terrible stiffness," and Anthea "look[s] at him [Hogan] like the first woman looking at the first man" (85). What Benson views as comic could be, in fact, a new world: "Are you a writer too?" Anthea asks Hogan (85). Their mutual recognition points to a world in which literary value no longer requires Benson's imprimatur.

    This emerging literary marketplace is, as the title of the novel indicates, "post-" colonial in that it divests masculinity and whiteness of literary privilege. Benson's writer's block stems from what is for him a surprising discovery: the saturation of his everyday life with riches obtained from the slave trade. As Benson researches the slave trade, its durée and its integration into the quotidian life and landscape in which he currently lives horrifies him: slavery "went on so long, I couldn't think of it just as an historical episode" (221). His home comforts, he realizes, depend on this history. His apartment in an eighteenth-century home "pleased and soothed him" with its "elegance" and "restraint," but this calm exterior is funded by "that fear the black people must have felt, taken from their forest homes, thrust into the open, exposed to the wide sky, the terrible surf" (52–53). Broadening his view, Benson sees the devastated urban landscape of Thatcherite Liverpool as poetic justice, a direct result of the city's role in the slave trade. Benson confronts a question Jane Marcus ponders— "who may write safely about whom" (58)—and he is silenced, forecasting the fate of some white male authors should their privilege be eroded by changing sociopolitical norms. Unsworth embeds this recognition in the novel's title, taken from the Cowper poem "Pity for Poor Africans."[16] Benson quotes from this poem during the novel, linking the privilege of authorship to the economics of slave trading.

This recognition leaves Benson with a story no one wants to hear. Although Suzanne Keen argues that Benson's personalization of historical responsibility creates "an incommunicable hyper-specialization" (116) that other characters in the novel do not understand, the responses to Benson's ideas suggest otherwise. Benson's assertion that current English people remain guilty of slavery's crimes alienates his intended readers: the educated, professional classes who might read novels of a serious stamp and lament England's historical role in slavery and slave trading. A history master judges as "fanciful" and lacking "a balanced view" (*Sugar and Rum* 42) a scene Benson has imagined about the formation of William Gladstone's political views: "It is quite conceivable that little William Ewart, out with his nurse," Benson has told him, "would have seen strange metal objects. . . . What is that, nurse? That is a branding iron, dear, so they would know who the slaves belonged to. And that is a pair of iron handcuffs, and that is a thumbscrew" (42). In the face of a resisting reader, Benson escalates his rhetoric, comparing the death tolls of slavery to those of the Holocaust (violating a cultural taboo that prohibits equivalences among genocides). The reader, as it were, closes the book: "Without replying the man began to walk away from him" (42). Likewise, Benson's casual remark that an eighteenth-century mansion was probably "built on the proceeds of the slave trade" draws a terse denial from the society matron who owns it (168). Benson's white readers resist acknowledging that current comforts rely on Liverpool's slave-trading past.

Benson's search for a more receptive audience, however, illustrates the limits of his revisionism and links him to Jiles's heroine; he is willing to speak for the subaltern but not with the subaltern. Benson seeks less resistant readers, "human creatures who would listen to him without offering insult or launching into rival monologues of their own" (14). His chosen readers are "mainly men, mainly black, mainly out of work" who remain mainly silent in the face of this narrative stream, emitting an occasional groan that Benson interprets as agreement (6). The groans, simultaneously physical and aural, may protest the imposition of uncongenial narratives without creating further vulnerability.[17] Evidence from one listener seems to confirm this possibility. Benson designates "a fattish, serene-looking middle-aged negro" (6) as an appropriately passive receptacle for his account of a suicide's symbolic meaning, but the man rejects

Benson's interpretative model: "You talking about stages. No stages there, man. When he jump off, that the end of the story" (7). Benson, in a move that anticipates the society matron and the history master, decides that his "smiling" companion is not feeling "very well" (7).[18]

One of Benson's Fictioneers, Elroy Palmer, confounds Benson's simultaneous desire to engage with slavery's history while also controlling how slavery is represented in literature. Palmer represents the postcolonial author of the future in his choice of genre: science fiction. Palmer impresses Benson with his "determination and a strong sense of literary vocation," but Palmer refuses filial models of influence (95). In this sense, his relationship with Benson mirrors patterns among modernist writers and their postcolonial protégés.[19] Palmer listens to Benson's feedback perfunctorily, anticipating praise and criticism as a kind of narrative trope: "He said nothing in reply to Benson's comment, merely nodded slowly in full agreement. There was a certainty about Elroy which was impressive" (95). Palmer also confounds Benson's desire for control by withholding parts of his manuscript and then wrong-footing him. Palmer illustrates the contingency of literariness, as Benson's speculations are inevitably wrong for Palmer's story. Benson suggests that killing a character, Jarrold, with a curved knife would be poetic justice, but Palmer asserts an alternative history in which "they talked a lot about it. . . . It had to be the right symbol. . . . He is killed by what he loves too much" (124). Jarrold, in other words, is killed not by resistance but by a deadly compliance. Palmer's evocation of a long discussion also suggests that these stories have circulated for a long time, perhaps even in plain sight. Like the buildings of Liverpool and the colonial British immigrants who have flocked to England, a postcolonial future is already present because of a colonial past.

While Benson genuinely *means* to help Elroy Palmer, he puts him off. Benson's judgment of the hero Zircon applies equally to Palmer: "Here was a man in the remote future, bubbling with lethal laughter, about to act, to break out, to restore the world" (125). The emphasis on "remote future" reassures Benson of a slow death for metropolitan cultural authority, but the Fictioneers move from story to action in the now.[20] Encouraged by their new narratives, the Fictioneers cooperate to resist dubious inscriptions of white English nationalism on local landscape.[21] When Benson tells them about a plan to reenact a medieval battle, the Fictioneers plan a protest beyond Benson's intentions, leaving Benson to stutter, "Now wait a minute—" (234). They become joint authors of the plan, and Benson must surrender his leadership to the cooperative imagination of the group. Although the novel foreshadows the "resurrection" of these nationalist efforts (246), it models the energies of a genuinely resistant literary culture.

This novel depicts literary culture under the sign of sugar and rum, but in Unsworth's canon *Sugar and Rum* figures as a time-out from the serious business of historical novel–writing. The book jacket promotes the novel as "tantalizingly semi-autobiographical" because this chronicle mimics the experience of Unsworth, who published a novel about the slave trade, *Sacred Hunger*, in 1992.[22] *Sacred Hunger* won the Booker Prize, instancing the well-worn ironies of a literary prize funded, historically, by plantation slavery (Huggan, "Prizing 'Otherness'" 414–15). The link between the "real" Barry Unsworth and his fictional counterpart invites reflection on the fetishistic consumption of historical fiction as a reification of colonial control. For example, the Booker Prize, which *Sacred Hunger* shared with Michael Ondaatje's *The English Patient* in 1992, has been accused of exploiting a market for the postcolonial "exotic" in both content and authorship. Graham Huggan claims that the apparent "*revisionist* critique" of empire in many Booker-winning texts "masks a *revivalist* ideology" that, in fact, reinvigorates the power dynamics of colonization in the postcolonial period ("Prizing 'Otherness'" 420, italics in the original). And yet, like Benson's "unwelcome" narrations of the slave trade into Liverpudlian history (Keen 112), *Sacred Hunger* seems like an unwelcome Booker Prize winner. It does not parley revision into revival, and it is not sexy. According to a review in the *Independent,* the novel, one and a half inches thick in paper and morose in tone, is "not really the sort of book one is inclined to pick up" (Rabinovitch and Quinn 17). The novel does not engage in the pyrotechnics of history and satire characteristic of Salman Rushdie's *Midnight's Children* (1981), nor the impressionistic romance of Michael Ondaatje's *The English Patient* (1992). Although the novel was televised, it did not receive either the treatment or the acclaim of the Hollywood film *The English Patient* (1996). Certainly, *Sacred Hunger* did not see a Booker-related sales bump equivalent to that of *The English Patient* (Todd 109).

With the sexy sell of *The English Patient,* we return to the broader issue of colonialism as exotic and erotic—and safely bracketed in the past. Jamaica Kincaid links this set of conditions to the realm of storytelling in her novel *Lucy* (1990). Lucy reflects on the possibility that the apparent personal dysfunction of adults may have sources beyond individual weakness: "Yes, I had heard of these people: they died insane, they died paupers, no one much liked them except other people like themselves. And I thought of all the people in the world I had known who went insane and died, and who drank too much rum and then died, and who were paupers and died, and I wondered if there were any artists among them. Who would have known?" (98) "These people" are not so much misfits in Antiguan society as people whose inability to articulate themselves as artists in a resource-poor society shatters them. Lucy is unable to say whether "there were any artists among" these tragic figures because the identifiers would not have been present. Kincaid's narrator echoes, empathetically rather than critically, V. S. Naipaul's litany "of failure: brilliant men, scholarship winners, who had died young, gone mad, or taken to drink" in *The Middle Passage* (35). Unlike Naipaul, Lucy uses her metropolitan experience to query the signifiers of poverty, madness, and alcoholism for their historical roots and ideological effects. Her final, melancholy question solicits a reparative response, a shift in ways of knowing that govern the reception of these tragic narratives, and a critical analysis of the tropes that dismiss these people as subjects for consideration.

2 Frustrated Drunks

Masculine Identity and
(Post)colonial Literary Ambition

"I was set to make my fortune within three years or get out," Owen said, "and here I am still beside this stinking river."

There was a reek of rum on his breath and his eyelids were reddish and inflamed.

—Barry Unsworth, *Sacred Hunger*

BARRY UNSWORTH'S Kurtzian narrator is a strange follow-up to Jamaica Kincaid's speculations about the systemic reasons for the apparent absence of Antiguan artists, yet Owen shares with the male subjects of this chapter a sense of disappointed entitlement and a practice of alcoholic self-medication as solace. Location provides variation rather than substantive difference in a general pattern of compensating for failed hopes with alcohol, which then becomes the reason for failure. Tragic alcoholism among (male) artists is a well-known trope; the loss of promise to alcoholism in the Caribbean merges with "gone native" and climatological stereotypes to insinuate that the location is more at fault than the man. Indeed, Lucy's ruminations state the general case for the characters to whom V. S. Naipaul introduces us in *Miguel Street,* to be considered in this chapter, as many of them are *artistes-manqués*—actors, sculptors, poets, firework designers—or visionaries. This chapter considers Naipaul alongside an unlikely comparator, Hunter S. Thompson; both launched their literary careers from the Caribbean and narrate their exceptionalism by disavowing alcoholic degeneracy, represented as endemic rum consumption. For both men, leaving the Caribbean is an essential escape from perpetual alcoholic time-out and access to literary currency. Looking more closely at the deployment of rum in the semiautobiographical novels *Miguel Street* and *The Rum Diary,* however, discloses relationships that must be foreclosed, investments that cannot be acknowledged, between male privilege and colonial ideology that require Naipaul and Thompson to adopt a paradoxically neocolonial *and* anticorporate stance.

Although Naipaul and Thompson may seem as far apart in literary origin and style as possible, their first novels to be written—neither of which was published first in their long careers—and their respective protagonists offer points of comparison. The autobiographical undercurrents in Naipaul's *Miguel Street* (written 1955, published 1959) and Thompson's *The Rum Diary* (written 1959, published 1998) retrospectively position each as origin stories for the genius who emerged from a Caribbean backwater onto the international stage. The authors share grand literary ambitions, a combative arrogance, and heinous sexism—in short, they are committed to male literary entitlement across racial difference. Their novels, despite distinctly different styles and genre, access this entitlement through coming-of-age narratives set against the features of Caribbean (under)development and (de)colonization. *Miguel Street* is a series of tragicomic vignettes, set in Trinidad during World War II after the American military had arrived; the young narrator negotiates his masculinity in the interstices of imperial competitors who also cooperate to maintain control over Trinidad. *The Rum Diary,* narrating a turning point in a young journalist's career, captures the overheated economy in Puerto Rico in the late 1950s.

The novels evoke the Caribbean islands in transition, highlighting their symbolic role as "a place of promising possibility" that is also a "dangerous crossroads" (Sheller 174) at historically specific junctures.[1] Naipaul's novel is set on Trinidad during World War II; the key impact of the war on Trinidad is the arrival of the US military and its money, which simultaneously creates opportunities unavailable under British control while reifying Trinidad as a possession to be traded between imperial nations without reference to Trinidadians themselves. As the character Edward states before becoming disillusioned, "And the Americans not like the British, you know. They does make you work hard, but they does pay for it" (185). The infusion of American money pushes the Trinidadian market into a small-scale boom-and-bust cycle, as Americans enrich and impoverish according to whim. The narrator's neighbor George capitalizes on American tastes by setting up a brothel in his house, but he is left penniless when the soldiers abandon his brothel for other "nice places" (35). In *The Rum Diary,* Thompson figures Puerto Rico as a newly opened frontier for ambitious American men, and he takes a dim view of viewpoints and behavior contrary to his desires. The novel, however, assumes the frontier is already closed: on arriving, the narrator, Paul Kemp, listens to departing passengers complain about the lack of "cheap beach-front" and threat of anticapitalist influence from "Castro and that crowd" (11). The ferment of the historical moment forces Kemp to recognize that he, like the Puerto Ricans he despises, is subjected to the demands of a neocolonial economic regime that refigures plantation as multinational corporation. Naipaul's narrator, by contrast, invests in this new economy by replicating colonialist attitudes toward Trinidad's people and culture.

Employment Precarity and Communal Drinking Rituals

The extensive description of masculine drinking rituals links economic uncertainty to underclass status in a colonial society. The men of *Miguel Street* are systemically underemployed, and each aspiration is thwarted. Bogart, from the first story, vanishes three times in search of work in British Guiana and Venezuela; Edward leaves for "Aruba or Curaçao" to work with "the big Dutch oil company" (198). The narrator suggests Venezuela to his mother as his route out of Trinidad (215). In *Miguel Street,* women have steadier employment and income and often support men, even when that income comes from prostitution, which the narrator depicts as emasculating the spouse. Popo, from the second story, does odd jobs but depends on his wife, "who worked at a variety of jobs" and was also "the friend of many men" (10). Young men like Elias dream of being doctors, but a corrupt examination system and limited opportunity reduce ambition to "driving the scavenging carts" (45). In "Until the Soldiers Came," Naipaul quotes variations of Lord Invader's calypso "Rum and Coca-Cola" to indicate that measures of masculine success are contingent, as the arrival of US dollars simultaneously offers the men of Miguel Street a glimpse of financial security beyond British control while inserting another level of competition in the form of well-paid GIs.

In *The Rum Diary,* Kemp keeps his sense of economic emasculation in check through the community of expatriates. White men seeking their fortunes in tropical places are generically romantic, "wild young Turks" seeking adventure and profit like himself, or tragic romantics, "working just long enough to make the price of a few drinks and a plane ticket" (2–3, italics omitted). As a white employee of an American newspaper, Kemp earns a "ridiculous salary" given the Puerto Rican exchange rate (42), and he is correspondingly infuriated to find this salary does not secure his physical or fiscal position. When he first arrives, Kemp finds the newspaper offices under siege by "some kind of wildcat strike" (16) led by underpaid local employees—the newspaper is employing scabs (36). At the bar with new colleagues, he hears speculation that "the paper was going to fold" (22). A mixture of racism and journalistic principle justifies his rudeness to a well-connected Puerto Rican official who excludes him from "parties that [he] would not have gone to in the first place" (46) and from useful government contacts. The figurative language Kemp uses to describe his feelings—"bothered" and "get on my nerves" (46)—forecast a rising physical discomfort with his precarious position. From the opening moments of the novel, male employment is provisional and temporary for most Puerto Rican people *and* most American white people, despite the differences racism makes to their respective employment prospects.[2] Kemp revels in overpayment; Puerto Ricans protest underpayment. Kemp believes promotional journalism about "The Boom" in Puerto Rico and therefore cannot understand why "Puerto Ricans at the airport" flee to New York (58). Kemp believes immigrating Puerto Ricans are "naive and ignorant" (58) about globalization, yet he sees no contradiction in fleeing when the newspaper closes. This blindness sets up an asymmetrical experience of emergent globalization and the contingencies of survival under its rule (to borrow language from López). This situation could make Kemp more empathetic and connected to Puerto Rican people; instead, it generates a panicked retreat to US comforts.

In this environment, rum has surprising effects, engaging Eve Kosofsky Sedgwick's potential for a reparative rather than a paranoid mode of reading that addresses the mediation of masculine privilege through colonial power.[3] Both Naipaul's sympathetic portrayals and Thompson's outlandish accounts fall within range of homosocial male bonding through drinking; examining the elements that physically jar participants marks reparative potential in these texts. Both authors steer a careful path endorsing these male rituals while inhibiting charges of alcoholism.[4] The first two chapters in *Miguel Street*—"Bogart" and "The Thing without a Name"—examine the boundaries and codes of homosocial drinking among the men of Miguel Street. "Bogart," titled eponymously for the focal character and the American actor he idolizes, immediately sites the novel as an investigation of masculinity as constructed, or performed, under external cultural influences.[5] Bogart the character, like Bogart the actor, is "quite the most popular man in the street" (11), and his home becomes the center of male bonding, even when he is absent seeking work in Venezuela. On his return, however, the calculus of male bonding has shifted to domination, as demonstrated by inappropriate consumption of a celebratory bottle of rum (13). Bogart drinks greedily, the narrator reports: "A long Madrassi shot of rum. Then another, and another; and they had presently finished the bottle" (13). *Madrassi* is a pejorative term for a South Asian, implying improper behavior; further, it is unclear whether Bogart takes three draughts in a row, or whether he takes more than his share in three rounds, thus denying the other men their fair share. His behavior is surprising and registered as a change in drunken comportment. His friends are "alarmed" because "they had never seen Bogart drink so much; they had never heard him talk so much" (13). The further revelation that his speech is "slightly American" (13) suggests that Bogart has reshaped himself to exploit like Americans rather than reinvest in his relationships. Bogart both acknowledges and accentuates the transgression by offering to "go buy another" (13)—a palliative action that nevertheless reveals his allegiance. Bogart's alignment with American domination, cued by the change in drunken comportment, fails when he cannot capitalize on American privilege: for actions the GIs take with impunity, he is arrested and imprisoned (14).

The second cautionary tale shifts the narrator's perspective on Trinidadian drinking rituals by inaugurating the theme of failed artistry among the men of Miguel Street. Popo rejects the drinking culture of Miguel Street; he is thus not "popular" with other men, labelled a "man-woman" because he does not adhere to rules of alcoholic sociability described in "Bogart" (19). Hat labels him "conceited" (19), a term Naipaul defines in *The Middle Passage* as expressing "the resentment felt of anyone who possessed unusual skills" (35), because "Popo had the habit of taking a glass of rum to the pavement every morning. He never sipped the rum. But whenever he saw someone he knew he dipped his middle finger in the rum, licked it, and then waved to the man" (*Miguel Street* 19).[6] The narrator deems Hat's dislike "unreasonable," indicating that he does not yet understand the important role drinking rituals play in masculine social norms (or perhaps the meaning of the gesture Popo makes). Popo's hoarding of resources typically shared makes him "feel good," but Hat stresses that it is not what you have but what you do with it: "We could buy rum too," he tells the narrator (19).

The young narrator is surprised when Popo adopts the typical male drinking habits of Miguel Street after his wife leaves him, rendering him economically dependent on communal networks. In adversity, he gains the support of the neighborhood, "an accepted member of the gang" who "smelled of rum" (21). The shift in Popo's relationship to rum is accompanied by violence. When Eddoes characterizes Popo as looking "Like he got no more rum," Hat "almost cuff[s]" Eddoes (20). Likewise, Popo threatens to "lay [his] hand" on the narrator for asking why Popo has ceased his artistic pursuits (25). The narrator decides he does not "like him when he was drunk" (21). Taken together, these stories illustrate for the narrator that the dictates of rum eliminate the possibility of art and that the possibility of recognizable art (rather than "The Thing with No Name") requires exclusion from the norms of homosocial drinking. As he matures, the narrator is unable to reconcile these poles, opting instead to sever ties.

Vocabularies of possession and sharing mark discussions of male drunken comportment in *The Rum Diary,* in which Kemp and his cronies twit the representatives of Puerto Rican finance capitalism by thieving rum. The novel begins with a nostalgic retrospective that establishes rum drinking as a coping response to the foreclosure of economic opportunity for enterprising white men. The prologue, "San Juan, Winter of 1958," sets the scene at Al's, a seedy bar where rum is "a dime a shot or fifteen cents with ice"—cheaper than a bottle of beer—and "a pleasant place to drink, especially in the mornings" (1, italics omitted). This scene reverses American drinking costs and values; beer is more expensive than rum, and rum is the characteristic drink of the island. The phrase "especially in the mornings" preemptively classes the narrative as alcoholic—who else drinks regularly in the morning?—and announces that this narrative violates middle-class drinking (and other) norms. At Al's, the congregants cannot afford prices in the "'New York' bars that were springing up" (2) for those employed by a corporatized government and industry complex. This multinational corporate structure refigures the operations of plantation slavery for a new era, as indicated by the fact that its representative "looked like he'd just stepped out of a rum advertisement" (27). The narrator disaffiliates from this version of colonization, but his desire for quick riches link him to the small-time fortune-seekers of earlier times, who persist in the cracks left by larger operations: "Like most of the others, I was a seeker, a mover, a malcontent, and at times a stupid hell-raiser" (5, italics omitted). The narrator, revealed as Paul Kemp in the body of the novel, aligns himself with an underprivileged group of white men situated between wealthy Americans and their Puerto Rican counterparts, and the mass of Puerto Rican people who are not benefitting from the postwar tourism development boom.

The disappointed protagonist and his cohort take revenge on corporate culture by absconding with the rum available at publicity events in terms that explicitly deny gift exchange and emphasize possession over consumption. Kemp justifies his actions based on the corrupt nature of these "thieves and pretentious hustlers" (70), frontiersmen whose ambitions are fundamentally different from his. Their philistine confusion of bodies and commodities, figured as "an orgy of rum" (70), updates the historical

Frustrated Drunks 63

pattern for sexually exploiting enslaved women and links to Hal Underhill's historical pornography. Under this guise, Kemp violates a corrupted gift exchange: the party as publicity event. He intends to "steal as many bottles of rum as [he] could carry" from each event and agonizes over the "painful socializing" that implies relationships he wishes to negate (71). When he reports that "sometimes there were as many as twenty or thirty" (71) bottles of stolen rum in his apartment, Kemp does not mention drinking the rum (though he must). Instead he and his compatriot Sala leave the stolen bottles at their apartment and "head for Al's" to drink according to their own masculine protocols (71). Kemp extols the "good feeling" generated by "a stock of rum that would never run out" (71). In emphasizing the sheer amount of rum and separating possession from consumption, Kemp appropriates the commodities at the base of colonialism as he disavows his desire for more power in that system.

Yet Kemp registers discomfort with even this level of passive-aggressive socialization: "After a while I could no longer stand even a few minutes at each party, and I had to give it up" (71). This emotionally flat, temporally imprecise admission counterbalances the hysteria Kemp displays in a scene, discussed earlier, when he thinks he will die over an unpaid bar tab. Kemp desires to maintain his privileges without acknowledging that he has them, investing him in American imperialism even as he professes to reject its corporate model. When Kemp, Yeamon, and Sala intrude on a beach bar for locals, Kemp characterizes the clientele as "tired and depressed" (80), but he is envious that these men "were driving big American cars" (82). As the group drinks, the manager confronts Kemp's friend Yeamon—Thompson's second alter ego in this novel—with the unpaid tab and an accusation about "drunk arrogant Yankees": "You think gringos drink free in Puerto Rico?" (83). Yeamon and Kemp, and their cronies, do, in fact, want to "drink free" in Puerto Rico, but they are made to recognize not the cost, but the real value of their bodies within the neocolonial regime. Kemp panics when he realizes that he is "being kicked to death in a Puerto Rican jungle for eleven dollars and fifty cents" of rum (83). When Kemp "scream[s] like an animal" (83), he is and is not "going native." This is a moment of surprise, in Sedgwick's terms, a point when the spurious architecture of white male privilege is exposed, and Kemp could establish a new set of relations with other subjected bodies.

Instead, Kemp exteriorizes this knowledge to the (not unreasonably) "angry mob" outside the police station after Kemp and his friends are arrested (85). Kemp's "surprise" (his word) that the observers do not attack registers the inaccuracy of his perception without engendering an impulse toward charity or empathy (85). More important, he decides to attribute the entire scene to drunkenness. During this episode, Kemp repeatedly assesses the intoxication of those around him: he hopes another reporter "had not been too drunk to recognize [them]" (87); some of the Puerto Ricans with whom he shares a cell "were drunk" (87); and he thinks the businessman who exerts his influence to free them "might be drunk" (89). These observations, though tonally flat, do the work of moving this scene into a time-out space, where the impact of the revelation can be safely forgotten.

Despite the disavowal above, Kemp continues to scavenge all the rum he can get throughout the novel to bolster his own position in this rum economy. Kemp's behavior at carnival elaborates on both Kemp's earlier carnivalesque thefts of rum and his terrifying encounter with his economic value during a barfight. Carnival on St. Thomas functions as a time-out within the larger time-out of Puerto Rico, but here a nervous Kemp joins in with Puerto Ricans, Swedes, and other Americans to circumvent the orderly distribution and consumption of commodities: "About two hundred people had looted one of the big liquor stores. Most of them were Puerto Ricans. Cases of champagne and scotch lay broken in the street, and everyone I saw had a bottle" (146). Kemp admits to a similar "lust for drink," but underlining his attempts "to rescue three quarts of Old Crow" bourbon is his sense of waste, particularly of high-value European liquors like champagne and scotch. Likewise, Yeamon has stolen "a magnum of champagne" (147). As is his habit, Kemp does not drink the looted liquor, unlike carnival participants who are "grabbing stray bottles and drinking them as fast as they could" (147). He hoards rather than shares, a behavior Thompson ironizes when Kemp explains that his "bag seemed to weigh about forty pounds"—an indication that Kemp is maintaining a useless investment.

These opening scenes establish the parameters for masculine drunken comportment in the novels and position the protagonists to disavow rum specifically and reify Caribbean islands as ahistorical alcoholic time-outs as they pursue modern masculinity. To pursue this storyline, both narrators strategically constrain female characters to prioritize homosocial bonding.[7] At beginnings of their novels, both authors narrate the presence and agency of women as severely constrained. In *Miguel Street,* women do not drink unless they are loose women. In "Bogart" and "The Thing without a Name," wives and mothers are mostly offstage or reported as present in the background. Bogart's wives are offstage, and the activities of Popo's wife are reported as asides, creating a focus on male interactions.

Women in "George and the Pink House" are prostitutes or abused family members.[8] Not until chapter 10, "The Maternal Instinct," does Naipaul focus on a woman (a prostitute), and only two of the twenty-five chapters feature female protagonists. White women are anathema, tricking men into marriage by pretending to be pregnant ("Until the Soldiers Came") or avidly consuming the emasculation of Trinidadian men ("The Coward"). From the beginning of the novel, the narrator intimates a network of female support, but the structural suppression of female agency is central to Naipaul's purpose: an exploration of homosocial relationships and contested masculinity in wartime Trinidad.[9]

The Rum Diary similarly positions women as marginal objects to the postcolonial field. Taking a cue from the frontier towns of the west, the narrator claims that "on any normal night a girl in Al's Backyard was a rare and erotic sight" (2). Kemp means white women, of course. Kemp subtly racializes his sole narrated sexual encounter prior to meeting Chenault. When he meets Lorraine—one of two named female characters in the book—in a casino, Kemp says she "claimed to be from Trinidad" and "had large breasts, a British accent, and wore a tight green dress" (31). Kemp's ratiocinations are a diagram of how white male privilege works: the word *claimed* drives an accumulation of details that question Lorraine's right to respect. To cement this representational advantage, Kemp introduces rum into the equation. Kemp amends Lorraine's suggestion of a "drive along the dunes"—romantic—to "Let's get some rum and drive on the dunes" (32). The sexual encounter that follows transfers desire and responsibility to Lorraine, whose orgasm is defined as "extreme" and nearly animal in "want[ing] nothing but the clutch and howl" (33). Kemp draws on traditions of depicting (Black?) women as sexually promiscuous and voracious, exposing a determination to insulate himself from any equitable relationship with a person from this region. Thompson doubles down by invoking racist stereotypes about the erotic charms of the Caribbean.

The sexual commodification Kemp engineers has everything to do with the history of plantation economy of which rum is a primary product, and it counterpoints the fetishized sexuality of the other named female character in the novel, Chenault. Thompson sets out the internal contradiction at the heart of fetishizing Chenault without entirely denying the thrill of possession. Her boyfriend Yeamon simultaneously fears that she will be "raped" by Puerto Rican men and threatens to "damn well let them have" her if she does not obey him (76). Sala's theatrically whispered comment that Yeamon "treats her like a slave" (79) voices the desired fantasy as critique. Resistance to the narrative Yeamon has created for her—as we will see writ large in *Wide Sargasso Sea*—leads to violence and imprisonment. When Chenault, "her face serious" (78), ventures an opinion about Mexico City, even the suspicion that she has a history independent from Yeamon attracts ridicule. With this move, Yeamon sidelines her from the companionable masculine consumption of alcohol and reveals his investment in commodifying and controlling her. Chenault—like George's daughter Dolly in *Miguel Street*—does not openly respond, but her actions, a "glare" and "a long drink" (78), communicate resistance. Yeamon understands the drink as appropriation of masculine resources, and he recasts it as submission: "Keep sucking it down—you're not drunk enough yet" (78). When Chenault openly resists, screaming at Yeamon to "Shut up!," he nullifies her protest using several forms of dehumanization. Yeamon slaps her, infantilizes her ("Go to bed"), locks her up, and then implies that she is a drunk; she must be prevented from "wandering around" before she "pass[es] out" (78–79). Like Antoinette's husband in *Wide Sargasso Sea,* Yeamon manipulates drinking norms to control women's bodies and stories and thus his access to the resources patriarchy affords him. Yet the beginnings of an alternate narrative emerge, one in which Chenault's purpose in coming to Puerto Rico is not entirely to play the role of sexy girlfriend. Thompson amplifies the anxieties generated by Chenault's noncompliance when, at the end of the novel, a suspicion of sexual relations with Black men requires manipulation of gender- and race-based taboos about drinking to manage an intolerable thought: that white women and Black people might willingly collaborate sexually and politically.

I Am Not an Alcoholic

Within these depictions of communal, sometimes excessive, drinking habits of men on Caribbean islands, Naipaul and Thompson must protect their protagonists from the stigma of alcoholism as an outcome of failed masculine role development. The authors must avoid both the opprobrium attached to "going native" and the intersections of such a narrative with changing Western theories and diagnoses of alcoholism in the 1950s and 1960s. While nineteenth-century discourses and treatment models understood alcohol abuse as a sin or moral weakness, post–World War II discourse on alcoholism had largely transitioned to a medical or disease model. While moral opprobrium was still attached to alcoholism, enlightened professionals and therapists shifted diagnoses to thwarted masculine identification. Alcoholism remained a man's disease, but therapy was familial, with wives and mothers sometimes identified as contributing to male illness by not supporting the man's self-image (Rotskoff 3–5, 77). Moreover, new definitions of alcoholism retained class distinctions by which alcoholism was a tragedy for middle-class professional men and further evidence of unworthiness among lower-class men. The stigma of alcoholism continues to have overlapping class, race, and gender implications for the midcentury middle-class professional man in a modernizing postwar economy. Alcohol abuse that could be labeled alcoholism, transgressing boundaries of normative male social drinking, still risks compromising the masculinity of the man in question. Thus, Kemp and the *Miguel Street* narrator must emerge as exceptional controllers of rum rather than typical consumers of it, framing an emasculating present as a dysfunctional Caribbean past.

Viewed from the outside (i.e., from a reader's perspective) many of the men in both texts might seem to verge on alcoholism, as their excessive drinking is regular and seems wasteful given their precarious financial situation. Like all addictions, alcoholism is grounded in metaphors of uncontrolled consumption and thus an improper subjection of the masculine self to commodity chains. Both narrators participate in the local male cultures of drinking, thus conforming to these expectations for masculine identity, yet both exhibit control over consumption that sets them apart from the group and offers each a different story. Thompson, in titling the novel *The Rum Diary,* courts this judgment: this quasi-autobiographical narrative models the self as a fiction of inebriation but recalling the definition of *rum* as "strange" suggests both alienation and uncanny truthfulness. Late in *The Rum Diary,* Kemp reports that rum is "one of the things [he's] tired of" (185), implying that ceasing—and starting—consumption is a matter of personal choice. Kemp's statement implicitly counters the hysteria of his drinking buddy Sala, who asks, "What the hell are we heading for, Kemp? . . . We keep getting drunk and these terrible things keep happening and each one is worse than the last" (166). Sala's statement presumes alcohol dependence for both men, but Kemp differentiates his habit from Sala's immersion. In addition, Thompson provides two portraits of confirmed alcoholics: Donovan, referred to as "a drunkard" (19) early in the text, and Moburg a "drunken bastard" who "looked sick enough to be in a hospital" and got so drunk he "pissed on the teletype machine" (26). By contrasting Kemp to these characters, the narrative deflects the classification of Kemp's excessive, habitual drinking as the same kind of addiction.

Naipaul's narrative consists of vignettes that offer potential patterns for the narrator's own plot, and by repeating short narratives in which excessive drinking is a prelude to violence and imprisonment, Naipaul intimates the difficulty of escaping this plot for men who live on Miguel Street. Yet the unnamed narrator of *Miguel Street* also differentiates this habitual drinking among members of his peer group and neighborhood from the alcoholic. Hat, the mentor figure in *Miguel Street,* points out the border when he calls Tony "a first-class drinking man, you hear" to differentiate his behavior from male norms (132). The narrator observes then that Tony's drinking is different from that of Hat and his friends, coming "to realize that the tall man [Tony] was drunk practically all the time" (132) rather than "in the ordinary fashion" (145). This distinction makes the narrator's own victory over drinking more impressive. The narrator announces that he "had become a first-class drinker" (215) like Tony: "I drank so much in one evening that I remained drunk for two whole days afterwards" (217). The narrator overcomes overconsumption with a "vow" that prevents both loss of status through unemployment or arrest and the stigma of medical treatment for a disease (216). He avoids being labeled an alcoholic by either internal assent or external judgment and regains control over both himself and alcohol as a commodity. The application of rational thinking and willpower implicitly differentiates him from both Tony, who cannot overcome his addiction, and the narrator's peers, who have no reported desire to shift their behavior.

These individual distinctions merge with cultural narratives that imagine the Caribbean as the drunken, disgraced past for a productive, modern future. At the end of these narratives, the protagonists trade up from an alcoholic culture. In *Miguel Street,* the narrator experiences his position in the commodity chain as physically painful: "I was drinking like a fish, and doing a lot besides. The drinking started in the customs, where we confiscated liquor on the slightest pretext. At first the smell of spirits upset me, but I used to say to myself, 'You must get over this. Drink it like medicine. Hold your nose and close your eyes.' In time I had become a first-class drinker, and I began suffering from drinker's pride" (215). The narrator of *Miguel Street* is not, initially, a manic participant in male rituals of expropriation and consumption; *confiscation* implies, here, endemic low-level corruption and the connection of "the smell of spirits" links possession with immediate consumption rather than the hoarding and husbanding of a Paul Kemp. Despite his reluctance, he masters the style required for masculine success: "We made wild parties and took rum and women to Maracas Bay for all-night sessions" (216).

It is only when his mother accuses him of "getting too wild" that he understands, first, that he is being consumed rather than consuming, and, second, that his behavior makes him vulnerable to colonial stereotypes of Caribbean men. When he transfers blame for his behavior to the culture—"Is just Trinidad" (217)—the narrator ironizes by deflection, for what might appear as deviant drunken comportment is normative, necessary, even required, by material relations between colonies and their colonizing oppressors. The narrator claims it is his job, as it were, to waste his resources—a move characteristic of Naipaul, who "represents and undermines his own authority and the nature of authority in general" (Coovadia 7). If the narrator professes some "disappoint[ment]" that in Trinidad "everything... going on just as before" after his departure (*Miguel Street* 222), then this situation is both the criteria for his own exceptionalism and the product of exploitative Western consumer desire.

In *The Rum Diary*, the immediate cause for Paul Kemp's abandonment of Puerto Rico is directly related to the employment precarity described earlier in this chapter and linked to the exploitation of tropical locales by US interests. The editor sells the newspaper "into receivership" to "Stein Enterprises of Miami, Florida" without paying outstanding salary due to his staff (195), and in response some of the journalists plan a vigilante attack. The journalists, including Kemp, are now in the position of the strikers seen demonstrating at the beginning of the novel, thus illustrating the precarity of even whiteness and maleness in maintaining economic entitlement as capital goes global. The attack on the absconding editor occurs at a garden party sponsored by "the Rum League and the San Juan Chamber of Commerce" (196). The sponsoring organizations would be, to Kemp's mind, interchangeable, as the Chamber of Commerce is certainly a rum league of businessmen in the pockets of American investors, but the pairing allies the modern trade association with the exploitative practices of an older rum league—plantation owners and slave traders. In this final depiction of monied Puerto Rican society, Kemp paints a picture of cyclical corruption, violence, and chaos in which time becomes timeless, an endless night: "The quiet deadly ticking of a thousand hungry clocks, the lonely sound of time passing in the long Caribbean night" (204). Puerto Rico fails to satisfy its promise as a *post*colonial modern frontier; instead, it reels drunkenly along, repeating colonial patterns under a new set of corporate investors.

The figure of Chenault would seem ancillary to this masculine psychodrama turned battle royal were it not for the fact that her participation in rum drinking raises white male suspicions that white women may collaborate with so-called others. When Kemp, Yeamon, and Chenault travel to St. Thomas for carnival, Chenault disappears after stripping and dancing naked at a party at the home of a local resident.[10] Kemp imagines that she will be gang-raped, and Thompson has indicated that he meant to titillate readers with the prospect of "an interracial orgy" (*Proud Highway* 261) in which Chenault is eventually "staked . . . out on a bed, a white, pink-nippled nightcap to wind up the carnival" (*Rum Diary* 161). Kemp's use of "nightcap" inverts the racial structure of exoticized sexual assault used by Underhill (see chapter 2), suggesting the fungibility of women and alcohol in the structures of colonial fantasy. Thompson intends a pornographic fantasy, but the alternative, that Chenault might have "enjoyed herself" (157), contradicts what, for Kemp, is the only possible story. Even before Chenault returns, Yeamon calls her a "bitch" (153) and "part nigger" (154) for dancing with a Black man, an action that links the Puerto Rican scene to customs of Thompson's home state, Kentucky.[11] "Any girl that runs off with a pack of bushmen is bad news" (180), Sala opines, reinforcing the circulation of racist stereotypes throughout American and Atlantic contexts.

Pointedly, it does not matter what happened *to her:* Chenault has raised specters of violated/licentious white women, Black beasts, and miscegenation that challenge white male privilege. On her return, Chenault has acquired color, "haggard and dirty," and shifted her subject position, looking, according to Kemp, like "she'd lost her mind" (169). She expresses a wish that her return flight "would crash," claims "I don't remember!" about events at carnival, and cries "for a long time" when asked what happened (173). Signs of trauma—possibly—but she never tells, and whatever the truth is, it will not be acceptable. Kemp characterizes her evasions as "malignant-sounding," but his suspicions say more about his white male privilege than Chenault's behavior (173). Again, Chenault offers no details except that "somebody bought" her a plane ticket back to San Juan (173), just stabs of emotion that echo, in form, her earlier protests against Yeamon's denial of her agency.[12] Without denying the possibility of sexual assault, I emphasize that the scripts Chenault's male observers follow do not depend on what may actually have happened, but on fantasies and fears generated by the combination of white women, alcohol, and Black or brown men. Even the suggestion of relations from which they are excluded, or do not form the principle beneficiaries, induces hysteria in Yeamon and an accompanying narrative hysteria from Kemp.

In the closing scenes, Thompson reestablishes the primacy of his story and Chenault's role in it by making rum the route to the heart of darkness.

By "shove[ing]" a drink into Chenault's hand before telling his story, he controls the terms. In this scene, Kemp confesses to being "a human suckfish," a hanger-on to the "sharks"—powerful men—but he reverses charges by naming Chenault a suckfish as well, and here Kemp is the shark (185). She returns to her strategy of sound rather than sense: she "giggle[s]" (185), later "shaking her head sadly" and "crying" (186). Her words, on the other hand, focus on practical matters—a plane ticket, the date of his departure—that Kemp can interpret as proof that she is a "suckfish," but which enable her escape. Her assent to sexual domination continues this strategy: "After a while I reached over and filled my glass again. In the process, I spilled some rum on my stomach and she leaned down to lick it off. The touch of her tongue made me shudder, and after a moment of contemplation I picked up the bottle again and spilled some rum on my leg. She looked up at me and smiled, as if I were playing some kind of an odd joke, then she bent down and carefully licked it off" (187). Chenault's agency here may be tightly constrained, but the overlap of this river of rum with the River Congo in Joseph Conrad's *Heart of Darkness*, which Chenault is reading, renders her destination, Kemp's crotch, a lesson about the relationship of male fantasy to colonial fantasy. By reacting as if Kemp is "playing some kind of odd joke," Chenault is clearly performing submission, which ironizes her compliance. The sexual relationship and the cozy domestic scene that follows encourages Kemp to believe Chenault is on board with his narrative, but she exits before he can stage his climax. Instead, he gets a letter which is a promissory note: they "will drink rum and dance naked" on his return to the United States, where he can visit her home in Connecticut (192). Chenault's offer to export Kemp's Caribbean imaginary to Connecticut rings hollow; like Kurtz's monomania, these fantasies cannot survive in a temperate climate.

As Chenault follows a river of rum to Kemp's penis, sexual and imperial fantasy unite to pleasure the white male body. The saturation of Thompson's novel with rum—from the title to the closing pages—suggests a community intoxicated by the past, if not addicted to the painful pleasures of identifying with it. Naipaul suggests a similar thralldom in his depiction of Trinidad as a place that induces passive assent to economic injustice: "Is just Trinidad. What else anybody can do here except drink?" (*Miguel Street* 216). The consumption of rum is affiliated with innocuous pleasure, shared solace, mob violence, assault, rape, corruption, thievery, and hedonistic celebration. In all the "white noise" produced by the presence of alcohol (Roth xviii), the economic bases for emotional and physical reactions pass for dissipation enabled by geography. The apparent social and economic dysfunction disparaged in Puerto Rico and Trinidad is, in fact, socially, economically, and narratively *functional*. Naipaul recognizes this when he deploys this figure as a necessity for the exceptional individual brown man's escape. This rhetorical move may seem unsurprising, given Naipaul's tendency to depict immigration as "a welcome escape from the degradation and misery of the Caribbean" that also percolates through fiction by Caribbean-born men of this period (Brown, "Geographies" 123), but this image of the Caribbean is also shared by the iconic American Thompson. Despite both Thompson's and Naipaul's attempts to contain this dysfunction in an imagined Caribbean time-out, it remains an engine for their success.

"I Remembered to Take a Bottle of Rum Superior for Chenault": You Take It with You

Thompson's Kemp, despite some anxious moments, leaves Puerto Rico determined to remaster his relationship to rum. Kemp finally manages to drink rum "on the house" (*Rum Diary* 204) and he packs a bottle of rum "for Chenault," implying that his strategic distribution of this commodity will enable the promised fantasy (203). The resurgence of Kemp's confidence in male privilege suggests the durability of delusion as well as the practical fact that masculinity, devoid of its attachment to any man, remains a putative entitlement to resources. For the narrator of Naipaul's *Miguel Street,* England may be a more sobering experience. Naipaul's narrator, anticipating English racism, maintains some critical distance from this figure; he refers to himself as "a dancing dwarf" and a "shadow" (222), suggesting that his occupation of masculinity as a privileged site will intersect with racial discrimination. The comedic invocation of "spilled milk" subtly links abjection of the mother(land) as a messy secret behind his escape. Yet, as a structural aspect of colonial relations both social and material, masculine privilege is both available and foreclosed; the "well-documented" patriarchal assumptions of novels of the 1950s Windrush generation that Allison Donnell enumerates require constant assertion and testing for maintenance (154).[13]

In these novels, rum is something to be superseded and abjected even as it fuels the melancholic masculine nostalgia that pervades these works. To illustrate this point broadly, contrast the association of rum with the past to the futurity of drugs. Hunter S. Thompson became famous for his drug-fueled narratives; *Miguel Street*'s narrator leaves Trinidad to study pharmacy—"drugs" (217)—on scholarship in England. In a sense, both protagonists trade a drunken time-out in the Caribbean for the sophistication of modern pharmaceuticals. They progress to advanced addictive commodities and literary glory simultaneously, relegating the islands and their tarnished commodity, rum, to the status of literary backwater. Thompson, known for what is now called New Journalism, chronicles the permissive, corrupt, hard-driving world of US politics and culture: a culture whose voracious appetite for drugs is matched only by its determination to blame the Southern Americas for Northern addiction. By contrast, the Puerto Rico of *The Rum Diary* is, by definition, a place to leave behind, and, by the logic of history, the novel is proof that Thompson emerged as the writer he is celebrated and reviled for being.[14] On the publication of *The Rum Diary*, he invited assessment as anachronism. According to Thompson, *The Rum Diary* was superseded by *Hell's Angels* and then by additional, more promising and profitable, literary enterprises. Thompson claims that the novel is out of time; to publish the novel, he tells Charlie Rose, he had to "dig up . . . forty-year-old history." Yet, he and Rose joke, the novel bears the signs of greatness—good enough to be "the great Puerto Rican novel," but not a Great American Novel.[15]

Reviewers corroborated this vision, commenting particularly on the levels of rum consumption as a signal of meaninglessness in Puerto Rican life that implicitly contrasts with the historical importance of later, drug-laced works. Nicholas Waywell calls the novel "remarkable for Thompson's presentation of a kind of stillness and frenzy intermingled, a sweat-drenched stasis caught in the rhythm of endless rum-soaked days," further noting that "the stupefying effect of the rum bottle on the narrative makes the quick, uneasy acts of love and intense, violent outbursts the more unsettlingly delineated."[16] *Publishers Weekly* comments parenthetically that "the amount of rum consumed would dry up a distillery" (Steinberg 72). As Donna Seaman observes, "Every scene is saturated in rum and sweat, and the action has a grindingly repetitive pattern, like a badly mounted ceiling fan on high" (173). However, critics attribute the excessive drinking to Puerto Rico's stifling environment rather than to a corrosive system of international investment.[17] By contrast, reviewer David Kelly explicitly connects the improvement of Thompson's style with the transition to drugs: "Drugs must have done wonders for Hunter S. Thompson, if we can go by his first novel. . . . There are no narcotics in this early work, and there is also none of the maniacal wit and deranged exuberance that roared through the *Fear and Loathing* books." He concludes, "If you are looking for the birthplace of gonzo, you won't find it here."

74 *Frustrated Drunks*

Miguel Street is the birthplace of V. S. Naipaul, Nobel Prize winner. Testimony from Patrick French's authorized biography lists the real people on whom Naipaul based his characters (153), and the novel's street setting is indebted to yard fiction, a legitimating move in the development of the West Indian novel (Nair, "Novel and Decolonization" 58). Like Naipaul, the protagonist leaves Trinidad to study in England. Although the protagonist of *Miguel Street* dislikes pharmacy as a subject, he latches onto the opportunity rather than remain on Trinidad to drink and womanize. England is the site of novelty, history, and civilization, emblematized by the lure of "seeing snow and seeing the Thames and seeing the big Parliament" (218). When the narrator coincidentally doubles back to his old neighborhood due to a plane delay, the fact that "everything . . . going on just as before, with nothing to indicate my absence" (222) both deflates his ego and justifies his departure by projecting an endlessly static future for Port of Spain. The city, and the island, are in "time-out," or out of time, in contrast with the narrator's movement outward and, literally, upward.[18] The men remaining on Trinidad, according to biographer French, "drink rum, and dream" because they have "a slim chance of moving out of the ghetto and destitution" (153). Like Thompson, Naipaul positions "drugs" as a historical and personal advance into a new commodity network, locating the world of habitual alcoholic intoxication in a contemporaneous Caribbean past.[19] Both the narratives and the authorial biographies associate rum with a degrading, unsuccessful economic past to be surmounted and jettisoned. While Puerto Rico and Trinidad remain historical backwaters, Thompson and Naipaul develop, respectively, into the father of a new literary genre and a commentator on colonialism and globalization worldwide.

Postcolonial White Male Fantasies

Joseph O'Neill's 2008 novel *Netherland* updates themes of precarity, migrancy, and alcoholic male bonding for the age of globalization. Set in the post-9/11 world, this novel undermines the narrative and social dominance of the white Anglo-European protagonist, pond-jumping Dutch equities expert Hans van den Broek, with a short counternarrative from van den Broek's sometime friend Chuck Ramkissoon, a savvy and ambitious Trinidadian immigrant. Ramkissoon's parable of the rum shop offers the longest, if not the only, sustained insight into Ramkissoon's consciousness—a sliver of first-person narration in 256 pages from a melancholic van den Broek, adrift as his marriage crumbles. In size and scope, Ramkissoon's tale reveals the impact of the narrator's socioeconomic dominance on narrative form. In this novel, O'Neill strides the scene of globalization, funneling the world market and migration networks through the streets and boroughs of New York, capturing what Benítez-Rojo might call "multidisciplinary maps of unexpected designs" (*Repeating Island* 3). By drilling into Ramkissoon's parable, the centrality of the first-person narrator shifts to reveal van den Broek's historical and current cost to others.

Critical discussions of *Netherland* focus on the role of cricket in the development of the friendship between Chuck Ramkissoon and Hans van den Broek.[20] After van den Broek's wife leaves him, taking his son with her to England, van den Broek seeks refuge by returning to his childhood sport, cricket. In New York, the game is largely played and organized by Caribbean, African, and Asian immigrants, and through them van den Broek meets Ramkissoon. Van den Broek delights in the shared purpose of the sport: male bonding. Although he and his teammates share the sport as an escape from "jobs, children, wives, worries" (48), the shared purpose masks the difference between van den Broek's cosmopolitan wealth and migrant precarity. The arguments of Claire Westall and Dennis Mischke, each of which emphasize cricket's recapitulation of structural inequities in twenty-first-century finance capitalism as a form of equitable access, address this distinction. Westall characterizes van den Broek's activities as "riskless risk" in the context of world-systems theory ("Cricket and the World-System" 289), while Mischke unpacks the ways cricket "fails to undo" the temporal inequities of van den Broek's financial capitalism and postcolonial positioning (105). Van den Broek can intellectualize the differences that mark inequity and privilege, but he remains unconscious of, and wary of recognizing, the price his character (literally and metaphorically) exacts from his friend and from the immigrant communities represented through the multiethnic cricket teams.

Examining the parable of the rum shop realigns global design as intimate relationships and narrative form. O'Neill documents a dynamic of whose story we care about that climaxes when Ramkissoon tells his story and van den Broek dismisses it. Simultaneously, this story refracts and lights up Ramkissoon's earlier efforts to call van den Broek's attention to the history of their friendship. The parable appears very late in the novel (page 242 of 256), well into the friendship between the two men, and just after van den Broek has dismissed Ramkissoon's business ambitions: "Get real," quips van den Broek with all the contempt of a successful commodities analyst (212). As an "explanation" for Chuck's unsavory business methods (248), Westall points out that the story "casts their difference in lifelong structural terms" as protection from risk ("Cricket and the World-System" 293), but Ramkissoon's parable is a more thorough-going refutation of van den Broek's homosocial fantasy because it signals their relationship as a commodity exchange on a continuum with other commodities extracted from the Caribbean by European and American companies.[21] As the story goes, young Ramkissoon is trapping songbirds in "one of the last virgin forests in Trinidad" (*Netherland* 243) when he stumbles into a marijuana cache; he knows the growers will kill him so he flees, crashing through a "cocoa plantation," "an abandoned tonka-bean estate," and "orange trees" before emerging at "a rum shop": "I tell you, I've never been so happy to see a rum shop in all my life. I stay right there, next to a bunch of guys shit-talking and drinking puncheon. Guys that make you feel safe" (247). Ramkissoon's characterization of the rum shop echoes Brana-Shute's finding than rum shops are a communal haven for economically and socially precarious men. Ramkissoon can "feel safe" in the shop because these men share his experience. By implication, this parable telegraphs the unspoken material relations that structure social relations between himself and van den Broek. This parable does more than reveal the transactional nature of their relationship; it renders visible the operation of van den Broek's white privilege, which has allowed him to erase differences between the two men depending on his own desires.

Retrospectively, this parable reactivates and connects Ramkissoon's intermittent but consistent efforts to contextualize the current relationship between the two men as a product of historical forces. Early in their acquaintance, Ramkissoon points out that van den Broek, through his Dutch ancestors, is part of "the first tribe of New York, excepting of course the Red Indians" (58). Ramkissoon gives van den Broek a book of *Dutch Nursery Rhymes in Colonial Times,* which tells of "all the slaves" on Manhattan (61). Van den Broek, dissociating his current wealth from this past, wonders, "What was one supposed to do with such information?" (154). After hearing the parable, van den Broek maintains outrage: "I wasn't interested in drawing a line from his [Ramkissoon's] childhood to the sense of authorization that permitted him, as an American, to do what I had seen him do. He was expecting *me* to make the moral adjustment" (248, italics in the original). In this moment, O'Neill connects the events of *Netherland*'s first-person narrative, in which van den Broek reviews how his childhood shapes his current situation, to the absent bildungsroman of Chuck Ramkissoon. Van den Broek has taken little interest in his friend's life story—shown when he attempts to help police investigate Ramkissoon's death but cannot provide useful information. Rather, van den Broek procures the pleasures of immigrant others, "the song . . . the rums and the Coca-Colas . . . Avalon's smooth skillful butt" (140). Van den Broek experiences intoxication as "homosocial pleasure," an intimacy wrought because drinking "dissolves self-consciousness and our sense of difference" (Roth 9). The parable of the rum shop offers a "moral adjustment" to the privilege of the white male narrator as a commodity stemming from a long history of extracting value from Caribbean people.

From this perspective, Ramkissoon's parable is a buzzkill. In fact, the friendship is a "look-like" friendship much as Indian whiskey, in the words of a food critic in the novel, is "look-like whiskey . . . stuff that almost tastes like rum" (*Netherland* 50). This false commodity trade results from van den Broek's misrecognition of the scene, his inability to connect his career as an oil and gas equities analyst (oil and gas are major Trinidadian exports) to a long history of trading Caribbean resources as commodities that produces both Ramkissoon and himself as contemporary subjects. Van den Broek deplores his wife's suggestion that he is "valuable" to Ramkissoon as a commodity rather than an individual "*you*" (249, italics in the original). In retrospect van den Broek admits that, because he "confined" Ramkissoon to an "exotic cricketing circle," he had, oblivious to his privilege, commodified their friendship (19). Ramkissoon's parable shows Van den Broek where he cannot be—in an authentic friendship with Ramkissoon—because van den Broek's presence in Ramkissoon's space arises from the fact that "*he could be there* . . . with every little resistance" (Said 7, italics in the original).

Ramkissoon's parable catalyzes the retrospective structure of the novel, suggesting that van den Broek's narrative can be read as an answer to the question he posed dismissively about the collection of nursery rhymes. While the novel's chronology ends with a happy family portrait, the white Anglo-European family restored after the terrors of 9/11, van den Broek begins his narrative of that story with a critique of narrative structure. He dislikes a reporter who treats Ramkissoon as a stock character— "murder victim" (6)—in a newsworthy "story," but he connects this result to his own casting of Ramkissoon as a "transitory figure" (4). "There's no such thing as a cheap longing, I'm tempted to conclude these days" (4), van den Broek writes as he begins this story. Understood in light of Ramkissoon's parable and his ultimate death—perhaps as a result of his lack of access to the financial resources that effortlessly support van den Broek—this insight frames this brooding, intelligent narrator as an expensive man to know. In fact, the only story he can tell is one of lost opportunity, of a past that could have been that was not, of the surprising recognition of a gap. *Netherland* demonstrates the cost of failing to read rum histories together.

3 Drunken Sluts
Protesting Colonialism and Patriarchy

> After you have gathered your material, use a fruit-press. It's the juices you want.
>
> —Sylvia Townsend Warner

IN THE previous chapter, I charted the ways rum signals a commitment to male privilege that resists movement toward postcolonial social structures. Middle- and upper-class women who appear to drink excessively—and sometimes at all—endanger their reputations as ladies, which means that their relationship to rum as a slave-produced commodity is doubly marked by the dangers of pollution and degradation. In short, gender norms for white women are also colonial gender norms that countersign the superiority of Anglo-whiteness. For women rendered "Other" by race, drinking is naturalized to confirm their deviation from respectability, as in the cases of Lally and Christophine (of *Orchid House*) and Lina (of *A Mercy*). In this chapter, another Christophine joins this group. In the figures of Julia Barnard and Antoinette Cosway, women's drinking challenges patriarchal power linked to rhetorics of white superiority, and these women must be controlled (Antoinette) and hidden (Julia) to retain imperial dominance.

Sylvia Townsend Warner's *The Flint Anchor* (1954) and Jean Rhys's *Wide Sargasso Sea* (1966) each explore the interlocking dynamics of gender and racial oppression under the aegis of nineteenth-century British imperialism. Both are set in the wake of emancipation in the British colonies, a time of social upheaval that parallels the upheavals decolonization caused during the 1950s and 1960s, when these novels were published. Rhys's novel is a prequel to Charlotte Brontë's *Jane Eyre* (1847), and Warner's *The Flint Anchor* is a family saga in which long-suffering wife and mother Julia Barnard begins her hard drinking with rum sent by her son Joseph from the West Indies. Both novels can be (and, in the case of *Wide Sargasso Sea*, has been) understood to articulate a protesting white female subject at the expense of Black West Indian—and particularly Black West Indian female—subjects.[1] Placing these novels into conversation through the depiction of female drunkenness suggests that transatlantic commodity analysis creates a reparative network of exchange among white women, enslaved Africans, and working-class women.[2]

When she sat down to compose *Wide Sargasso Sea,* Jean Rhys was no stranger to the polysemic possibilities of the word *rum;* she deployed it to code the operation of a gendered Caribbean imaginary in her 1934 novel *Voyage in the Dark* (Nesbitt, "Rum Histories" 309–10). She had expanded her understanding by 1945, when she composed the story "Temps Perdi," a series of three vignettes set, successively, in rural England, prewar Vienna, and the Carib Quarter in Dominica.[3] Juxtaposed, the trio of vignettes link the murderous present with colonialism's originating violence against indigenous people. The narrator is troubled by her ability to make sense of these connections and her inability to communicate them as part of a historical narrative. The solution, however, is rum: "But when you have drunk a good tot of rum nothing dismays you; you know the password and the Open Sesame. You drink a second; then you understand everything—the sun, the flamboyance, the girl crawling (because she could not walk) across the floor to be photographed" (274).

The hyperbole of "nothing" and "everything"—a totalizing system of oppression and privilege—contrasts with the microscopic detail that locates the Carib woman "crawling" toward her sole opportunity to be seen. Although this passage suggests rum's soporific effects by anticipating *Wide Sargasso Sea*'s Antoinette exclaiming, "I have been so unhappy for nothing, nothing" (116), Rhys's prose also suggests a new epistemology. What is the "password" and the "Open Sesame" that may allow readers to link three locations and situations represented as separate and unrelated? Is there another way to look at this photograph? The narrator recognizes another way of understanding the relationship between geography and history, one that makes the experience of gender and disability in the Carib Quarter crucial to the Eurocentric depiction of World War II. The individual experience of a girl weighs heavily in the background. Establishing explicit and implicit links between populations deemed "lamentably alien" (Said 207) to colonialism's male beneficiaries, *Wide Sargasso Sea* and *The Flint Anchor* rewrite a past that cannot end differently in order to suggest that it could have—and, more important, could have given rise to a different future.

Wide Sargasso Sea and *The Flint Anchor* exploit the links across the categories of gender, class, and race to figure the recruitment of white women in what Spivak calls the "imperialist narrativization of history" (897) and the emergence of a pluralized economic network—a forerunner to recent ideas of a Global South—that shifts these investments. Neither novel engages the polysemic dimensions of the word *rum,* but each affiliates rum with white English femininity to suppress the protests of women and reinvigorate white male dominance. Antoinette Cosway becomes a stick-figure madwoman, ready for insertion into *Jane Eyre,* but her reduction to a stock character evacuates Rochester, who becomes, in *Wide Sargasso Sea,* a nameless colonialist husband rather than the romantic hero Jane loves.[4] In *Wide Sargasso Sea,* Rhys plays out the scenes nineteenth-century readers might have imagined based on Rochester's testimony, in *Jane Eyre,* that his first wife is "at once intemperate and unchaste."[5] Antoinette's husband indulges in easy explanations of unfeminine behavior when he accuses Christophine of making Antoinette "dead drunk on bad rum" (*Wide Sargasso* 155). In *The Flint Anchor,* Julia Barnard names herself a drunkard, replacing the stock character her husband desires with one less flattering to his biographical constructions. That she typically drinks rum seems a matter of convenience rather than significance, but her husband's generalized temperance rhetoric—"*Wine is a mocker, strong drink is raging.* . . . So Solomon testified" (*Flint Anchor* 93, ellipsis and italics in the original)—merges with his abolitionism to blame his wife's dissipation on "Joseph's rum."[6] These novels are both historical train wrecks because the outcomes are faits accompli (the headstone for a good father and the backstory for *Jane Eyre*), but tracking how privileged white female characters begin to understand and repair the effects of their privilege allows another route to the present.

"Good Shot of White Rum in That": *Wide Sargasso Sea*

Late in part 2 of *Wide Sargasso Sea,* Antoinette tries twice to exceed the role established for her in *Jane Eyre* by discussing the role of economic necessity in her story. She seeks to recognize her husband as someone other than a nameless English patriarch, and she also seeks to be recognized as someone other than a drunken Creole wife. Her failed efforts are framed, even undermined, by the apparently unavoidable presence of rum. Antoinette seems to understand the danger presented by the drink, just as her husband perceives the advantages it may confer. He has replenished their rum—"The decanter of rum was nearly empty so I . . . brought out another bottle," we are told by him—but Antoinette refuses to drink (130). To tell her story, "she poured herself a drink, touched it with her lips then put it down again" (130). The "touch" of rum prompts a narrative that prioritizes financial insecurity rather than a melodrama of threatened white femininity. For example, the husband suggests that Antoinette's mother was "lonely and unhappy," but she amends his explanation with "and very poor" (130). Her attempt to address material conditions fails when her husband offers her a glass of rum and she "push[es] the glass away so roughly that it spill[s] over her dress" (132). As the rum soaks in, the husband rejects Antoinette's story: "I began to wonder how much of all this was true, how much imagined, distorted" (133). The rum that stains her dress stains her story, foreshadowing the futility of Antoinette's effort to explain how her mother's poverty led to perceived madness and promiscuity. At the end of the scene, Antoinette gives up trying "to make [him] understand" (135), and he has begun shaping her into *Jane Eyre*'s madwoman: he calls her Bertha for the first time. Under the sign of rum, Antoinette's alternative narrative cannot be carried forward.

Antoinette's second attempt to humanize her marriage is both a greater success and a grander failure: in this instance, the reinforcement of gender- and race-based alcohol taboos marks her successful challenge to the dominance of white Englishmen. Antoinette and her husband argue violently after he retaliates for her alleged use of an obeah love potion by sleeping with the mulatto servant Amélie. The husband again tries to use rum to his advantage because it affirms his self-image as English male husband/father/colonizer. "It was rum I *chose* to drink," he says, and then remarks on the transformative power of the alcohol: "I waited a second for the explosion of heat and light in my chest, the strength and warmth running through my body" (144, italics added). He perceives the rum as invigorating to his body, as something that corporealizes his power as a white Englishman; even though this power results from external conditions, the effects are concrete and immediate. Under these conditions, he puts Antoinette in her place and reminds the servants of theirs by countermanding Antoinette's demand for a drink with the order to "mix me a good strong one" (145) before attending to his wife's earlier request. No longer masking power with chivalry, the husband asserts his place in the household hierarchy.

In the standoff that ensues, Antoinette gains the power to narrate when she gains control of the rum bottle and forces an economic history lesson into her husband's ears. When "she dart[s] to the table and seize[s] the bottle of rum" (146), she intervenes in her husband's version of events. Antoinette eviscerates his claim to be more humane than the original, slave-owning planters he despises. "You abused the planters and made up stories about them, but you do the same thing," she tells the husband, referring to his relationship with Amélie. "You send the girl away quicker, and with no money or less money, and that's all the difference" (146). He avoids the subject of money, shifting instead to a moral argument about abolition as a "question of justice" rather than addressing Antoinette's charge of sexual exploitation (146). Antoinette explains, after another shot of rum, that "justice" had been denied to her mother. She also has the strength to challenge the name Bertha as an attempt to dehumanize her. "You are trying to make me into someone else . . . that's obeah too" (147), she says, laying bare the false binary between "black magic" and the "white magic" of colonialism.

Although this scene shows the potential to use a product of imperialism to critique imperial ideology, neither Antoinette nor her husband can ultimately overcome the script established by history. Under rum's influence, neither can maintain a critical stance that might forestall the imposition of the *Jane Eyre* plot. Antoinette bites her husband as he attempts to wrest the bottle from her control, the bottle breaks, and "the smell [fills] the room" (*Wide Sargasso* 148), overpowering both Antoinette and her husband. Antoinette is reduced to curses and sobs as she yields to the narrative *Jane Eyre* created for her. Wielding a smashed rum bottle with "murder in her eyes" (148), Antoinette has become Bertha Mason Rochester, madwoman.[7] When both characters lose control of the rum bottle as a site of negotiation, their destinies as colonizer and colonized subject are confirmed.

In Rhys's hands, Antoinette's reduction to the stock character she plays in *Jane Eyre* results from a failure to understand her white privilege as contingent on plantation economics and her unwillingness, ultimately, to divest herself of that privilege. The tool that enables the literary repositioning (Antoinette to Bertha) is a product that requires her compliance with subject positions crucial to the reproduction of English imperial dominance: rum. She sidelines herself in her narrative under the influence of rum, blinding herself to her economic interests by substituting cultural or moral imperatives that serve colonizing interests. As Judith Raiskin points out in *Snow on the Cane Fields* (1996), Antoinette "has been educated, trained, and bribed not only to serve but to identify with colonial and patriarchal interests" (139). Psychologically, she invests in her status as a privileged white woman and resists understanding the economics of her position. For example, when Antoinette complains about her marital woes, Christophine proposes an economic solution, suggesting that Antoinette, "a rich white girl," can exploit her privileged position and "walk out" (*Wide Sargasso* 110). Confronted with these economic realities, Antoinette uses racism to avoid acknowledging that her supposed privilege rests on economic disempowerment. She capitalizes on Christophine's belief that "England" may not exist to label her nurse an "ignorant, obstinate old negro" and dismisses her arguments as a failure to understand English customs (111–12). Even after Christophine reminds Antoinette of her aunt Cora's fury that no legal settlement "protected" Antoinette financially in her marriage, Antoinette remains allied to her privilege as a white wife. After she drinks a rum-laced cup of coffee she ceases thinking critically about what the memory of Aunt Cora means: "When I had drunk the coffee I began to laugh. 'I have been so unhappy for nothing, nothing'" (116). This effect is repeated later in the novel when Christophine reports, "As soon as she has the rum she starts raving that she must go back to you" (155). Rum lulls Antoinette's sensitivity to material conditions, and she not only acquiesces to her dehumanization but also enforces Christophine's.

Ironically, the husband also follows the script to become the stock English gentleman, recognizing that his self-image depends on strategically maintaining and denying his reliance on economic power. Initially, he appears as overwhelmed by rum as Antoinette, having "stumbled back into the big candlelit room which still smelt strongly of rum" (150). Although he tries to maintain the pose of an English gentleman with Christophine, she too forces a narrative into his rum-befuddled ears. Under the influence, the husband acknowledges the economic self-interest at the root of his actions, admitting Christophine's charge that he married Antoinette "for her money and . . . take[s] it all" (152) to sustain his social position in England. He balks, however, at recognizing that his economic motivations subject him as they do Christophine and Antoinette. When Christophine suggests that they negotiate a financial settlement that distributes financial control equitably, he "no longer felt dazed, tired, half hypnotized, but alert and wary, ready to defend [him]self" (158).[8] Here, Christophine's shift from social to material relations violates codes that are both gender- and race-related: finances belong to the world of white men. For a Black woman to analyze the conditions of production that subsidize the husband's position denaturalizes and thus endangers his unmarked identity as white Englishman. No longer intoxicated, he reasserts his economic interest through a combination of race and class norms. "Of course, that is what all the rigmarole is about" (158), he thinks when Christophine mentions money, accusing her of the economic pettiness characteristic of a wily servant. The "rigamarole" is, of course, the rhetoric he uses to mask his own economic commitments. The possibility of another, more ethical narrative based on shared economic conditions is laid out, but rum marks the easy redirection of this potential through the imposition of racial stereotype.

In rum, Rhys embodies the long history that shapes the immediate situation and responses of the characters. To Baptiste, a Black male servant, the husband intimates that he now realizes how to manipulate the paradox represented by the rum bottle. The husband contemplates the rum that filled him with "strength and warmth" earlier, seeing it as a tool for maintaining his sense of self:

> Baptiste appeared, looking towards Antoinette's silent room.
> "Have you got much more of this famous rum?"
> "Plenty rum," he said.
> "Is it really a hundred years old?"
> He nodded indifferently. A hundred years, a thousand all the same to *le bon Dieu* and Baptiste too. (163)

The husband first redirects Baptiste's concerned gaze away from Antoinette and toward himself, establishing his control. The husband claims the asset with a question that is really a command: "Have you got much more of this famous rum?" Baptiste responds concisely, which is to say uncooperatively, so the husband demands further detail that implicitly supports English domination. Baptiste's apparent indifference belies the humiliation of forcing the acknowledgment of a hundred years of slavery.[9] It is unlikely that Baptiste is indifferent to historical time, which recently transformed slavery into emancipation, but the husband's assertion to Baptiste that "a hundred years, a thousand all the same" dismisses any claim to agency Baptiste gained from emancipation. The husband wants the rum to be "a hundred years old"—in other words, produced during the time of slavery, a time when the husband imagines the English enjoyed complete control. But he also wants all time to be "the same" under the sign of rum. The husband deracinates the history that empowers him, naturalizing the hierarchies of race and gender, to recenter himself in the historical narrative.[10] The presence of rum monitors the strategic denial and acknowledgment of material conditions essential to English dominance.

Rum is both the means and the end of enforcement for the husband. Drinking, he composes a disingenuous letter, all innuendo and suspicion, to his father about his marriage. Rum also helps him reorganize relationships to maintain his position at the expense of Antoinette's. He reports, "I drank some more rum and, drinking, I drew a house surrounded by trees. . . . I divided the third floor into rooms and in one room I drew a standing woman—a child's scribble, a dot for a head, a larger one for the body, a triangle for a skirt, slanting lines for arms and feet" (163).[11] The limited characterization offered to Antoinette through this system appears in the schematic drawing; her only distinguishing feature is the "triangle for a skirt," which reinforces femininity as central to her subjugation. That the husband depends upon exercising his legal authority is clear from an exchange as the couple leaves Coulibri for England. Antoinette explains that she had promised a young Black servant that "we . . . you—would take him with you when we left" (171). Her shifting pronouns show her struggle to adapt to the position she has been assigned. "I certainly will not," her husband responds. He notes to himself, "And looking at her stiff white face my fury grew" and demands of her, "What right have you to make promises in my name? Or to speak for me at all?" (171). The connection of "fury" to Antoinette's mask-like "white face" reflects the husband's determination not to recognize his own mask and role. Antoinette's response is a reassuring catalogue of negated statements: "No, I had no right, I am sorry. I don't understand you. I know nothing about you, and I cannot speak for you. . . ." (171, ellipsis in the original). In addition, the choppy sentences verbally resemble the husband's stick drawing: simple lines from a character without any depth, feeling, or humanity that need be recognized by the emerging hero of *Jane Eyre*.

Although the main plot of *Wide Sargasso Sea* does not offer a way out, linking rum to two other beverages in the novel, the obeah love potion and gin, suggests an alternate reading based on joint recognition of economic subjection and a new understanding of self-interest. Superficially, both the potion and gin signify the debased otherness of, respectively, Black people and working-class people. They are inappropriate for wealthy white women like Antoinette. Antoinette's decision to use obeah on her husband appears, first, as race betrayal and, second, as treasonous native resistance to British authority. However, as Carine Mardorossian's "Shutting Up the Subaltern" (1999) and Sue Thomas's *The Worlding of Jean Rhys* (1999) demonstrate, this interpretation of obeah is a product of colonial ideology rather than a disinterested representation of African-based spirituality.[12] Further, such an interpretation refuses to historicize obeah as a spiritual practice that developed in slave communities, communities that existed because Europeans wanted a cheap labor source for the plantations. Like rum, the obeah potion is a product of imperialism. Reading the potion in the context of other products of imperialism diffuses its exotic otherness, but not its significance. Rather, the potion and rum similarly represent colonialism's power to shape subjectivity by shifting between material relations and cultural representations. The potion is not a singular sign of betraying otherness, but part of a larger strategy of justifying, through stereotypes about race, the continued exploitation of Black labor.

Gin offers a third coordinate in this analysis, one that connects the economic oppression of Antoinette and Black people in the West Indies with that of the working-classes of England. Gin has historically been associated with the degradation of the working classes, effects captured in William Hogarth's famous illustration *Gin Lane* (1751).[13] Grace Poole, Antoinette/Bertha's keeper at Thornfield Hall, drinks gin and loves gold. In *Jane Eyre,* Grace's liking for gin resembles the West Indian liking for rum; she indulges to forget "the coercive exploitation of labor . . . set within a highly contentious social hierarchy" in which she has little or no power (F. Smith 126). Rochester claims her alcoholism is "owing partly to a fault of her own, of which it appears nothing can cure her, and which is incident to her harassing profession" (Brontë 326). Rochester illogically melds character and employment into a tautology in which Grace's "fault of her own" is a product of nursing and vice versa. Rochester also considers Grace, like Christophine, to be degraded by her interest in money: "Grace will do much for money," he remarks (317).

Antoinette reinterprets Grace's obsession with money once she shares her gin, although she initially shares Rochester's disgust. Antoinette puzzles over Grace's seemingly obsessive behavior, remarking on the way she "holds a gold piece in her hand and smiles. Then she puts it all into a little canvas bag with a drawstring and hangs the bag round her neck so that it is hidden in her dress" (*Wide Sargasso* 179). But Grace's actions parallel Aunt Cora's attempt to secure Antoinette a minimal degree of economic independence in her marriage. Aunt Cora gives the new bride "a little silk bag" containing her rings and tells Antoinette, "Two are valuable. Don't show it to him. Hide it away" (115). One of the rings is gold, consolidating the link between the two valuable bags. In the final section of Rhys's novel, a stolen sip from Grace Poole's glass of gin allows Antoinette to rethink her cultural disgust as economic coalition: "When she is snoring I get up and I have tasted the drink without colour in the bottle. The first time I did this I wanted to spit it out but managed to swallow it. When I got back into bed I could remember more and think again. I was not so cold" (179). If Antoinette "wanted to spit it [the gin] out," this visceral response may be her last unconscious effort to retain her privileged status as a white, colonizing female subject. This desire now appears insane, given the economics of character development in the novel. When Antoinette manages to swallow this "truth," she finds that sharing Grace's drink clears her confusion, allowing her to "remember more and think again" about her relationships with Christophine, Aunt Cora, and Tia. Moreover, she recognizes that "gold" has significantly shaped her experience: "I heard a clock ticking and it was made of gold. Gold is the idol they worship" (188). Antoinette retrieves the story of her incapacitation and thus learns "why I was brought here and what I have to do" (190). For Antoinette, gin proves rum's undoing.[14]

Rum's "Mocking Rejoinders" in *The Flint Anchor*

In Sylvia Townsend Warner's *The Flint Anchor*, rum appears at strategic moments to index the events of a provincial domestic plot to the concerns of empire. Under the sign of rum, two classic Victorian characters, the paterfamilias (John Barnard) and the angel in the house (Mary Barnard), become avatars of imperial selfishness. Warner formally announces the West Indian context for *The Flint Anchor* when, early in the novel, the eldest son Joseph becomes a plantation manager in the Indies rather than joining the family business, Barnard and Sons. This event is more than a violation of paternal dictates regarding career choice; Joseph also flouts John Barnard's abolitionist beliefs by participating in an economy his father believes to be corrupt. Joseph's decision forces his father to choose between maintaining a claim to moral superiority or to economic control; John chooses economic control, at some cost to his reputation as a just and moral Englishman. "For all that talk about sugar and slavery," the townspeople claim, Joseph "was whipping the blacks on an island in the West Indies" (38). The reference to "sugar and slavery" implies that John had actively supported the abolitionists' sugar boycotts for humanitarian reasons.[15] This possibility is confirmed in the name of John's youngest son, Wilberforce, born about 1830, who was probably named for the prominent abolitionist. Thus, Joseph's economic independence, "a salary and a house of his own" (32), leaves his father "mortified" rather than grateful (33). To hide the fact that his son flouts both his economic and cultural authority, John Barnard permits his reputation as an abolitionist to suffer.

In violating John Barnard's careful barrier between morality and economics, Joseph sets a narrative of beset English manhood in motion in which his father defends England's civilizing mission against the rapacious desires of others at home and abroad. By naturalizing economic disempowerment as a matter of race, class, and gender, John avoids confronting how financial self-interest promotes his self-image at the expense of others. This strategy is apparent from his reaction to the "consignments of delicious West-Indian produce" (44) Joseph sends home as peace offerings. To John, these foods have already "imperilled [*sic*] Joseph's salvation" (45), and he will not endanger his own by consuming products from such an economic system. The women of the family appall him with their practicality, accepting and enjoying the West Indian produce without, apparently, a qualm. In John's mind, their behavior signifies their innate moral, physical, and intellectual weakness; it is also distantly implied that John associates their appetites with racial stereotypes. Judging the women as morally weak prevents him from acknowledging that women's economic dependence prohibits the luxury of discriminating among resource providers. John's discomfort with the "delicious," then, masks an anxiety that his character relies more on the ability to provide resources than on any innate superiority.

Into this general context, Warner introduces the demon rum. The rum shakes John's self-image temporarily, but he reinterprets rum's significance according to temperance ideologies of womanhood to bolster his position as patriarch. Surveying the contents of his wine cellar in preparation for an important dinner party, John is confronted by empty rum bottles, "a ranked assembly of bottle rumps, and another beyond it, and beyond that another" (93). The whiff of the scatological ("ranked" and "rumps") in the prose carries his earlier discomfort with the "delicious West Indian produce" squarely into the realm of saturnalia, an a priori "mooning" of John's explanation of their meaning. Reasoning through and dismissing the proper modes of rum consumption—rum punch and Julia's "medicinal" dosage—John stops short of following the drain on his resources to its actual source, his wife's alcoholism. He substitutes another explanation:

> *Wine is a mocker, strong drink is raging* . . . So Solomon testified, though John Barnard had never found it so; but because he was immune to that temptation, he was not justified in putting it in the way of others. The Madeira might be medicinal, but rum, rum in such quantities! . . . Joseph's regular consignments now seemed direct interventions of Satan, mocking rejoinders to the tracts and baby clothes sent out so regularly to the labourers on the sugar-cane plantations. He should never have allowed Joseph's rum to enter the house. Better still, he should have closed the cellar when he became a family man. If he had done so he might by now have set up the Temperance Union which was so badly needed in Loseby. . . . God had not prospered Anchor House with a wine cellar in its foundations. Could it be that Ellen's port-wine stain was an indication, a writing on the wall? (93–94, ellipses and italics in the original)

Attributing the effects of rum to "Satan," John employs the standard tropes of temperance rhetoric, but the narrative tracks his strategic denial that this unsanctioned use of resources represents the agency of others. John infantilizes women, Black people, and children separately and collectively, making them his moral responsibility and thus justifying his control of resources. The empty bottles are a judgment on him as a patriarchal subject because he has failed to protect the welfare of various, less responsible "others." Thus, Julia's alcoholism is a result of her husband's failure to shield her feminine weakness rather than a response to being objectified as "a model wife and mother" (239). Ellen's birthmark is a sign of his moral failure rather than a problem for *her*. Even the "tracts and baby clothes" are evidence of his failure to enlighten the West Indians.

The rum bottles are "an indication, a writing on the wall," but not always or necessarily as John thinks they are. By pursuing the links between the passage above and other parts of the novel, we can find an alternative script functioning under this overpowering narrative. The "mocking rejoinders" of rum for "tracts and baby clothes" assert an alternate economy in which groups of relatively disempowered characters barter symbols of their oppression. First, the baby clothes link Julia to West Indian women as reproductive workers with little control over their output. Julia has borne eleven children, and she seems resigned to the knowledge that her years of service earn her a life that is "in its way, no worse than a nun's" (27). Her suffering is not the same, but incompetent patriarchal control of reproductive assets infuriates her. Most of her children, she later asserts, have been "snubbed and ignored and *mismanaged*" (240, italics added) because John favors one daughter, Mary. At birth, Julia calls her "a creditable little Miss Barnard" (25), but she becomes a loss in the marriage market. What John explains as a moral desire to preserve Mary, his "angel," from contamination and consumption by "worms" (25) works out as a poor economic choice, a nearly incestuous desire not to trade on Mary's value in the marriage market.

The apparently incongruous exchange—rum for baby clothes—highlights ethical problems in the exchange economy. On the one hand, the exchange links merchant-class child-rearing in England to the commodification of babies in plantation economies; it ups the ante on Julia's oppression by reminding us that the children of slaves were saleable property. But this inequity has multiple dimensions. John Barnard's injured sense of altruism arises from his position within the colonial world system; on this trade he has lost value. Yet the items sent were made by the women of his household, labor he arrogates to profit himself. The return gesture, rum from the plantation, also derives from exploited labor, but the enslaved people do not send it. Alongside John Barnard's exchange the laborers make another trade. Baby clothes are both inappropriate to a labor force denied its progeny, but they might also recognize that trauma. In the exchange of rum and baby clothes, there is both acknowledgment of connection between English and West Indian mothers and a delineation of limits.

Secondly, the "tracts" exchanged for rum similarly correlate, without collapsing, working-class oppression and racial oppression. The conditions under which the tracts are produced link slavery in the colonies to workhouse exploitation in England. The tracts are "done by pauper children, who also coloured the illustrations to the Moral Tales. They were learning habits of industry and forwarding the Lord's work by working unpaid, but many of them were too young to be neat, and by the end of a day they lost interest and painted blue maws on crocodiles and rosy faces on Negroes singing hymns under the lash" (*Flint Anchor* 51). The tracts carry messages beyond those of Christian charity and endurance formally announced by their narratives. Through their inattentive painting, the children ironically reveal the oppression of workers exploited in the name of England's civilizing mission. The transposition of skin color links the working-class poor, child laborers, and Black West Indians in a global pattern of exploitation. The situation of neither "unpaid" group is particularly "rosy." The children create a phantasmagoric worldview in which they are metaphorically "Negroes" singing under the lash of Christian charity. Yet the presumed inability of young children to articulate this metaphor deliberately robs the image of easy equivalence. Instead, the image remains suspended, critically balanced between the pathetic and the ridiculous, allowing the real possibility of connection between "pauper children" and "Negroes" without assimilating them.

These incidents, dispersed through the early parts of *The Flint Anchor*, coalesce when John discovers that Darwell, a servant and Julia's drinking companion, is an alcoholic. The Darwell incident is a classic Victorian set piece featuring a stock character, the servant who drinks, in which one might expect the expulsion of the guilty party by an outraged patrician family. After the doctor departs, having treated Darwell's delirium tremens, John starts the expected scene: "Did no one suspect this?" Instead of dutiful expressions of denial, "He saw that everyone but Mary knew or suspected that Darwell drank" (236). Only Mary joins the cast of the melodrama. "Papa! You must send her away," she tells her father. "I can never be easy while she is in the house. I think she ought to go to prison"

(236). The other characters refuse to follow John Barnard's narrative lead, derailing a Victorian script that will consolidate patriarchal power (countersigned by female moral purity) at the expense, literally, of Darwell's financial security. Under very controlled conditions, Julia rejects the privileges of white upper-class womanhood; she identifies with Darwell by calling herself "a drunkard" of twenty years' standing (239). Julia refutes each excuse John Barnard trots out to protect her, forcing an exposure that he needs her complicity to support his own reputation. Moreover, this avowal allies Julia not only with Darwell but also with the West Indian population: as Darwell's drinking companion, Julia must share "the spicy breath of Joe's plantations" with her servant (232). Like the smell that fills the rooms in *Wide Sargasso Sea*, the "spicy breath" of rum momentarily settles over the Barnard home, couching its middle-class respectability in the horrors of slavery.

Mary, representing the uncritical white Englishwoman as consumer, revels in her consuming power, a pleasure that arouses her father's disgust. In the fallout from Darwell's illness, the text offers a physical parallel to Mary's moral outrage: "She was rosy with excitement and ate enormously at dinner" (*Flint Anchor* 236). Mary's "rosy" complexion and large appetite figure her as a monstrous consumer; this English rose thrives on the pain of others. Her complexion, perversely joined to the "rosy faces" the orphans paint on enslaved people, links her self-satisfaction to the consumption of slave labor (51). If John felt her birth was "free of tax or charges against deterioration" (24), her cost is exacted now. John Barnard's sudden inclusion of Mary in his general misogyny, as palpable as the husband's in *Wide Sargasso Sea*, might excite pity were it not for John's deflection from the economics of Mary's character to business concerns. His strategy is "a safety valve" because "the business was doing very well" (290). John Barnard substitutes legitimate business concerns for unpleasant knowledge of domestic economy.

As the only unredeemed character in *The Flint Anchor*, Mary provides a cautionary tale of oblivious white womanhood. Within the novel she lives on, clueless to her implication in the economics of imperialism, playing her part as loving wife and dutiful daughter to the hilt. Even John falls victim to her script. He can admit that he is "a bad father" (305), but his request for a simple gravestone—only his "name, and after that, 'Lord, have mercy on me, a sinner'" (314)—is overwritten by Mary, who replaces his text with a fulsome tribute to "a devoted Husband and Father, an example of industry, enterprise, and benevolence to his native town" (3). Mary, in her role as compliant, indiscriminate consumer is presented here as an extreme, but if she is filtered through the perspectives of critics like Spivak and Mohanty, she is a norm. She illustrates what it means to reproduce the scripts of imperialism: she revels in the limited role assigned her and then is made to take much of the blame.

In the "three maiden sisters, reputed to be horribly learned," who rent Anchor House at the end of the novel (308), the correspondence between Julia, Darwell, the orphans, and the enslaved persists as a matter of aesthetic design. One sister paints, choosing "everyday objects" and depicting them "exactly and as though no one had ever set eyes on them before" (309). Her subjects include a crab, "a tangle of rusty ships' chains," and "an old net, thrown over the arm of the lay figure" (309). These images suggest a still life, building meaning from juxtaposition rather than narrative flow, and lateral rather than forward movement in the crab's characteristic gait. The "tangle of rusty ships' chains" implies antiquity, misuse, and neglect: perhaps the "tangle" of cultures and relationships created by the British Empire's dominance at sea; "chains" are both essential to maritime travel and iconic for slavery. A "lay figure" is an articulated dummy used to practice drawing: the inanimate human form figures a process by which subjects acquires identities. Posed among things, the body acquires meaning from the items around it. By concluding with ekphrasis, Warner asserts art as work, as a composition as dependent on the flexibility of the artist as the interpreter.

The Flint Anchor and *Wide Sargasso Sea* filter concerns about decolonization by considering the consequences of abolition, offering historical "juicings" of the period following emancipation.[16] At a time when whiteness, and white femininity, were problematic representations in both West Indian literatures and politics, these novels portray the limited effects of protest from white women embedded and invested in colonial power for their own sense of identity and agency. Reading the role of rum in these two novels accentuates relationships between oppressed groups suspended across space to generate a resistant community that could be representative of a Global South that could already exist. The political potential of these narratives rests in alcoholic timeout, largely unheard even as it is voiced. To the degree that rum poetics can produce a rum history for these novels, later women writers from the Caribbean point out the limits of these reparative efforts and surface a Southern response.

The Wives' Revenge: "Rum Sweet Rum"

Through the name of a main character, Dolly, Rosanne Kanhai's short story "Rum Sweet Rum" (1999) has tacit links to female characters in V. S. Naipaul's *Miguel Street,* in which there are two Dollys: George's daughter, who "giggle[s]" and "burst[s] into tears" but never speaks (27, 35), and Hat's wife, whose mercurial behavior arouses neighborhood speculation (208–9).[17] These Dollys, by virtue of Naipaul's strategy of limiting female speech, express their resistance in actions and sounds. In Kanhai's story, set outside the city after the war, Dolly acquires the speech and agency her predecessors lack, emerging from the cane field—the site of so much sexual violence—to invent a future using rum. Dolly's counterpart, and the story's narrator, is one of her employers, a newly married woman who recalls that she "could be a maid myself" (5) as she adapts to her role as upwardly mobile middle-class working mother and wife. The act that seals their cooperation is silent: Dolly "point[s]" to a bottle of rum and the narrator allows her a swig (5). In that moment the narrator violates all of her mother-in-law's strictures on "how to train a maid, how to break them of their bad habits, how not to give them bad habits from the very beginning" (4). As the story progresses, the narrator remains uncomfortably complicit as Dolly takes items from her house and drinks (and replaces) the rum (11), countering the criminalizing gaze of Dolly's other employers, who are always on the lookout for theft. The narrator tempers the significance of the interaction by reducing its cost and emphasizing its appropriate use by women: "It was not expensive rum. I kept it there to season meat" (5). Yet a "strong" smell of alcohol pervades the apartment, indicating that this exchange is more of a libation, blessing a shared enterprise (5).

This illicit contract violates communal borders established by class/caste and cosmopolitan standards that require transnational class affiliations to trump cross-class gender solidarity. This aspirational cosmopolitanism is represented by the Churchill-Roosevelt Highway that bisects the novel's settings, concatenating local social structures with familial development goals that read as middle class across cultural and national lines. When Dolly meets the narrator, she emphasizes their geographical proximity and social distance: "She pointed, 'Look, you could just see the top of my house from here. That is where I living.' She leaned over the banister, her face tilted upwards, her eyes focused beyond the Churchill-Roosevelt Highway to a distant point on the horizon. I came forward, stood beside her and leaned with her, both our shadows long and sideways in the morning sun. I looked where she pointed but could only see cane tops stretching to the sky" (3–4).

Despite Dolly's assertion of proximity, the narrator sees "only . . . cane tops," a thought that indicates the irrelevance of Dolly's life to her middle-class employers except as it pertains to her work for them. In an inversion of Jameson's modernist-imperial aporia, Dolly locates herself in the space of narrative invisibility, "a distant point on the horizon." To see her life, the narrator must lean out spatially and socially, repositioning herself. The Churchill-Roosevelt Highway that runs between the narrator's apartment building and the cane fields separates Trinidad's postwar future (suburbs, working women, professionals) and an agricultural past. Named for the leaders who agreed to station US troops on Trinidad during World War II, the highway links Fort Read, an American base, with Port of Spain. At the time, road construction "bisected rural communities" and uprooted local farmers whose crops were in its path; the completed road was reserved solely for military use (Jaggassar). In the story, it separates those who benefit from postwar development and the peasantry subsisting as the economy transforms. The narrator has been enlisted to progress while Dolly has been left behind "in the cane" ("Rum Sweet Rum" 4). In the opening encounter between the two women, rum is already center stage, linking past and present exploitation to the production system that creates rum from cane.

For Dolly, the combination of rum and poverty allows the larger community to naturalize her experience of domestic abuse. The details of her life are familiar: as her family grows, so does her husband's "drinking" and "beatings" (7). He spends his pay at the rum shop, beats her when drunk, and steals her money to spend on rum, and Dolly's efforts to support the family only intensify the abuse.[18] Fingers himself has been fragmented and dismembered by the labor system: the fingers he loses on the job and the leg he injures while drunk make him useless as a laborer (16). Dolly's is a typical story of poverty and dysfunction as a sign of moral unworthiness that excuses community and institutional inaction. It is, moreover, "husband-and-wife-business" (8). This official story has been told, the narrator notes carefully, in the police officer's "large notebook" with "his writing all over it" (12), with the compliance of middle-class women.

Observing the treatment of Dolly and tacitly supporting her, the narrator reflects on domestic violence from which she is putatively protected by class but is equally dangerous to all women. After the police officer assures an outraged housewife who has accused Dolly of theft that Fingers will "fix she up" (12), the narrator wonders about an overheard incident in which her own mother was beaten by her mother-in-law; while the narrator "pretended not to hear," she now "wondered if my mother had wanted me to hear" (13). The mother-in-law's physical beating to force compliance with male dominance corresponds with the use of state institutions to ensure that Dolly is beaten by proxy. Listening to these official scripts, the narrator considers "what kind of message" she offers her sons and husband through quotidian compliance with her mother-in-law's rules (8). As a result, the narrator makes a significant exchange by giving Dolly "a bed my husband's uncle had made for him when he was a boy" (15). The concentration of male pronouns ("my"; "him"; "he") and subject position markers ("husband"; "uncle"; "boy") in this sentence registers the narrator's determination to divert patrimonial inheritance to support female agency—her own and Dolly's.

As the narrative progresses, rum shifts from primarily an oppressive substance to primarily a liberating substance. Earlier we saw that the narrator's acceptance of Dolly's terms liberates them into a cross-class alliance, and Dolly does use rum to celebrate in her free time, taking "rum and a chicken to curry" on an excursion to the beach (16). Yet she suffers not only from drunken beatings but also from "yellowish" (9) eyes and limited appetite (13), symptoms of alcoholic hepatitis. These symptoms also link to the tradition of the zombie, or *soucriant,* but Kanhai clearly blames Dolly's diseased condition on rum—both in an immediate sense and as its history shapes her current position. Dolly turns this set of conditions to her advantage, complying with the terms to liberate herself. Dolly plans to murder her husband with the commodity that currently and historically subjects her and Fingers: "I done have it plan. Is Indian cocktail for Fingers. You know what is that? Is phosphono, the medicine we does put in the crop to kill the weeds. I will put it in his rum. When he smelling the rum he wouldn't know the difference. . . . And he done drunk already. How will he know?" (10). The "Indian cocktail" fuses old agricultural products, sugar and rum, with a modern agricultural chemical, phosphono, breaching the Churchill-Roosevelt divide by connecting the oppressive economic priorities of the past with those of the present. Dolly executes her plan, trusting to conventional wisdom to mask her crime. As a former neighbor reports to the narrator, "Police say like he kill himself. Put poison in the rum and make Indian cocktail" (17). Fingers's reputation silences suspicion—though the "like" could indicate some reservations. The neighbor encourages compliance from the narrator by coercing agreement ("*You know* how that man used to drink!"), using imperatives

("He *must* be get tired of living"), and reiterating police preference for the easy explanation ("*you think* they will make a case for that?"; 17, italics added). In Kanhai's narrative, rum transitions from instrument of torture to instrument of feminist liberation across class borders, and by the end of the story both characters have left the scene of the crime. In their absence, this narrative raises questions about cross-class cooperation as a potential function of a Global South. "Rum Sweet Rum" illustrates local cooperation between two women, and the narrator's transgression of respectability in her treatment of servants counters patterns that align the wealthy classes transnationally.

Land of Love and Drowning: From Danish Krone to Yankee Dollars

The failed promise of US influence comes under direct attack in Tiphanie Yanique's *Land of Love and Drowning* (2014), which deploys "Rum and Coca-Cola" as a utopian vision unfulfilled, belied by racist and imperialist exploitation in US and colonial territories. The negative effects of the relationship between the US Virgin Islands and its new owner as of 1917 emerge early, as the US policy of prohibition destroys the business of the family at the center of this novel. Like Rhys's *Wide Sargasso Sea,* Yanique's novel juices a prior work to rectify the stereotypical portrayal of Caribbean people. In this case, the target is Herman Wouk's *Don't Stop the Carnival* (1965), in which islanders live in a state of "endless carnival" that frustrates US profiteers (5), not unlike Thompson's *The Rum Diary.*[19] Wouk mixes satire of "white people charging hopefully around" with a background of local color that excludes the Virgin Islands from history and productivity: "Today is like yesterday, and tomorrow will be like today . . . the idea is to take things easy and enjoy the passing time under the sun" (4). Yanique explores how this caricature of endless time-out impacts the family history of two sisters, Anette and Eeona, for whom the arrival of US control only shifts the locus of male dominance.

Through the narrator, Anette, *Land of Love and Drowning* also links to *Wide Sargasso Sea.* Anette's mother shares a name with Rhys's heroine, whose mother is named Annette. In one sense, *Wide Sargasso Sea* is about a happy, sexually fulfilling marriage driven off course by imperialism; *Land of Love and Drowning* similarly contrasts a promised "sweetness" between the United States and the Virgin Islands to pornographic exploitation of Black bodies (84). Like Antoinette, Anette understands that her story counters dominant historical narratives and anticipates the need to credential herself. Anette asserts her authority as "the historian of this family" and as a historian: "Teacher of history at the Anglican school. . . . If anyone know the history is me" (9). Nevertheless, Anette understands that history is a representational form that proposes a version of facts, "a kind of magic I doing here" (9). Her notion of history as "magic" evokes both the devastating impact of obeah, as perceived by British authority, on *Wide Sargasso Sea*'s plot, but Anette proposes instead a transformation through the addition of other stories to the historical record.

The relationship between rum and Coca-Cola, as synecdoches for the Virgin Islands and the United States, has been central to Anette's family since 1917. The prospect of becoming American initially excites Virgin Islanders, but the reality of Prohibition—which outlaws a crucial export, rum—damages rather than strengthens the economic position of Owen Arthur Bradshaw, father of Eeona and Anette, who "had always shipped rum" (*Land of Love* 4). This relationship appears to shift during World War II, when the song "Rum and Coca-Cola" symbolizes the pleasure of equitable personal relationships as part of a joint military enterprise. The pleasure comes from mixing "both," according to Anette: "The Caribbean is the rum and America is the cola and we in the Virgin Islands is both so everything sweet, sweet, sweet" (147). Rum and Coca-Cola is a libation for "sweet" relations untainted by racialized sexual exploitation by the Coast Guard intent on policing women's "rummy underwear." Only later does Anette realize that the sweetness masks continued exploitative behavior, this time in the form of artistic theft: "Is much later we hear 'bout the Yankee Andrews Sisters thiefing the song" (147).[20] This episode, situated at the midpoint of the novel, is its fulcrum, and from there the sisters enact, with limited success, resistance to sexual and economic oppression rooted in rum and Coca-Cola.

Eeona, the elder sister, experiences abuse ratified by patriarchal power generally (her father) and the expression of that power through European (Danish) and US systems that further victimize Black women. The psychological machinations that her father, Owen Arthur Bradshaw, uses to justify sexually abusing Eeona are tightly bound to his submission to economic constraints forced by the United States. To maintain his business, Bradshaw acquiesces to an uncomfortable exhibition at a private party among business associates: a young girl, "very afraid" and very like Eeona is "tied up with lace and silk" for a demonstration of a Gauss ball (3). The allusion to punishment of enslaved women, with the soft-porn "lace and silk," merges male erotic pleasure with female terror. To accommodate himself to the spectacle, Bradshaw "jostle[s] the warm rum in his glass and listen[s] to the wind" (3). Rum requires the continued abuse of girls in the name of masculine sexual and economic desires, which the pronunciation of Eeona's name—"He Own Her" (308)—announces. Eeona begins to break this cycle when she is jostled by a rum and Coca-Cola. Her relationship with McKenzie (Kweku Prideux) begins with "a warm rum and Coca-Cola, for he, too, had heard the song" (161–62). In the novel, this scene precedes Anette's discussion of the song by a few pages, but the framing indicates that he trades on Eeona's innocence. She "did not know the song the Andrews Sisters would steal" (162) and is thus vulnerable to exploitation. As "she sip[s] her warm drink," Eeona drops her guard and, like Antoinette, indulges in fantasies of marital bliss: "Wouldn't she enjoy hearing it [his name] after her own given name?" (162). By contrast, McKenzie drinks "calmly" during intercourse (63) and manipulates her body for his pleasure. When he spills his drink on her, she awakens to her uncomfortable position: "He turned her head to the side, so he could spill rum and cola onto her shoulder and then suck it off. She saw through the bushes. . . . Another man and woman moving against each other like the slamming of the waves. That woman was looking at Eeona. That woman was looking like her. And that woman was grimacing, her naked back to that man's shirted belly" (163–64). The spillage shifts her perspective, showing her an imperfect mirror that makes her see that her story, with variations, is routine. Eeona sees how she will be looked "at" as well as what she looks "like" in the eyes of a(nother?) suffering woman. Eeona attempts to get out of this story, disrupting the flow of rum. As the glass is "shattering about her face and head" (164), she gasps and grasps again for the fantasy that marital propriety can be hers: "The bed . . . I want the master bedroom" (164). But the "master bedroom" contains only a "mattress on the floor" (164).[21]

While Eeona's scene of resistance is domestic, Anette politicizes the abusive behavior of US investors and the constraints they place on access to pleasure. She uses rum and Coca-Cola as the symbol for a political protest. This practice continues her earlier commodity analysis of the song, and her sense of US injustice has been sharpened by televised reports of civil rights protests.[22] Anette, angered that her family is cut off from "their own common beach history" (296) by the decision of a "white woman" who violates local custom, starts the Beach Occupation Movement and Bacchanal (BOMB). The mélange of political, military, and hedonistic words, culminating in the acronym, explodes distinctions that mask usurpation with the regulation of private property. "Beaches must be free," she claims, echoing a US ideal to ground their right to protest.

Anette's "swim-ins" (315) position themselves semiotically between the sit-ins referenced in the text (324) and the love-ins of later in the decade. At these protests, there are "coolers of rum and Coke" because the events are "bacchanal" and "serious business" (315).[23] Her actions invoke African and Caribbean syncretic traditions of rum as a libation that promotes community, marks sacraments, and can be the prelude to violent uprisings against exploitative masters (F. Smith, 157–67). In identifying with the civil rights movement, she reveals the false promises made to US citizens and connects her protest to internationalized resistance to racism and neoimperial economic exploitation.

The use of rum and Coca-Cola in *Land of Love and Drowning* is not simply convenient set-dressing, but an engagement with commodity forms that transport ideological content across space and time, as well as through bodies. Yanique forecasts this effort in the early pages of the novel as part of Anette's discussion of history. When Anette admits that "this ain true history. . . . Is just a story I telling, but put it in your glass and drink it" (33), the drink in question is as yet unknown. Retrospectively, Anette calls on her readers to put some thought into what they are drinking and discover where it came from.

4   Libations 1
Spirits of Change

> Cause the heights was cold and our breath making feathers
> Like the mist, we pass the rum. When it came back, it
> Give us the spirit to turn into murderers.
> I lift up the axe and pray for strength in my hands
> To wound the first cedar. Dew was filling my eyes,
> But I fire one more white rum. Then we advance.
> —Derek Walcott, *Omeros*

PHILOCTETE, WALCOTT'S speaker in this section of his epic poem, knows his audience: tourists. His representation of folk culture teems with stereotypes of drunken primitives assaulting trees as part of a ritual blessed by shared alcohol consumption. "Fire" and "advance" conjure organized violence, but the words belie a spiritual conjunction between men and nature.[1] This homosocial bonding is cooperative rather than competitive, with rum as the libation that sacralizes the effort. Philoctete's evocation of violence drifts toward the topic of this chapter, an exploration of the delegitimization of political resistance by exploiting rhetoric surrounding drunkenness.[2] By building on Anette's insistence that a "bacchanal" is "serious business," this chapter considers the political action through the figure of libations.

The first of two chapters using libations as a figure to render legible relationships that are glossed over, this chapter is also a shift between analyses of rum that illustrate the colonization of interpersonal dynamics to those that offer a critique of colonized institutional structures. This chapter looks at the positioning of rum texts that narrate communal resistance to colonial or quasi-colonial governments, and it documents the dismissal of political protest as drunkenness to discredit resistance. The next chapter registers these operations metacritically, tracing the consequences of a professional habit of ignoring rum in literary studies. Both chapters identify scenes of reading in which rum both marks and deflects engagement with historical economic patterns as formative for the consumption of texts labelled as Caribbean.

In this chapter, the figure of libations stresses that, despite decolonization as a process intended to separate West Indian colonies from England as independent nations, English and West Indian societies remain structured by a shared historical context. Libations are closely related to liberation in Caribbean cultures because they have precedents in antecolonial, preslavery origins: the African societies from which enslaved people were taken. These ceremonies directly or indirectly challenge colonial economies that enslaved African peoples by reconnecting to a precolonial past. Drawing on African cultural traditions akin to Western ideas, slave rebels used oath drinks when they "strengthened alliances and reaffirmed individuals' community obligations" (F. Smith 163). Unlike so-called Dutch courage, however, these oath drinks also had a spiritual component, invoking gods and ancestors as guides and advisors (164–65). As a libation, rum draws on spiritual traditions in which alcohol drinking or pouring invokes or appeases spirits or ancestors, an African tradition that survived and became part of a syncretic Caribbean culture (164–67). The use of rum at funerals and weddings, carnival, home building, or home demolition continues to be current practice across the Caribbean (Japal and Benoit 8) and Latin America (Mitchell 7). These practices translate easily across cultures. The practice of marking holidays, or the return of the master, with alcohol would not have been unfamiliar to people newly captured from Africa (F. Smith 161–62) or Anglo-Europeans (Gusfield 404; Burke qtd. in Adler 385). As obvious as it is to say, enslaved people, the local plantocracy, and the English at home shared traditions of using alcohol to mark celebrations, transactions, and pledges, establishing a common ground for interpreting—and misinterpreting—these scenes.

As such, these latter chapters focus on texts associated with the Caribbean and normalized as subjects for Caribbean literary studies. The strategy of interpreting these texts as products of the Caribbean enables a double focus in which rum is an inflection point for both the interpretation of political resistance as dysfunctional chaos and for the economies of reading that allow such interpretations to proliferate. This chapter refutes Phyllis Shand Allfrey's depiction of Black protesters as easily dissipated with the application of "rum and water" (151). Two of the three novels featured in the chapter take place in West Indian islands, and in George Lamming's *Water with Berries* the protagonists are planning a revolution in their fictional homeland, the island of San Cristobal, while in exile. All three center on political movements that resist local governments that, despite increasing local control, cannot be called decolonized. Walter Castle, protagonist of Earl Lovelace's *While Gods Are Falling* (1965), uses rum to analyze an apparent disengagement of peasant communities from politics. In George Lamming's *Water with Berries* (1971), Derek, an actor in London and a conspirator for revolution, rapes an actor onstage after a bottle of rum releases memories of a history of British oppression. In Sylvia Wynter's *The Hills of Hebron* (1962), Moses Barton establishes a separatist community. When he is temporarily institutionalized, his conversations with Dr. O'Malley, the alcoholic superintendent of a Jamaican asylum, are a series of missed opportunities for political empathy between representatives of colonized populations. The figure of libations marks lost potential for political change—political change that could have produced an alternative and perhaps more ideally postcolonial present, but did not.

"There Must Be Some Significance in That": Time-Out as Protest

In *While Gods Are Falling*, Earl Lovelace critiques neocolonial reification of colonial economic models by playing on the meanings of *rum*. Published just after Trinidad and Tobago were granted independence from Britain in 1962, *While Gods Are Falling* intertwines rum with the nativist impulses of the Party of National Importance to fictionalize the critique Frantz Fanon makes in "On National Culture" (1961). Protagonist Walter Castle, unhappy in his low-level white-collar job, frets that promotions are based on political loyalty rather than merit. In the process, he remembers the analysis of party politics offered by Mr. Reggie, a wise man who represents peasant knowledge:

> "This Party card can be rum," Mr Reggie said. "A strong drink to stimulate you to action. But you can become so drunk on it that you could believe that you could whip the world. But when the effect wears off . . . There is that time when the effect of the liquor wears off. You have to guard against that time, Soscie."
>
> "It's Mack," Soscie said.
>
> "Too many Macks," Mr Reggie said. "Too many Macks expecting something for nothing, expecting to have things the easy way. Too many Macks taking this Party card as something to wear in their button-hole." (*While Gods* 119, ellipsis in the original)

Mr Reggie elides the adjective "rum" and the noun "rum," turning rum into a metaphor for the intoxicating effects of political hierarchies. The first sentence of the passage calls for the adjective: "rum" describes the Party Card, an indicator of entitlement rather than commitment, as ideologically suspect. The party card, however, becomes the alcohol, "a strong drink to stimulate you to action." It intoxicates, leading to unrealistic expectations of "whip[ping] the world." Mr. Reggie invokes typical management practice on plantations that produce rum, implying that the Party of National Importance replaces one hierarchy with another. He distrusts the party's cronyism as another manifestation of colonial exclusions based on race. To be "drunk on it [rum]" is to be enmeshed in a system that recapitulates colonialism as decolonization. Soscie pushes back by individuating the problem to single bad actors when he claims that "it's Mack," but Mr. Reggie insists that Mack is a phenomenon of which there are "too many" rather than a singular instance. Mack takes his position for entitlement "to have things the easy way," yet a government official foils him by pulling rank. "Party Card" holders, Mr Reggie implies, claim to eradicate corrupt colonial politics, yet they reinstate them for their own benefit. Postcolonial politics are like rum, "a strong drink," in that they promise "rights and privileges" long denied (106), but Mr Reggie warns that the intoxicating effects will "wear off" (119). "The effect of the liquor" of racist Western values is inevitably, historically, there. As Walter reflects on his political ideas, this debate helps him understand alternative forms of political action.

Mr. Reggie's stance counters the Party of National Importance's investment in periodizing colonialism. Party leaders claim, "Gone is our colonial past" (106). They want to erase the shame of colonization with a return to precolonial origins: "The bow and arrow was used by our Carib ancestors. . . . by our African and Indian ancestors on the mother continents. . . . Today, we use the bow and arrow as our symbol to slay colonialism and ignorance, to slay immorality in public affairs and narrow-mindedness" (107). The emphasis on "ancestors" and "the mother continents" asserts a unity undermined by historical fact, as Caribs, Africans, and Indians have formed social relations out of the conditions of extermination, enslavement, and indentured servitude. Colonialism makes this symbolism possible. Frantz Fanon repudiates this ahistoricism when he claims that assertions of precolonial purity "serve as a justification for the hope of a future national culture" by silencing resistance under the conditions of slavery ("On National Culture" 170): "They fought as well as they could, with the arms that they possessed then," he concludes (167). Fanon historicizes struggle and its forms, asserting a need to look not only at armed resistance but also at "silence and passivity" to recognize political work.[3]

Using Mr. Reggie's *rum* metaphors, Walter Castle puts Fanon's ideas into play to create a resisting West Indian consumer. He begins, as Mr Reggie does, with amorphous desire: "The root of our problems" as human beings, Walter claims, is that "we want" (*While Gods* 101). Walter analyzes his wants—materialized as the desire to be promoted—as potentially a function of a colonial legacy mimicking Englishness rather than as independent desires. He contrasts his habits to those of his hometown, a peasant village called Nuggle: "The people at Nuggle work hard all week and when they get paid on Saturdays, they go to the rum shop, or go and gamble under the old house by Mack. They don't seem to think about doing anything else. And when it's Christmas they want to have their houses stocked with rum, and they want rum for Carnival . . . There is something in that. There must be some significance in that" (102, ellipsis in the original). In terms of MacAndrew and Edgerton, the people of Nuggle live in perpetual time-out, a repetitive cycle of work and hard drinking that is anthropological rather than historical. Walter repeats the "some" at the end of the passage, seeking to create "significance" from a set of behaviors usually assigned obvious meanings (lazy, unproductive, drunk). In seeking to read the peasantry otherwise, Walter politicizes the peasantry in familiar ways. Selwyn Cudjoe argues that "democratic sentiment" of Caribbean literature seeks "to stress the surging activity of the masses from below who are catalytic" (269), but here inactivity is the site of resistance. Walter rejects class stereotypes by ascribing agency to people in Nuggle who "work hard" and then choose how to spend their money and their leisure time. According to Walter, the rum drinking consciously resists the protocols of industriousness that relied on slavery.

As a caveat, it is important to understand that Walter's musings are part of an argument between him and his wife, Stephanie. She advocates for upward mobility and appropriate consumption; according to her, "living" means "money," "improving," and "success" (102–3). She thinks Walter has a case of sour grapes: "Because you didn't get the promotion, you're trying to say that position is not important? From one extreme, you want to move to another?" (104). She becomes the mouthpiece for complicity, playing the role Fanon assigns Mayotte Capécia in *Black Skin, White Masks,* that of the Black woman with "white" values. Such figures require a wary approach; taking them at face value risks recapitulating systems that silence women's political participation. Romanticizing drunkenness as critique—the risk Stephanie points out—is not the same as recognizing efforts to "[fight] as well as they could, with the arms that they possessed then" (Fanon, "On National Culture" 167). Yet that vague "something" in the passage above forces the debate into a place between Stephanie's and Walter's positions: What is the "something" strange about this peasant lifestyle? Can excessive drinking be reimagined as grass-roots economic resistance to the legacies of colonialism? Who gets to decide what models of "living" means as decolonization precedes? The word "something" forces a pause, asks for an analysis of drunken comportment in its historical context rather than a gloss on Caribbean imaginaries that either celebrate rum drinking as carefree essence or vilify it as endemic sociocultural dysfunction.

"Souvenir Size": The "Black Beast" Returns

If Walter Castle attempts to open a space for a semiotic analysis of rum, George Lamming slams the door shut. His novel *Water with Berries* literally performs the impact of rum's history within the larger frame of a text that is itself a rewriting of Shakespeare's *The Tempest*.[4] Although the bottle of rum that appears in the novel is "souvenir-sized," it has an outsized effect on the plot because it inspires actor and displaced political activist Derek to rape a white female cast member onstage. The scene echoes Caliban's attempted assault on Miranda as revenge upon Prospero (*The Tempest*, 1.2.345–47) and confirms the worst fears about Black male sexuality. Lamming's detailed descriptions of the rum bottle fetishize it as a commodity: it intoxicates Derek and bends to its desire an entire audience of theatergoers, who consume this performance. The onstage rape is horrifying not only because it signifies over the female body, but also because of the violent cascade of conflicting signification it produces.[5]

Lamming frames the rape as an inevitable outcome of turning a man into a corpse. Derek's experiences as an actor capture the effects of discrimination suffered by Black British people in the 1960s. Despite early success as the Moor in *Othello*, Derek subsists on bit parts that reflect, to his mind, his position in English society. His current role is a corpse. As corpse, his body grounds the action; the discovery of his body by the ingénue engenders the action. Derek's death gives the play life, mirroring his sense of life in England, where nothing changes "except the timing of the body's fall from the bench" (*Water with Berries* 237). Even as a corpse, though, he must work to make his Black body unthreatening, especially in the presence of "the girl" who plays the ingénue (237). Derek recalls a discussion with the director about whether, for the purposes of verisimilitude, the corpse should have his "eyes open": "My back is to the audience before the fall. Eyes open if you like. Better keep them closed for the girl's sake. It's the girl's début. She's just fresh from drama school. Eyes closed" (237). The first sentence is spoken by Derek, and the second is the director's response, but the remaining words could be the director's chivalrous second thoughts, or Derek's self-censorship. This recollection demonstrates the careful policing—internally and externally—of Black bodies in England and the toll such self-conscious performance takes on immigrants and their incomes.

In this context, rum's status as an intoxicant and its role in colonial economies engenders resistance to and the reification of these oppressions. Derek needs a drink to acclimate himself to his role, much as Anna in Rhys's *Voyage in the Dark* (1934) uses drink to ease herself into prostitution—"A thimble of liquor might have cooled his nerves" (*Water with Berries* 235)—but "the little phial of rum" (235) produces very different results. The bottle evokes memories, images, and symbols that speak to his position as a colonized subject:

> It was the little bottle all right. . . . He took it up and gave it a look of applause. It was souvenir size, almost the shape of his thumb. He glanced at the little ditch of space that opened round his trouser leg; then looked at the miniature bottle again. It might have been a toy ship that had got sunk. It was a generous double in any pub; but he didn't want to drink it now. It seemed a pity not to let it last. Souvenir size. Growing up from his hand like a swollen thumb. He was smiling. (237)

"Souvenir," French for memory, places Derek's current position in the context of personal and historical memory. Critics such as Helen Tiffin have made similar claims; as she notes of this novel, "the contemporary West Indian is still deeply enmeshed in the toils of that history" (39). Rum, however, intensifies these identifications and emphasizes the materiality that meshes bodies, products, and profits. The two references to a "thumb," one of the distinctions between men and apes, evokes racist caricatures of Black people, suggests deformity, and alludes to the hypersexualized masculinity attributed to Black men. Instead of meeting the promise of "discovery" and "magic" (*Water with Berries* 238), England's ship of state has diminished Derek's sense of self. The bottle miniaturizes colonialism as a consumer good, a "toy ship" that alludes to the Age of Exploration and the Middle Passage as key features of England's economic growth. The bottle connects a history of colonization to Derek's immigrant experience in England. Derek's sense of self is fully contingent on colonization: thus, Derek sees his childhood "swimming through the neck of the bottle" (238).

Under the influence of this rum history, Derek simultaneously protests his condition and meets the racist expectations of his white audience. He becomes both less and more himself. Even if, as Supriya Nair and others explain, the rape protests colonialism, "the black man as rapist is hardly a radical breakthrough against . . . stereotyping" (Nair, *Caliban's Curse* 67).[6] Rum incites a signifying chain that links Derek's actions not only to history of the Caribbean, but to the history of the representation of the Caribbean that enables colonial exploitation. As Lamming describes it, Derek's performance dredges the Caribbean unconscious of the audience. The rape "seemed to go on forever, as though there would be no end; as though there could be no end to this unholy wrath which had erected the corpse from its bench. . . . Some hurricane had torn her pants away, as the body struggled to split open her sex. And the audience saw it, almost watched it, as though the girl's scream had manacled every witness to his seat, made impotent by their lack of warning before so uniquely brutal an assault" (*Water with Berries* 241–42). "Forever" ties this rape to mythological time, abstracting concrete historical violence into a perpetual colonial agon. Images of hurricanes and revivified corpses (zombies), disseminated along a chain including evocative verbs ("manacled") and adjectives ("unholy"), position the Caribbean imaginary as a representational onslaught that terrorizes subjects into submission. "The girl's scream" announces a collective trauma as colonialism recruits gendered and racialized bodies to perpetuate its work. Derek thus retrieves not his humanity but "the privilege of the beast" (242). The audience, "manacled" to the same historical contingencies, equivocates the national threat of this "body" as a threat to the national homeland, "some dragon of legend" (242) that St. George defeats. The chain of signification linking a girl "fresh from drama school" to the psychomachia of nationhood has, simultaneously, a logic and an instinctiveness that intoxicates, a signification stew that resonates with the anti-immigration rhetoric typified by Enoch Powell's 1968 "Rivers of Blood" speech.[7] The audience's collective conclusion that "some monstrous shadow was spreading through the land" (242) registers a shift from act to ideology, a slur—or slurring—that substitutes hysteria for logic, with a symbolic logic that makes more violence against women "a logical event in this process of 'disalienation'" (Da Silva 173). Despite Derek's ability to read the miniature bottle of rum as a representation of the links between economic exploitation and cultural ideas, he remains intoxicated. Similarly, the audience, which "saw" and "almost watched," is subject to the contingencies of this commodity chain from a different point of view.

"Spiritual Shackles":
Drinking and Abstaining in *The Hills of Hebron*

Lovelace offers a linguistic, and Lamming a performative, critique of rum as a commodity that structures a set of material relations. Sylvia Wynter offers a transactional critique in her novel *The Hills of Hebron* that rivals, and precedes, Rhys's *Wide Sargasso Sea*, in its obsessive attention to rum's presence. In *The Hills of Hebron,* asylum director Matthew O'Malley drinks rum while conversing with temporary inmate Moses Barton. Barton, who seeks to establish a separatist, fundamentalist community in Cockpit country, has historical roots in charismatic religious leaders like Alexander Bedward and the Maroons.[8] The scenes with O'Malley occupy limited space in the novel, but his interactions with Barton are a literal and figural time-out from the main thrust of the narrative. Wynter is an unusual figure in West Indian writing of the 1960s, and her work offers an important corrective to work by white West Indian women authors and by male West Indian authors whose names are more familiar.[9] Extant criticism largely contextualizes the plot of *The Hills of Hebron* in debates about gender, national literatures, and nation-building during the 1960s. These critics argue that the novel critiques "the prioritizations of race or gender that have governed decolonization discourses" (Harrison 163) by narrating the suppression of West Indian women in and the homosociality of drives toward sovereignty. As in *Water with Berries*, heterosexual rape is a key trope of colonization *and* decolonization—a signifying practice that empowers men through female bodies "without giving voice" to women as subjects (Toland-Dix 71). Reading the O'Malley-Barton scenes into this conversation connects the novel's local arc to global, recurring economic structures of colonialism. Wynter emphasizes the suppression of shared material relations in favor of competitive rhetorical relations. Literal intoxication becomes figural intoxication as Barton discovers words of power.

The conversations between Barton and O'Malley can occur because of the ways colonialism distributes its subjects. O'Malley, a failed Irish drunk and a disgrace to his English wife at home, becomes—routing through Said's "flexible positional superiority"—a medical authority after shipping out to Jamaica. Barton, devoted to his religious vision of a self-sustaining community, figures himself as the Messiah and allows himself to be crucified by his followers. Each is deemed dangerous and incompetent by British authorities, respectively metropolitan and colonial. Despite a privileged position in the class hierarchies of Irishness, O'Malley chafes under the expectations of Englishness, embodied by his wife, "an English girl from the minor aristocracy" (*Hills of Hebron* 142). O'Malley is "the second son of a landed family," educated at Cambridge, and expected to have "a brilliant career" despite his Irishness (141). Instead, he becomes an alcoholic because he cannot meet the standards of English masculinity implicitly required by his wife: "Her sterling qualities of patience, consideration and self-discipline which aggravated his own lack of character, drove him to drink" (142). The wife's characteristics represent cultural and national traits, which the narrative labels "all that she stood for" (142). Although O'Malley does not share the narrator's clarity on this issue, he understands his current exile to emanate from contingencies of his wife's position. He becomes more "fluent" and "passionate" as he drinks (142), and his plan to write "a manifesto against colonialism" degenerates into *ad feminam* invective: "He wouldn't be a drunk for the rest of his life, as his wife expected, as she wanted him to be, the bitch" (146). In Wynter's hands, O'Malley is cartoonish, a belligerent Irish drunk whose political analysis is personally motivated blarney, but he is also a subject of colonial rule who struggles to assert himself against British power, represented as a "girl" who can dominate him.

Like O'Malley, Moses Barton has an ambivalent relationship with white male power; he seeks to usurp colonial authority by establishing a separatist religious group isolated from colonial administrative control. Barton's apocalyptic visions of a world renewed are deemed "lunacy" (131) after he attempts to fly to heaven, promising to "return with a fleet of golden chariots driven by white angels, dressed in tunics with gold buttons" (127). The literalness of the vision generates evidence that Barton is mad; however, Barton's liberation theology remakes the world. Kelly Baker Josephs has seen this madness as productive, arguing that "Wynter locates madness as a positive space from which to imagine new ways of being in an emergent postcolonial Caribbean society" (48). If Barton's "white angels" show that he has internalized a Christianity designed to maintain white dominance, the quasi-military outfits his angels wear may recall the uniform of Toussaint L'Ouverture, leader of the Haitian Revolution. As the chosen vessel of leadership, Barton seeks to establish authoritarian rule over his new community, demonstrating his investment in the patriarchal structures that have served colonial administrators well.

References to rum occur frequently in scenes between O'Malley and Barton, thus emphasizing that the meetings—framed by the presumption of Barton's madness—are also polite, and politely ironized, exchanges between gentlemen.[10] Rum or being drunk on rum is mentioned ten times in as many pages, with a growing insistence that the beverage shapes O'Malley's discourse. Wynter specifies the type: "The doctor was drinking white rum that morning" (144); "the doctor [. . .] sipped his white rum thoughtfully" (144); and "white rum always heightened O'Malley's feelings of persecution" (144–45). Drinking "white" rum may signify O'Malley's racial privilege, part of the Jamaican settler elite, but it also exposes his difference, as rum drinking would have been less common among white people, who preferred imported, more expensive alcohols.[11] The routine consumption of rum fuels O'Malley's anticolonial ravings. As he speaks, the narrative notes, "he poured himself some more rum" (146), and, later in his analysis, "he gently stirred the rum with a teaspoon" (147). He needs the rum to keep going: "The doctor stood up, crossed the room and took out another bottle of rum from the wall safe" (148). Rum fuels the anticolonial, antihierarchical analyses O'Malley shares with Barton about "the island's white minority . . . educated black and brown 'natives'. . . . all things Irish . . . the English" (145), and this information becomes vital to Barton's political aspirations.

However, the negotiations are more complicated than a simple conversation over drinks, not least because of the asymmetrical relationship between white doctor and Black patient. Natasha Barnes claims that "something considerably less asymmetrical emerges from the mutual desires of both men to inhabit the psychosocial space of the other. Within the mutuality of this desire comes the symbolic refiguration of each man's social position, and something of a spectacle of equality is produced" (156). This equality remains spectral, I argue, because of the rum that intoxicates them, causing each to misrecognize shared oppression and seek competitive advantage. This misrecognition occurs despite and perhaps because of Barton's refusal to drink with the doctor:

> The doctor was drinking white rum that morning. For the sake of protocol he drank out of a teacup. The Prophet sat in a canvas chair opposite him. Moses did not drink. He invariably refused the doctor's offer of a "cup of tea." He wanted to keep alert, to learn all he could from this white man whose mind seemed to encompass the world. Moses was always astonished at the number of words the doctor had stored away inside his head. With half those words, the Prophet thought, he could hypnotize the whole island into doing his bidding. So, while the doctor talked, Moses noted words that seemed weighty and valuable, and later, in bed, repeated them over and over to himself. (*Hills of Hebron* 144)

Barton, in refusing to drink, rejects the "protocol" of the exchange, even though the doctor, as the authority figure, can maintain the fiction of equity and propriety. His refusal disavows both unstated protocols of Englishness and masculinity. The "teacup" and false "cup of tea" invoke English civility as well as the global reach of the empire, substituting one colonial commodity for another in a repeating pattern of trade. O'Malley invites Barton to manipulate alcohol rituals into a subversion of racial hierarchies through a mutual recognition of oppressed masculinity. Sober and "alert," Barton makes a different exchange: information that "seemed to encompass the world." Barton nominally cooperates but his goals for the conversation are hardly antihierarchical or even anti-imperial.

In these conversations, one-sided as they are, Barton hears statements about patterns of colonial exploitation as rhetorical tools and tropes. Wynter captures a moment in which economics becomes ideology. Barton is interested in "words," and particularly words that can "hypnotize the whole island into doing his bidding." Barton frames the words as a good investment that will profit him; he considers that he can accomplish his goals with "half" the words, saving the remainder for future use. He describes words as material things, "weighty and valuable," to exchange for goods. Less struck by O'Malley's lectures on "their common condition" as "colonials" (143), Barton latches onto the racialization of "the concept of man creating God in his own image" to manipulate the faithful (148). The rhetoric recycles into material conditions as well, as Barton thinks "the Lord had shown to Moses a way in which he could obtain from the government the legal right to the land which he would call Hebron" (153). Barton learns from a man he sees as a representative of colonial authority the discursive forms of social control essential for his planned community. The old master's tools will build the new master's house.

Thus, the phrase "spiritual shackles" (143) applies more thoroughly to this encounter than its obvious association with Barton's religious creed might imply. It has the resonance with slavery of the verb "manacle" Lamming uses in *Water with Berries* and a reference to the "spirit" that facilitates and frustrates communication between O'Malley and Barton as colonized subjects of the British Empire. Although he recognizes the critique of colonialism, Barton never considers the possibility that O'Malley's diagnosis of his condition as "paranoia" induced by British colonization (142) may be partially accurate: Why believe a drunk, racist Irishman? O'Malley, for his part, protects his reputation and status by confiding his political analysis to a convicted madman. Both are conscripted by rum to repeat an old story. This legacy frustrates the good in O'Malley's attempt to connect with Barton as well as in Barton's desire for an autonomous Black community, leaving an uncomfortable sense that some potential for social justice and cross-cultural understanding has been spirited away.

The scenes featuring rum in these three novels of decolonization are brief interludes. The central narrative arcs are more concretely devoted to the organization of social life and political institutions as the British Empire recedes, yet they invite consideration of how these texts will be circulated and consumed, how readers will comport themselves in the face of these intoxicated performances. Looking through rum leads to expected readings, recirculating stock elements of Caribbean imaginaries through their established routes. West Indian nationalists are greedy, violent, dysfunctional, or some combination of the three, so their claims are illegitimate; often they are simply drunk, so their claims are illegitimate. White people from the United Kingdom are mostly passive observers of this pathetic drama, who bear no responsibility for conditions in the West Indies. Women are symbols to be signified over and through, often simultaneously complicit and victimized.

Looking at rum as a product with the historical power to structure relationships suggests the difficulty of finding alternative routes into a postcolonial future. The occurrence of rum in these novels frequently activates vocabularies of investment and value, as in *The Hills of Hebron,* and the more generalized forms of desire, "want," in *When Gods Are Falling.* Chains of signification reference "ships" as well as the tools of control, "shackles" and "manacles," that enslaved African people to the emergence of modern trade routes and production formats. The careful observation of patterns of reference around this commodity reengages Simon Gikandi's "basic assumption . . . that before we deal with the 'post' we have to interrogate its antecedent from all possible theoretical and cultural positions" (*Writing in Limbo* 255). In this and prior chapters I have tried to suggest that the iconic status of rum enables readings that focus on the intersection of subjects across vast distances and implicate readers—particularly Anglo-American, mostly white, readers—as uncritical consumers of these narratives. If we take evidence from texts written after the period roughly designated "decolonization," the movement of the colonial period into history has not ended the force of the relationships that enabled its diverse forms and processes. In the wake of a decolonization that has not emerged as "post-," writers have become more self-conscious in deploying commodities as sites of contest rather than simply a "symbol of the Caribbean." This phenomenon is apparent in such texts as *Land of Love and Drowning*, "Rum Sweet Rum," and *Netherland*. Michelle Cliff's *Free Enterprise* (1993) partakes of this phenomenon in a fictionalized transnational history of slavery that also accounts for a traumatic transnational phenomenon contemporaneous with the novel: the global AIDS crisis.

"Carib Blood Running into the Rum": Queering Rum Histories

In the face of political setbacks, a utopian conception of the future may be less effective than a melancholic one, and each of these novels ends by recuperating some political momentum and mourning lost potential. Lamming's *Water with Berries* is, perhaps, the least hopeful: after Derek commits rape and Teeton commits murder, "they were all waiting for the trials to begin" (249). Trials suggest both individual criminal proceedings and a long, shared period of suffering that includes "all" of England and San Cristobal, Lamming's invented West Indian island. In *The Hills of Hebron*, Barton's widow Miss Gatha cradles her grandchild, the product of a rape her son committed, as rain soaks drought-ridden Hebron. Miss Gatha sees that the baby is "perfect," but she wonders to her companion Kate whether "the sins of the fathers, then, had not been visited on the children?" (315). The interrogatory punctuation challenges the declarative syntax, thus leaving "the fabric of her forebodings" (315) intact even as tears mark her apparent belief that this child—never definitively gendered—signals a different future for Hebron.

In *While Gods Are Falling*, Earl Lovelace continues the meta-analytic strand of the narrative to reflect on reading as an act of interpretation and consumption requiring awareness of one's positionality. Walter Castle has transformed his analysis of rum into "something" of significance, a politics that thinks globally and acts locally. As the novel closes, Castle and his wife approach a community political meeting. Although the characters are only shown approaching the meeting, the narrator endorses their belief that it is a "fine night"—a phrase repeated three times—for the "wild hope" that a grassroots political community will develop (253, 255). The novel's concluding scene begins by evoking a second-person "you," which challenges and invites readers to identify with, to participate in, to relate to, this community and its aspirations. This "you" consuming the text echoes with Bruce Robbins's ruminations on the "you" hailed in commodity sagas and confronts readers with their positionality in relation to this text. *While Gods Are Falling* is not coy about the grinding poverty in Trinidad and Jamaica or the racism of the English, nor are the political motivations of the protagonists obscure. Scenes with rum suggest that the apparent dysfunction of Trinidad's postcolonial politics and consumer behavior is a rational response to rum conditions.

The title of Michelle Cliff's *Free Enterprise* refers ironically to a free-market capitalism rooted in the slave trade as well as to the enterprises of freedom the novel fictionalizes. These retellings explore the contributions of women to John Brown's raid; Cliff focuses on Mary Ellen Pleasant, who financially supported John Brown, and Annie Christmas, a supporter of abolition who abandons her home in Jamaica to support Brown's raid. Critical analysis of this novel highlights Cliff's method of rewriting standard national histories as transnational, embodied, and polyvocal.[12] Critics do not substantially include the character Captain Parsons, a homosexual Black man, in their accounts, but his narrative suggests a queer rum history leaking into and out of Cliff's already polyvocal text. Not only does Parsons directly engage the slave trade, but his death reaches backward, to the genocidal effects of colonialism on indigenous peoples in the regions, and forward, to the anxieties surrounding contact with blood during the AIDS crisis of the 1990s. This plot counters critical emphasis on Annie's bottle tree, clinking with products signaling "a variety of spaces that reflect colonization in the new world" (Dunick 39), with images of leakage and flow across categories of oppression.[13]

Initially, Captain Parsons's politics seem familiar: he resists slavery and slave trading, and rum symbolizes its horrors. Disguised as a slave trader, Captain Parsons runs a Robin Hood–like pirate operation that frees African people from slave ships and thwarts the Royal Navy that protects the trade. Captain Parsons enjoys the symbolism of toasting a British boarding party with "a dram of the finest Jamaican slave-made rum" before murdering them (112). This encounter figures some standard tropes surrounding rum: a casual dismissal of cruelty as business, the transfer of blame to oblivious consumers (notably, American), and bonding over apparently shared purpose through a toast. His efforts also align with Cliff's project of demonstrating slavery's oppressive ubiquity across a multinational terrain.

Cliff suggests Parsons's political aims are much broader in a scene where British troops attack him and his companion, "a sympathetic Carib," in a tavern. The Carib man dies, and Parsons is arrested and enslaved "for being in the wrong place at the wrong time" (115). Parsons and the anonymous Carib are up to something that is political: "In the tavern they had been talking about what drove them, how they kept on despite all they had witnessed, all they looked forward to. To each other they admitted despair, to furious brainstorms, dulled only barely by rum" (118). The narrator claims Parsons and the Carib are caught up by chance, but Parsons is already an enemy of state-sanctioned slave trading, guilty of murdering British troops. Such affiliations tend to link "sympathetic" to political sympathies, particularly as the Caribs—like the Arawaks Cliff mentions early in the novel—are the original victims of European colonization. From the height of the slave trade, then, Cliff traces a bloody path back to the earliest enslaved people.

But the imagery of the encounter between Parsons and the Carib is also homoerotic, such that "a sympathetic Carib" might be a potential sexual and political partner. The two were "falling into love," and the language of the quotation cited above could describe the stress of hiding transgressive sexualities and the stress of hiding transgressive political agendas. Does each drink to cope with "despair" and "brainstorms" associated with the horrors of slavery, ironically solaced with the products slaves produce, or to cope with the discrimination and criminalization of same-sex relationships? When Parsons describes "the Carib blood running into the rum on the tavern floor" after the attack (115), Cliff evokes abolitionist imagery in which sugar and rum contain the bodily fluids of injured slaves. The contemporary context for Cliff's novel, published when fears about HIV transfer through bodily fluids were reaching a peak, queers this image to include gay male bodies that leak and disintegrate as officialdom watches.[14] In the description of rum and blood bleeding together, Cliff resists what David Harradine calls "rationalisation" of images by violating the operation of abjection across race, gender, and sexuality (70). Thus "Captain Parsons could not weep for him in front of these men [British soldiers]" (*Free Enterprise* 115) because leaking bodily fluids *in sympathy with* the Carib might generate murderous (racial? sexual?) anxieties on the part of his captors. In this image, rum bleeds the social into the material, melding politics and love, the rational and the affective, to capture the losses suffered by bodies whose suffering has been erased by history: Carib, slave, queer.

The anonymous Carib dies in *Free Enterprise* with only Captain Parsons to mourn, invisibly both to officials within the text and to interpreters outside the text. This scene links *Free Enterprise* with Cliff's earlier work, which engages sexual oppression as inseparable from racial oppression. Failing to account for this enduring concern as it appears in *Free Enterprise* overlooks the complexity of Captain Parsons's political alliances to focus on racial issues. Likewise, Cliff includes women pirates in her narrative as sites of sexual noncompliance. Short scenes featuring Anne Bonny and Mary Reade ironize the use of heteronormativity—pleading the belly to avoid hanging—among women who fail to comply with either gender or sexual norms: "It's a rare woman who suckles on the scaffold. Yo, ho, ho, and a bottle of rum" (111). By linking the devil-may-care attitude in pirate drinking songs to the exigencies of survival on the sexual and economic margins, Cliff implies that piracy was at best a precarious refuge for sexually nonconforming women, but she suggests that the systems driven by rum create complementary avenues for resistance.

Free Enterprise continues Michelle Cliff's transformation of her narrative style from a predominantly realist mode (as in *Abeng*) to a highly self-conscious fragmented style that summons connections with purportedly nonfiction discourses. In this novel, Cliff opposes a "the majority unconscious" content with "the official version" of history through a carefully patterned fictionalization of historical figures (16). The tavern scene is one of libations poured for a joint cause and a history remembered; intervening critically to mark that site, and its loss, has been a purpose of this study. This novel builds a web of connections across oppressed groups that, without oversimplifying the tenacity of the links, attends to the silencing of one group in service of a unified narrative. The novel also targets institutional activities that ratify "the majority unconscious," among them the "convocations, colloquia . . . dissertations" that perpetuate the silencing of queer trauma (16).

5 Libations 2
Reparative Models in Literary Criticism

> Since the texts are there, to be explained, interpreted, accepted, dismissed, the interpreter replaces the writer; the critic displaces the creator.
>
> —Sylvia Wynter

GIVEN THE tragic losses depicted in *Free Enterprise*, it may be surprising to learn that this novel contains a more positive depiction of rum than is usual in Michelle Cliff's work. Her tragic, and often scathingly ironic, figuration of rum as a scourge contrasts strongly with Paule Marshall's use of rum as a catalyst for authentic connection, healing, and pleasure. The previous chapter has proposed that rum poetics can track alternative understandings of postcolonial politics that are latent in narrative reifications of colonial hegemony, thus creating opportunities for relations that move toward the reparative. These readings figure broadly as libations, interactions indexed by the sharing of alcohol to consecrate joint purpose. This chapter shifts slightly to focus on works that invoke libations critically, as a subject of analysis within the text, and examines a corresponding silence on the subject among literary critics. These expert readers—literary critics—countersign a textual economy that actively works to ignore the implications of rum as it circulates in discourse.

Both Paule Marshall and Michelle Cliff refer to rum repeatedly in their works and call attention to its role in the history and economy, past and present, of the Caribbean. Moreover, their best-known and most frequently studied novels—*Praisesong for the Widow* (1983) and *No Telephone to Heaven* (1987), respectively—contain gripping scenes in which rum is a central element. In Marshall's *Praisesong*, a ritual prominently featuring rum transforms protagonist Avatara (Avey) Johnson by reconnecting her to her past. In Cliff's *No Telephone*, Christopher, enraged that his employer Mas' Charles will not lend him the money to settle the ghost of his grandmother, murders his employers and then rapes the wife's corpse with a broken rum bottle. Critics analyzing *No Telephone* and *Praisesong* often focus on whether the protagonists of these novels decolonize themselves, overcoming the oppressive forces of colonialism in structuring their lives, identities, and bodies. No Telephone generates suspicion, since the protagonist heals her divided soul only in death, while *Praisesong* has elicited readings that explore the reintegration of Avey Johnson's fractured self by restoring her African roots. Critics situate these discussions within systemic forces of globalization, represented by multinational industries like film/entertainment (*No Telephone*) and tourism (*Praisesong*), as they interact with the slave-holding past.

Due to the central presence of rum in these scenes, scholarly writing about these scenes, and these novels, mentions rum. In this chapter, I compare what critics do or do not say about rum with what the literary texts say about rum to understand how literary critical discourse participates in a broader economy of (not) reading it. The arguments in this chapter are less about which literary critics ignore rum in these specific cases than identifying a professional habit. This habit—what David Kazanjian, drawing on Foucault, calls "a discursive regularity that governs what can be said and what cannot be said" (79)—has already been exhibited in literary-critical analyses of sugar, professional book reviews, and broad-based Caribbean studies texts.[1] Examining how the word *rum* diffuses through literary-critical writing, without itself becoming a subject of analysis, identifies habits of reference that contribute to a broader pattern in which rum is present but unaccounted for.

The figure of libation reconstrues the relationship between literary texts and critical scholarship to recuperate interpretive energy toward reparative ends. Under these conditions, I invoke libation as a figure rather than a delimited practice associated with rituals. These texts contain libation scenes as well as scenes that generally sanction a relationship by sharing rum. The figure of libations emphasizes communality of purpose and joint obligation, often with reference to ancestors or across generations, implying that to move forward the past must be incorporated into and reconciled with future actions. Such rituals are fraught within local social groups; they become even more so across perceived national, racial, and sexual boundaries. From a rum poetics perspective, libations are not necessarily comforting fictions; they often mark uncomfortable facts about the past that persist in the present and require reckoning. These reckonings—actual, failed, or unrealized—allow speculation about what the future can look like if we read rum histories as accounts that could have been different but were not.

Paule Marshall: Rum as Libations

Paule Marshall uses rum in her work to connect people affectively and politically: characters who do not drink rum are usually overinvested in versions of a neocolonial status quo in which lighter-skinned, Anglo-affiliated people retain power. However, the results of communing under the auspices of rum are not obviously transformative or progressive. In fact, a melancholy resignation to the difficulties of forging equitable futures pervades scenes containing actual and implied libations. In the context of Marshall's treatment of rum, Avey Johnson remains an outlier, despite her apparent knowledge of customs pertaining to rum, because she consumes it rather than communes through it. The undigested, if you will, appearance of rum in critiques of this novel that focus on Avey's transformation and healing signals the limits of political engagement across cultures of the African diaspora.

Early works like *Brown Girl, Brownstones* (1959) and "British Guiana" (1961) associate rum with positive identification with Caribbean geography, embodied pleasure, and resilience under punitive colonial conditions—which extend into the immigrant Bajan community of Brooklyn. In *Brown Girl, Brownstones,* Suggie struggles with unemployment and the puritanical attitudes of other Bajan women (among them, Selina's mother), who mask or deprecate the pleasures of drinking. In bottles of rum, Suggie recalls "a cane field at night with the canes rising and plunging in the wind, hearing again the ecstatic moan of the lover inside her" (29), a reclamation of cane fields from a history of exploited labor, violence, and sexual assault. After Selina shares a glass of rum with Suggie, in defiance of her mother's assimilationist philosophy, Selina "carrie[s] the sun inside her" and recalls this moment during her own sexual arousal, scrambling both heterosexual and colonial scripts. This polyvalent movement of desire enables Selina to withstand racist encounters at college and abusive elements in her relationship with Clive. Shared libations allow Selina to claim her body for her own pleasure and knowledge through positive, though distanced, identification with Barbados. This identification, however, is neither romanticized nor nostalgic: Selina remains attuned, politically and socially, to the racist and colonialist systems that shape both her own and her parents' generations.

In "British Guiana," rum suggests alternative modes of community and identity, rooted in geography, that are repressed and proscribed by a combination of local and colonial custom. Gerald Motley appears to be a garden-variety alcoholic, compensating for failed ambition with rum, but he is kin to Captain Parsons of *Free Enterprise* in that his alcoholism protests, even contests, heteronormativity as a function of colonialism.[2] In this case, the proscription against homosexuality in English culture overlaps with local proscriptions associated with caste, and the enforcers are women rather than British troops. Motley's drinking starts when he is prohibited from accessing "the self he had long sought" in the "pleasures" of the bush by Sybil, his female lover (74). Uttering "a protective cry," Sybil places her female body between Gerald and "what could have been a vision of himself" (75). From the relationship between Gerald and his protégé Sidney and Gerald's tacit admission to "foolish" behavior (124) late in the story, it is clear that the bush is the site of homosexual desire. The bush, like the cane fields Suggie recalls, figures the geography of the Caribbean as a site for definitions of desire and pleasure that exceed the racialized sexual codes used to police Caribbean subjects and appropriate their pleasures, and their bodies, for other uses. Sybil's "protective cry" restores Motley to heterosexual masculinity and career "success" following colonial rule (75): Gerald becomes "the first colored man in the West Indies to hold this high a position in broadcasting," according to his boss, who owns the radio station and "the large sugar estates" (73). The imposition of heterosexual norms as a function of broader assimilation to British values coincides with Gerald's increased and steady drinking.

For Gerald, rum supplements a gap between homosexual desires and English models of masculine success that he cannot overcome, though the story offers mild hope for a more tolerant future. Gerald's relationship with Sidney is thus consummated, insofar as it is consummated, through rum. After Sidney drinks from a rum flask, Gerald "felt the warm place Sidney's hand had rested . . . tasted Sidney there" (109). By contrast, when Gerald later pours Sybil "a drink from the flask he and Sidney had used," Gerald "avoid[s] looking" at her body (114). This story of compulsory heterosexuality resonates with the coercion Antoinette's husband uses in *Wide Sargasso Sea*, as Sibyl's enforcement of sexual norms relies on unstated assumptions about "natural" male behavior. The story also compares to *Wide Sargasso Sea*, which leaves traces of relationships that could have been, in that it presumes Gerald's death (126). However, "British Guiana" ends with a precarious sense of hope. Earlier in the story, Gerald Motley's commitment to cross-caste relationality—tolerated by his social equals—takes the form of sharing drinks. Gerald Motley likes "to drink rum and shout politics with the stevedores" (71), and this political alliance may be with working-class people, with the sexual subculture of "trade" among sailors and working-class men, or some unarticulated combination of both. With his social equals, he can propose the wholesale destruction of Georgetown with "the rum stinging his throat" (98). At a waterfront bar, he distributes "expensive whisky" to commune with thieves, pimps, and betting agents: Is seeking "the intimate press of their bodies" a political or a sexual desire, or does he join oppressed groups for common purpose using an alcohol that represents the repression under which they labor (104–5)? Thus the final image of Sibyl, "holding the paper cup of rum, bearing it gently between her hands as if the ash of his [Gerald's] life was dissolved there" (127), continues the oppressive protective closeting of Gerald's desires, but it also—with some irony—constitutes an anticipatory libation for a future in which Sibyl challenges hierarchies of color, class, and sexuality to help Sidney achieve his ambitions.[3]

This is not to say that Marshall uses rum to transform a bad (rum?) history into a progressive and just future in which diversely oppressed classes form an intersectional coalition for justice. What rum can point to is the negated presence of alternative ways to construct relationality that could be but were not activated as resources to support more empathetic inter- and intracultural relations. Suggie's evocation of cane fields as a source of pleasure, for example, empowers her as a sex worker. She counters not only colonialist sugarcane poetics as identified by Tobias Döring but also sugarcane imagery that naturalizes Black women as sexually available, as seen in texts like Austin Clarke's *The Polished Hoe* (2002) or Nicolás Guillén's poetry. But Suggie's transmission of resilience to Selina does not solve Suggie's problems or prevent Selina's difficulties with her lover Claude. Gerald Motley is not only dead but "neuter" at the end of "British Guiana" (126): the story humanizes a statistic, telling the story of one life among many ruined by concatenating oppressive forces that drive Motley, in this case, toward compulsory heterosexuality. Marshall's rum poetics points to the ways the past could have been different but was not, charting a history in which national progress could have diverged from neocolonial models.

These early depictions pave the way for Marshall's more sustained engagement with rum and notions of progress in her novels *The Chosen Place, the Timeless People* and *Praisesong for the Widow*. Written and published after the first Caribbean Federation failed, *The Chosen Place, the Timeless People* (1969) directly addresses notions of appropriate national development. The plot examines the conflict between development projects managed and created by US-based organizations, in an uneasy alliance with local elites, against local resistance in a rural, impoverished area known as Bournehills.[4] From the outside, the resistance of

Bournehills residents to assistance appears counterproductive and even self-destructive. Local elites deride Bournehills as "someplace out of the Dark Ages," a money pit, ungrateful, and obsessed with a forgotten slave revolt (56–59). In other words, Bournehills exists in time-out because it refuses to progress beyond the squashing of Cuffee Ned's revolt by British troops. The one thing the people do have is decent health and unembarrassed sexual desire: the doctor reports that "the damn place is a natural sanatorium" (58), and the residents call sex their "only sport" (57). Thus, the novel sets up the residents of Bournehills as successors to Suggie and Gerald Motley, both of whom regard neocolonial iterations of colonial ideology (whether they come from the United States or England) as anathema to their self-determination.

In *The Chosen Place, the Timeless People,* Marshall figures the distinction between neocolonial assimilators and communal resistance through two commodities: sugar and rum. This distinction appears first at a cocktail party to welcome the advance team for the development project, Saul and Harriet Amron. Saul notices that the men, to underscore their alliance with English class hierarchies, are "drinking imported whisky, scorning as a matter of status the local rum, which was excellent" (53). The emphatic modifier "which was excellent" undercuts local claims to discernment and implies that local elites are mimic men rather than authentic selves. Saul's beverage choice also aligns him with Merle, who asks for "rum and water, . . . none of that fancy stuff you people down this end drink for style" (66). Harriet's choice is unstated, but she joins the women in the drawing room who drink "sherry or Coca-Cola" (69) to maintain feminine propriety. Saul understands and identifies with the local culture; Harriet, a philanthropist whose fortune descends from slave trading, aligns with elites whose views conform to her own. This distinction triggers the implications of an earlier contrast: Harriet Amron relishes a bird's-eye view of Bournehills as the plane circles to land while Saul sleeps off "the rum [he] had back at the last place [they] stopped" (22).

Marshall associates the neocolonialist perspective with sugar, as a product that structures bodies in relation and in community now through the economic structures of the past. Sir John Stokes, who represents the British-owned corporation that has controlled most of the sugar production on the island, quips, "It's always a bit of a shock, don't you know, to realize that the thing that sweetens your tea comes from all this muck" (222). The "muck" refers indeterminately to both sugarcane trash and the workers. Merle announces to Saul that sugar "runs in our veins," producing "a nation of diabetics" (85). Since Marshall positions the nightclub

Sugar's as a kind of omphalos for international trade, the world's citizenry traverses Sugar's/sugar, internalizing and circulating its economic diseases. With its diverse clientele, tolerance of perceived vice, and walls bulging with the commodities of colonial trade (including a teddy bear that could reference Teddy Roosevelt's shenanigans in Cuba and Panama), Sugar's shows "how things stand on this side of the island" (78).[5] While Merle might seem to celebrate diversity and pleasure, she means that "this side" reifies colonial systems in neocolonial forms. Lyle Hutson characterizes Sugar's saturnalian atmosphere as "the one truly egalitarian institution we have on the island" (79). Saturnalia, the carnival, requires a dominant order and is a temporary release—both are strongly associated with alcoholic time-out. Thus, Hutson's "egalitarian institution" preserves the caste system of which he is part. Moreover, nightclub owner Sugar, though presented as a cipher, is reputedly American.[6] The mystification of Sugar's origins attests to the mystifications that successive modes of empire use to deflect historical analysis of current conditions and to the networking of subjects through the trade and consumption of commodities.

Rum, on the other hand, orients community and cooperation toward the future by surfacing past resistance in the present. In Delbert's rum shop and grocery store, the men pour libations of rum prior to debating the facts of Cuffee Ned's slave revolt and the viability of Saul's efforts (*Chosen Place* 125).[7] Saul's experiences in the rum shop lead him, eventually, to understand that helping the small-acreage cane farmers maintain production when Kingsley, the large cane processor, abandons them is more relevant to the community's needs than a project he might bring in. When Saul explains that he felt "a sense of renewal" (259) and "love" (318) after attending a ritual pig-killing, Merle identifies "love" as a product of shared libations. While Merle is not unaware of the problems alcoholism causes, here she advances its mediating properties:[8]

> "And rum," she added. "You were good and salt. I tell you, you seem determined to become as big a rummy as anyone in Bournehills . . ." Then, a speculative note sounding in her voice, she said, "But maybe that's how it had to be." She was suddenly serious. "Maybe if someone like yourself, someone from Away, as we put it, ever really hopes to understand us, he has to become a little like us, slightly mad as people in town say we are and as you were sounding on our way over here; and taking his rum regularly. Rum's our elixir of life in Bournehills, did you know that? Oh, yes, [. . .] we're preserved in the bloody stuff down there. The whole place. Preserved." She drank from her glass. (318–19, ellipses in the original)

Saul describes emotion; Merle counters with digestion. If rum is "our elixir of life," the definition of that life according to outsiders is "slightly mad" for resisting economic progress and harping on "that old-time business" of slave rebellions (59). Rum is also an acknowledgment that colonialism has been "preserved" structurally and is a shaping factor in current social and material relations. To "become a little like" is both to acknowledge the limits of identification with those descended from the enslaved population and to support economic and cultural self-determination as a right. Merle confirms Lyle Hutson's earlier declaration about Bournehills's intransigence: "It's not, you know, that it can't change, but rather, one almost begins to suspect, that it chooses not to, for some perverse reason" (62). What seems "perverse" or, as Merle says, "slightly mad" to outsiders results from an insistence on reparative relations based on an ethics of "understanding" that everyone is "preserved in the bloody stuff"—this rum history is acknowledged as shared.

In a confrontation between sugar and rum, sugar wins, illustrating the hegemonic qualities of colonialism's economic and social legacies. This is evident at the cane-processing plant, when fortification with rum does not enable Ferguson, representing the workers, to confront Sir John Stokes, the business owner. Saul, observing, sees that under Stokes's "challenging" gaze, Ferguson physically cannot speak even though he is "straining to do so" (221), a contrast to his "passion and force" when speaking "in the rumshop" (222). Ferguson had prepared for the confrontation by drinking rum, a ritual already normed in this novel: "He had taken a few drinks to give him heart, and he stood waiting in all his lean tensile grace and authority on the platform above the two noisy wheels, his breath, his whole person, gave off the faint redolence of rum" (219). This "faint redolence" suffuses the scene, but, as in *Wide Sargasso Sea* or *The Hills of Hebron,* it literally chokes resistance, in both Ferguson and his libation-sharing ally Saul. Stokes assumes Ferguson is drunk and that Saul, a fellow white Anglo-European, assents to this script. Saul, "shaken and white-faced" and silent, temporarily shares the bodily and mental position of Ferguson as a result of sharing libations.

If Saul's experience of Ferguson's emotions "as intimately as if they were his own" results from entering into relation with the men of Bournehills through rum (222), his wife, Harriet, maintains a racial distinction that plays out through alcohol imagery. Harriet joins the Bournehills carnival band like a disinterested ethnographic observer and wifely good sport. The Bournehills band brings the same theme to carnival every year, a reenactment of Cuffee Ned's revolt. Harriet, unlike the local elite who consider the obsession with the past unseemly, considers it quaint. She will learn a dance and wear a costume. After she has "proved herself" (292), she will return to her position, literally above the fray, by joining Saul in "the air-cooled American-style bar one flight up" (291)—"air-cooled" and "flight" recall her view from the airplane—from the parade route. In the bar, screened by "drapes shutting out the street below," she will drink a "civilized" martini that will "cleanse her throughout" (293). Harriet's martini-thinking generates an overwhelming response from rum's histories. Harriet is separated from the Bournehills band and surrounded by a "raucous green-clad guerilla band from the Heights"—urban, Black, noisy, paramilitary (293)—and her sensory revulsion takes the form of objectionable commodity use: she is "choking on the smoke from their cheap cigars, engulfed by the smell of their heavy sweat-soaked uniforms and the rum they had been drinking from the canteens at their waists" (293). The "green-clad guerilla" with a cigar evokes Fidel Castro specifically and mid-century Central American and Caribbean revolutionaries generally. The parade synchronically compresses diachronically sequenced resistance to colonial exploitation, implicitly joined in purpose by libations.

The flasks of rum sanction their joint purpose just as the libations at the site of Cuffee Ned's rebellion do, but Harriet cannot distance the guerillas as she can the resisting slaves. What, for Harriet, seems a quaint custom emerges as an immanent future in which whiteness no longer guarantees privilege. As the band sweeps Harriet toward the sea, she reacts with terror—not unlike Paul Kemp in *The Rum Diary*—to the idea that the mechanisms that reify white female US privilege might no longer function. She realizes that her color had not registered as a marker of privilege: the group had not "really *seen* her" as white, even with blonde hair and skin tanned but "nonetheless white" (*Chosen Place* 294). Her fear of being mistaken for Black or brown evolves into a more mortifying possibility when she realizes that the next generation, the younger participants, "disregard . . . her as if she wasn't there" (295). Comically, she asserts the civilizing mission as the reassertion of appropriate consumption: "They needed—the whole unruly lot of them—to be bathed, their mouths scrubbed clean of the tobacco and rum smell, and put to bed" (295). Harriet wants to put the band in time-out.

It is—not at all ironically—Harriet who must be rescued, babied, and sent to bed after a long shower (297–99). Structurally, her experience resonates with the well-known scenes on Carriacou in Marshall's *Praisesong for the Widow* in which Avatara (Avey) Johnson receives care from island citizens who—superficially—have no reason to succor a woman who has previously exhibited little empathy for them. *Praisesong* is well known for Avey Johnson's traumatic yet healing bout of seasickness on her journey to Carriacou (an island off the coast of Grenada) to attend the Beg Pardon. Her humiliating loss of bodily control figures a recognition of the Middle Passage as generational trauma,[9] the climactic event in a series of digestive problems signifying Avey's regurgitation of American middle-class values, which Marshall portrays as implicitly white.[10] Avey is guided through this illness by Joseph Lebert, the rum shop owner and trickster figure who invites her to attend the Beg Pardon, and the women of Carriacou, who wash, feed, and soothe her after her illness. Avey, unlike Harriet, reconnects with her ancestral history and survives; Harriet refuses accountability and is swallowed by the sea her slave-trading ancestors used as a graveyard. On the face of it, Harriet Amron and Avey Johnson have little in common, but Avey, when initially attacked by indigestion on the cruise, does fantasize about drinking "a glass of white wine" (*Praisesong* 25) on the "nonstop flight" that will return her to New York "shortly" (23); these speculative fantasies are italicized in the text to mark them as such. Between the well-documented color imagery in this novel and Marshall's history of alcohol symbolism, Avey's identification with a beverage associated with feminine refinement and cleanliness signals an unrecognized investment in "white" middle-class American values that is not erased by her experiences in the Caribbean.[11]

In *Praisesong*, commodity analysis slips into the background and consumer behavior moves to the forefront as Marshall examines the ethics of consuming the Caribbean. While Avey Johnson attunes to the consumption of racist spectacle while on the cruise, she is less aware of her willingness to consume the Caribbean to strengthen her African American identity (emphasis on both parts of the adjective). Thus, while Avey shares rum in the context of libations, the limits on her ability to share a purpose with the people of Carriacou affirm her position as an American consumer who can use the contemporary Caribbean as a product. Even as Avey identifies a shared historical wound from enslavement, she replicates reading strategies that encourage passive consumption of contemporary economic disadvantage. Rum poetics traces these edges as they appear in the text and then are replicated by critics. Despite the discomforts Avey experiences because of Joseph Lebert's invitation to travel to Carriacou, the experience is narrated as awaiting her as a special customer. As Avey approaches the rum shop, the "cool dark" interior is "like a hand extended in welcome" (157), and the proprietor Joseph Lebert instantly "s[ees] and underst[ands]" exactly how to serve the specific customer Avey (171). Avey deflects her active choice to enter a traditionally masculine domain; not only does she claim to be drawn in "without her having anything to do with it," but she later explains that she "failed to notice" the sign indicating the building's purpose (157). In positioning herself as the oblivious consumer, Avey meets her match in Joseph Lebert, whom Patricia Stuelke reads as an image for "Reagan's vision of the lost precolonial capitalist" who actively participates in the capitalist tourist market that caters to Northern tourists like Avey (133). His "cryptic nod" as Avey drinks reads as the trickster/guide's anticipation of Avey's cure and the trickster/capitalist's satisfaction at reeling in a customer. Their dialogue about the drink he serves allows speculation about the nature of the relationality established:

> "Coconut water?" she asked, pausing after the first swallow. . . .
> He nodded. "Fresh out of the shell."
> "And . . . ?" She was frowning slightly.
> "And a drop of rum, oui," he said. "But not from those bottles you see there," he dismissed with a wave the half-dozen bottles of white rum on the shelves across the room. "I put a little Jack Iron from Carriacou in yours. Is the best. I don' give that to everybody."
> Rum and coconut water, a standard in the islands. She had had much stronger versions of it in other places. Nevertheless she almost instantly felt that first swallow of the drink soothe her parched throat and begin to circle her stomach like a ring of cool wet fire. Eagerly she raised the glass to her lips again. (174)

This scene establishes Avey as an expert consumer, able to identify ingredients by taste and a poor mark for shifty purveyors. Why is she "frowning" as she drinks? Is it the effort of identifying the alcohol or a suspicion that she is being plied with alcohol? Why does Lebert claim that she is getting the "best" that he "don' give . . . to everybody" before she expresses any opinion about the drink? What is the point of stating that the drink is "a standard in the islands," but a weaker version of what is available "in other places"? The dialogue performs Avey's power as consumer over the local producer, but it also marks this interaction as performance in which the mythical trickster is now a savvy small-businessman who flatters tourists that their hedonistic impulses are rational purchases. Avey drinks "eagerly . . . again"—evincing desires to consume she is unable to control.

Avey's fantasy of consumer discernment intimates her attitude toward participating in the Big Drum/Beg Pardon. She connects with a more authentic self explicitly contrasted with her prior assimilation to middle-class American values, but her attitude about the role of alcohol in the ceremony undercuts her relationship with the people of Carriacou. At the Big Drum, rum is the ceremonial libation. Libations mark the beginning of the ceremony: "Outside the house, ... the ground at the four corners had been liberally sprinkled with rum from a bottle of Jack Iron" (213). Moreover, the drums that summon the ancestors are made of "small rum kegs" (234). As the ceremony progresses, Marshall fuses the text rhythmically by exploiting the potential of *drum* as a kangaroo word containing *rum*. She further fuses product and ritual by using *rum* as a synecdoche for *drum*—"The rum kegs followed suit" (237). The words rumble in the text, a linguistic hum that saturates the ceremony with the implications of rum in the history and the present of the celebrants.

Avey, however, distances herself from the trance-like atmosphere by judging the drunkenness of her hosts. Set in the context of Marshall's general sympathy toward rum drinkers, Avey is an outlier: a sympathetic protagonist who violates the spirit of libations. There are "two or three bottles of the rum they called Jack Iron" around which "most of the men were congregated" (234). Avey notes that "the eyes of the men were already mystical with Jack Iron" (235)—a remark that presumes that the men are more interested in getting drunk than in the ritual itself. She undercuts the seriousness of the ceremony by attributing the appearance of the Old Parents in animal form to loss of inhibition, describing "a hard-back beetle ... zooming drunkenly (from all the Jack Iron imbibed earlier)" (238). The general drunkenness makes Avey's failure to imbibe—she drinks only "soft drink[s]" during the Big Drum ceremony (243)—more than caution after her recent illness. She joins the ceremony to commemorate a shared past, but she only partially shares their purpose.

Thus Avey's desire for what Carriacou can do to help her reclaim the past coexists uncomfortably with her desire to remain separate from Carriacou's recycled present. Invoking T. S. Eliot's "Preludes" (1934) by calling the ceremony the "burnt out ends" of an ancient tradition, Avey meditates on the scene's belated insufficiency before recognizing the "tenacity that she suddenly loved and longed for" (*Praisesong* 240). Even as she recognizes the dignity of survival, she resists incorporating the intervening history—enslavement—into this model by evading a commodity analysis of, for example, rum kegs. Although her eyes are drawn "repeatedly to the rum kegs that served as drums ..." (240, ellipsis in the original), she does not, as the ellipsis indicates, pursue the implications. The kegs reinforce the presence of history on Carriacou—a history present in modern adaptations in the ceremony like "the bottle-and-spoon boys" who make music using traditional musical instruments and agricultural implements, "maracas and shak-shaks, bottles, cowbells and hoeblades," as well as items associated with later phases of industrial production, like "the heavy iron hub of a car wheel" (242). Cheryl Wall claims that these instruments demonstrate "the determination of a people to beat out the rhythms of their culture even when the drum was prohibited" (205). The significance of their positioning "to one side" in Avey's depiction of the scene may mirror her unconscious desire to bracket the knowledge of the effects contemporary economic arrangements have on material conditions and opportunities for younger generations. These tools and products insist on continuity and relevance in the relationship between the United States and the Caribbean: Carriacou is not solely a place to locate a shared past.

At a conscious level, Avey understands the difference between her "real" New York middle-class existence and the "product" Carriacou she has experienced, but her expression of this difference does not produce an ethical change in her relations with people on Carriacou or, potentially, younger generations of African Americans in New York. She has assets she can use to assist her friends in Carriacou; for example, she leaves with letters for Rosalie's "children in Canada to be mailed from the States. They would reach them faster that way" (253). Her description of Carriacou as she leaves uncomfortably mirrors the fantasy with which her adventure began:

> Everything fleeting and ephemeral. The island more a mirage rather than an actual place. Something conjured up perhaps to satisfy a longing and need.
> She was leaving Carriacou without having really seen it. (254)

Carriacou is a product she has created, not a real place where people live and work—and while Avey's recognition of fantasy (if not paradisical) points to self-consciousness, it also places the island in the realm of myth, out of time. The placement of Carriacou in the deep past rather than the recent present strengthens Avey's claim to agency in the now. She arrives in Grenada ready to correct the perceptions of a local taxi driver: "She would sit him down, take off his mirrored sunglasses, and the straw cowboy hat and explain it" (254). On her return to the United States, she envisions forcing her message on young African American professionals: she would "tell" them "before they could pull out of her grasp" (255). On the one hand, Avey assumes her role as elder; on the other, she has become . . . imperious?

In considering Avey's future actions, we are far from her initial encounter with Joseph Lebert in the rum shop. But Avey herself refers eight times to the encounter in the rum shop as the turning point in her quest.[12] The referencing becomes a "discursive regularity," to use Kazanjian's terms, that marks as yet incomplete internalization of the lessons of Grenada and Carriacou. Avey worries at this moment by referencing it, echoing in narrative terms the chime of *rum* and *drum* during the ceremony. Critics replicate this discursive regularity by using rum and the rum shop as an orientation point in their analyses without addressing these elements explicitly. Barbara Christian and Joyce Pettis Owens both cite the use of "rum keg" drums (Owens 129; qtd. in Christian 82), but each critic emphasizes Avey's connection with precolonial African pasts without considering how locating this mythical past in Carriacou might affect the present. Elizabeth McNeil also makes passing references (194, 199, 200, 201), but she also devotes a paragraph of analysis to the rum shop scene, emphasizing its function as "a comic opening" (193) without reflecting on the specificity of the site to Caribbean cultures. Other critics include the rum shop to set scenes: Jane Olmstead, for example, remarks that Avey "is fainting from heat when she sees Lebert Joseph's small rum shop, stumbles in, and is offered a drink" (260). Similar versions include "she stumbles on a wooden shelter, a rum shop" (Rogers 85), "whose rum shop Avey stumbles into" (Sandiford, "Paule Marshall's" 386), and "the rum shop owner she meets on the island of Grenada" (Brown-Hinds 112).[13] The assonance in "stumbled" and "rum" in three of these appraisals denotatively attributes chance to the encounter, but the chiming creates a background hum. Pervasive but unprocessed, rum cues a more complex set of relations Avey could establish but did not, a suppressed connection between her renewed agency and her consumer choices in Carriacou.

These references to rum are economical, a shorthand for getting to elements of the text deemed more important to Avey's journey. Given Marshall's long-standing use of rum to image modern Caribbean communities that account for the past, however, such economy needs unpacking. Balancing critical histories of *Praisesong* that emphasize the transformative benefits of Avey's reconnection to her past with a close reading of her consumption of rum reveals a seam between Avey as focalizer of a realist narrative and critical discourse that overlooks the neocolonialist aspects of Avey's consumption habits. Rum poetics bridges a gap between critiques of the novel as a "black feminist literary fantas[y]" (Stuelke 119) that reifies the Caribbean as "the locus of spiritual, mythical power"

(Nair, "Expressive Countercultures" 84) and analyses that celebrate Avey's transformation into a modern political agent. The cultural influences in *Praisesong*'s "polyphony" are "uncountable and catholic, are native and creole, African and European and homegrown" (Cartwright 141), but critical emphasis on the ways the Big Drum/Beg Pardon reunites Avey with a repressed African past obscures the Caribbean islands as sites of political agency and retains them as subject to American patronage. Consuming the Caribbean as an avatar for Africa, Stuelke and Nair argue, respectively, "helped consolidate the neoliberal order" in the 1980s Caribbean (Stuelke 120) and silences systemic protest against "predatory capital" (Nair, "Expressive Countercultures" 85). In *Praisesong*, Marshall's metaphors of digestion and indigestion obtain in discussions of critical reception as much as in the narrative. Rum poetics traces the costs to Carriacou of an extractive economy of reading that limits accounts of the Caribbean background to Avey's transformative journey—without, I hope, invalidating the importance of either Avey's healing process or the voluntary coalition between groups whose ancestors were enslaved. It establishes material relations between segregated zones of critique, furthering the decolonization of critical practice by redistributing the sites of critical labor.

Michelle Cliff: Broken Bottles, Violated Libations

Michelle Cliff, as seen in earlier discussions of *Free Enterprise,* understands the political potential of rum as a libation, but compared to Marshall she is savage in her representation of rum's devastating legacies. In the paired bildungsromans *Abeng* (1984) and *No Telephone to Heaven,* excessive rum drinking represents generational effects of enslavement on family and communal history for her protagonist Clare Savage. The abuse, misuse, and weaponization of rum hums through these narratives, peaking early during a brutal murder and performing a bizarre anticlimactic role in *No Telephone*'s final scene. Paradoxically, Cliff explicitly compares rum to religion as opiates for the masses yet excoriates those who flout the symbolic contractual element of libations.[14] For example, in *Abeng* the failure to pour funeral libations for her son causes his mother, Hannah, the village obeah-woman, to become mentally ill. This communal sin arises from another: the exclusion of Clinton from village protection because of his sexuality, which leads to death by drowning (63). The community withdraws the usual voluntary assistance with the funeral, refusing "to assist [Hannah] in the rite of laying the duppy at peace" (63), which requires libations as part of burial. Hannah must rely on hired help to fulfill the customary obligations:

> She bought two bottles of white rum, one for each of the men, and told them to be sure and pour a drink for the duppy before they took a drink themselves. But they ignored her, emptied the bottles into themselves, and fell into the grave, singing a song about a woman in Montego Bay. So Mad Hannah buried her son alone the next morning—when it should have been done at midnight.
> On the third night after the burial she saw his duppy rise from the grave. (64)

The substitution of transactional exchange for voluntarism, followed by sacrilegious appropriation of libations, intensifies the violation of communal norms. The violation transforms Hannah into Mad Hannah, depriving the village of her services as obeah-woman as punishment. Features of this episode foreshadow the betrayal of Christopher by his employers in *No Telephone to Heaven*. Christopher, a houseboy for Paul D.'s family, murders his light-skinned employers after Paul D.'s father dismisses Christopher's request for money to settle the duppy of his long-dead grandmother.

Considered rationally, Hannah's madness and Christopher's murderous rage are irrational: duppies are the stuff of folktales. Indeed, when Hannah, institutionalized, seeks to explain "her son and his incomplete and dangerous burial" to "the people in charge—the light-skinned educated people" (*Abeng* 66), they dismiss her. Likewise, Christopher's request to his employers for money to bury his grandmother, thirteen years dead, location of her remains unknown, seems ridiculous. When Christopher, drunk, awakens them in the middle of Christmas night to ask them for money after seeing his grandmother's ghost in the rum shop, dismissing his concerns as "nonsense" (*No Telephone* 47) seems reasonable. For Christopher, the result of being "more and more black-up from the white rum" on an empty stomach (44) is ancestral connection, and his employer's denial violates holiday custom, when masters typically distribute gifts to servants and tolerate drunkenness. As Christopher reasons, "Backra people could be soft around de Chrismus—dem who was so mean the rest of the time" (45). The contrast between "soft" and "mean" registers emotionally and economically, suggesting that for Christopher this request functions as low-level saturnalia, an impertinence allowable because it confirms the usual order. From Mas' Charles's perspective, refusal may appear reasonable, and Christopher's subsequent actions sociopathic.

These examples of violated libations, and the extreme harms that result, exist on a continuum with other uses Cliff makes of rum to indicate how histories of colonial exploitation thread through Jamaica's social fabric. The modes of rum consumption and exchange track microeconomics, the intimacies and intimate exchanges of macroeconomic systems. In *Abeng*, rum signals both the extractive and selfish effects of plantation slavery as they were practiced in the past and persist in the present. Clare's paternal great-grandfather, Jack Savage, faced with declining revenues from sugar, opts for the other mode of capitalism: waste. He guzzles resources that could fund an alternative future to protest the loss of his position as a wealthy West Indian planter. He "began every day by opening a rum bottle—rather, by having it opened for him—and having it poured into a crystal decanter, and thence into a crystal goblet. It was rum from his own sugar cane, aged in wooden kegs, and poured into dark brown bottles bearing the name SAVAGE and the motto from the family crest: MIHI SOLICITUDO FUTURE—TO ME THE CARE OF THE FUTURE" (31). Likewise, the aunt and uncle who raise Boy, Clare's father, "were drunks. Not mean drunks, just sodden and soppy alcoholics" who "talked all day and all night of family" (42). Though Clare's father, Boy, escapes the alcoholism, he continues to promote the family brand: submission to English superiority. As "a traveling liquor salesman for a British distillery, peddling Beefeater gin and Haig & Haig scotch to hotels and rumshops" throughout Jamaica (24), Boy encourages psychological and economic investment in cultural hierarchies indebted to colonialism.

Where the example of Boy Savage's family demonstrates a systemic betrayal of Jamaica's future, Clare's maternal family, the Freemans, demonstrates intimate betrayal in the form of household economics. Though suspicious of Boy Savage because he is an "inheritor of bad traits and a liking for rum" (130), a "family joke" (137) indicates that the Freeman men are equally prone to waste. Clare's maternal grandfather drank the profits of his small cane crop, impoverishing his household and treating them with hot cross buns that he has, "in the darkness and in his drunkenness," mixed with lumps of horse manure (137): rum lays waste to social relations in the present, surfacing the sins of the past.

At this point, Cliff's deployment of rum appears straightforward, an image for the defilement of intimate and generational connection as a legacy of colonialism. Cliff expands her critique of patriarchy as a norm that may stem from imported European social codes but has long been internalized and made native to Jamaican gender roles. In the treatment of Harriet, a nonoperative transgender woman ostracized as a "battyman,"

Cliff's approach recalls Marshall's critique of compulsory heterosexuality in "British Guiana," where norms for sexual behavior are impervious to the critiques readily made around race and capitalism. *No Telephone*'s Harriet laments a code of masculinity that excludes her, making her "more welcome" in the Caribbean "stage set" of a tourist bar than at "a rumshop in Matilda's corner" (121): "Now, if they had *any* sense of irony, or history, they would call this place Triangle Trade and be done with it. The tourists them would never get the joke ... them would probably think it some sort of sailor's preference back then" (120, italics in the original). Harriet articulates a paradox: that northern tourists evince a kind of liberal tolerance for gender nonconformity abhorrent to many Jamaicans, yet they are ignorant of the historical implications of consuming colonial-themed interior design. The Caribbean imaginary promoted by tourism encourages selective contextualization of Jamaican history, creating a "stage-set" that leaves out details like "whips and chains"—echoes of Unsworth's *Sugar and Rum* here—necessary to create the world they enjoy (*No Telephone* 121). Harriet's allusion to the stage not only foreshadows the conclusion of the novel, in which Jamaica's history is likewise sanitized for a Hollywood film, but also recognizes the ironies of anticolonial political actions that continue to dehumanize other others—in this case, transgendered people. The price for gender nonconformity is the loss of male community in the rum shop, yet for Harriet's interlocutor Clare, and for most Jamaican women, the rum shop has always largely excluded them based on gender. In this scene, Harriet's exclusion is the felt loss of a natural right (male friendship in the context of local alcohol customs), rooted in her embodiment, that might or might not verge on the political. Since rum shops were sites for political organization, however, the failures of inclusion suggested here imply larger political frames and tacitly advocate for what we would now call an intersectional approach.[15]

Harriet's critique of Jamaican bar culture is one of three deployments of rum within *No Telephone* in which characters consciously critique rum's role in culture, politics, and economics: characters look at rather than through rum and see an explanation for current conditions in Jamaica. Harriet's use of ironic contrast stands in the middle of two additional instances of commodity critique, both from perspectives that lack credibility in the world of the novel. Early in the novel, a character named John D. renders the ethics of rum consumption in political terms: "John D., who dreds his hair and whose daddy teaches African studies at the university, had brought the ganja with him. He quite seriously denounces rum as an 'imperialist' drink. 'Lef' it wid the touris', man.

Have some talawa smoke. Is Rasta grass dis. Pure Jamaican gold'" (21). The quotation marks ironize John D's claim that rum is an "'imperialist' drink." As in Christopher Moore's *Fluke* (2003), a faux Rastafarian offers an instantly discredited economic explanation. Yet Rastafarians endow marijuana with spiritual powers based on its association with "peasant lifeways" correlating to a rejection of capitalism (Benard 92). Cliff rejects the notion offered by John D. that economic protest is simply a matter of consumer choice. *No Telephone to Heaven* operates in a complex economic present in which the past unavoidably makes its impact known; the rebel group in *No Telephone* could not finance its activities with marijuana sales to the United States without the economic histories in which contemporary smuggling positions itself—right down to the "war on drugs" their actions ironically embody.[16]

The second instance of commodity analysis telescopes the effects of the multinational film industry into transactions at a local rum shop. Two visiting film executives, one English and one American, both "whitemen" from the bartender's perspective (200), compare inadequate cocktails to the broader consumer experience of filming in Jamaica. In this scene, Cliff telescopes in from the global to the regional to the local to show how macropolitical legacies of imperialism shape mundane interpersonal insensitivities. The northern privilege of the film executives plays out through the local, strongly gendered, alcohol culture of the rum shop. The executives lament the local rum shop's inability to produce a daquiri: "Christ . . . if they can't make a bloody daiquiri, how in hell are they going to provide us with what we need?" (201). The bartender, "used to men ordering their rum straight," has difficulty producing "a tourist drink" (200). The executives speak as if the bartender cannot hear them; the bartender pretends he has not "heard any of the conversation" (203).

Consumer and laborer are in proximity but only the laborer, the bartender who was "hard-pressed" to meet their demand (200), acknowledges the social and material relations that enable the presence of the executives in his rural rum shop. The historical conditions for executive privilege are displayed in this encounter, as the American executive references his experience filming in postcolonial Cuba, the Congo, and Haiti to reassure his partner that Jamaican authorities will come through because they have been "tied up by the IMF" (201). The executives speak of the history that enables their presence in Jamaica, much as Sir John Stokes in *The Chosen Place* acknowledges the commodity chain that leads from soil to sugar, but they similarly fail to acknowledge the corollary relation between their privilege and the conditions under which the bartender labors. In this case, the bartender has his revenge: he overcharges them, of course, and he points to their—implicitly effeminate—solipsistic consumerism by offering to prostitute his mother and find a "cure fe your cancer" as they leave (*No Telephone* 204). In this context, the difference between a daiquiri and straight rum is the difference between an identity comfortably supported by consumer choice and one structured by accidents of race and national origin. The bartender's parting shot—likely unheeded by his privileged clients—delineates the economic conditions that allow the filmmakers to be, simply, themselves.

At this juncture, Christopher, now mentally ill and known as Da Watchman, arrives in the rum shop, portending the crystallization of a rum economy in the novel's climactic scene. The juxtaposition of scenes in which rum is a conscious site of reflections with those where rum is a site of unmarked inflection offer trenchant insights into the operations of colonialism's legacies. The bartender, in the former case, may win a battle for readerly sympathies—who wants to be those clueless white guys?—but Hollywood executives win the war when the Jamaican government machine-guns its own citizens for interfering with their efforts to sell the country as a film set.[17] The final scene represents the power of rum to organize bodies to perpetuate colonialism beyond the moment of "post-" colonial nation formation. The government warns the US-based crew that the boundaries between art (a film for which real military helicopters are props) and life (the military attacks the rebels protesting the film's misappropriation of Jamaican history) will be breached: the crew shelters in a trailer and "Someone opened a bottle of rum and passed it hand to hand . . . waiting for this to pass" (207). What is "this" to the film crew as readers of the scene? Black-on-Black violence? Proof of Jamaica's inability to meet the needs of a modern market? Government corruption typical of the region? The crew's position echoes that of Cowper's antipathetic consumers, anxious but compliant, stupefying themselves as slave owners used rum to accustom the enslaved to their position in the commodity chain. Here, rum measures the privilege of "waiting," making the attack a kind of time-out, from the perspective of the crew, in the progress of their film. The film crew is not only implicated in this scene of (literal and representational) violence, but also essential to it. They are, to loosely quote anthropologists MacAndrew and Edgerton, the drunks neocolonialism allows, and the rum a blasphemous libation.

What would it mean to think about criticism of *No Telephone*'s early murder and rape scene through this lens, using rum to identify areas of passive consumption in scholarly reading? The murderer, Christopher, now known as the Watchman, dies in the attack like Clare, bringing their parallel quests to accommodate the maternal to violent ends. As noted above, Christopher is drunk on rum when he murders Mas' Charles, his family, and the housekeeper; the narrator implicates rum as the catalyst of the violence, for Christopher's "passion calmed and the rum wore off" after the murder (177). A rum bottle is Christopher's supernumerary weapon: after Christopher machetes the housekeeper and slits the throats of the family, he uses a broken rum bottle to mutilate the daughter, castrate the father, and rape the mother, leaving the bottle in the mother's vaginal opening (49). Yet critics who analyze this scene tend not to incorporate this extra element into their analyses. For example, Nada Elia uses the phrase "drunk with rum and sadness" to introduce the murder of Paul's family (69), without pausing to consider what that juxtaposition implies. While Wendy Walters registers the intersection of abstract concepts and material goods—"the exogenous (Europeanness) is constructed by a reliance on colonialism, for example relying on the indigenous nature of sugarcane to Jamaica" (30)—subsequent analysis speeds through quotations containing references to rum without acknowledgment that this commodity might expand her commentary on sugar (30–32). Joel West is one of few critics who recognizes the bottle's importance on a continuum of the commodities hoarded by the family: "Even the broken rum bottle that Christopher uses to sever his employer's penis and to violate his wife's vagina post-mortem is an ideologeme, representative of the sugar cane and rum trade that served to enslave the Jamaican people even after the plantation system was abolished."[18] The alignment of the scene with Freudian psychoanalytic patterns makes Ramchandran Sethuraman's 1997 article "Evidence-Cum-Witness" particularly useful in unpacking the translation of Cliff's deployment of rum as site of critique into a cypher in scholarly work. Sethuraman theorizes "a problematic link between the two disciplines" of psychoanalysis and postcolonialism (250) by analyzing a doubled pattern of gazes in this scene. Sethuraman uses the theory of castration anxiety to show how the doubled narration of the murder (first through Paul's eyes and then through Christopher's) denies mastery to the light-skinned Paul without making Christopher's protest legible unless we "learn and cultivate a different mode of reading identity" (266). Sethuraman's drive toward a different mode of reading identity (the aim of rum poetics) expands when the item that fills the lack (the rum bottle) becomes part of the critical narrative.

Essentially, Sethuraman replicates Paul's reading strategy by looking through rather than at the rum bottle, but rum returns, like the repressed, in the textual weave of the article's discourse. Sethuraman asserts that Paul attempts to master his fear of castration first by disavowing his father's severed penis and secondly by revealing his mother's castration, citing the "gesture of pulling out the rum bottle" from his mother's vagina as a telling moment (262). At the very least, the rum bottle is a site, as West notes, where readers could hear a resisting subaltern voice: Christopher castrates the father and denaturalizes paternal authority as such by replacing it with a product that structures Mas' Charles's familial and societal position. The scene also frames a masculine psychodrama that fails to account for the doubly oppressed role of Black women in the cycles of production and reproduction that slavery demanded. Looking at the rum bottle, then, furthers the intimate connections Sethuraman seeks to make between psychoanalytic and postcolonial theories. Sethuraman speaks of the link between young Christopher's lack of phallic control, manifested as a fear of uncontrolled urination in front of his employer and revenged in the "defiant piss on their wall" he takes following the murders (267). Expelling rum as urine, Christopher offers an anticolonial antilibation in the form of waste to mirror the failure of Mas' Charles to acknowledge either their personal relationship or the socioeconomic forces that position them in that relationship.[19]

This lapse, this inability to read, manifests as a rational break in Sethuraman's argument, where rum is doing some work without explication. To coronate his analysis of the doubled gaze, Sethuraman elevates his prose: "Is it gratuitous violence that Cliff recklessly subjects us to in going over the same heinous crimes from two different perspectives? The question becomes all the more compelling in the light of Christopher's revisiting the dead bodies to obliterate them further with the jagged edges of the rum bottle" (265). Sethuraman does not elaborate. The paragraph breaks, jumping to a theoretical discussion about "the socializing and civilizing ends of the novel and the nation-state" (267) and never returns to explain what is "compelling" about the rum bottle. In the context of an argument based on castration theory, this rhetorical flourish glosses when it should delve. This gloss, part of the discursive regularities around rum I trace here, belies Sethuraman's goal of "another, more interesting tale that begs to be told" about the relationship between postcolonial and psychoanalytic discourses (254). In other words, this tonal shift marks the break Sethuraman seeks to mend—right at the point where racial and gendered privilege position readers to confront the cost of an imagined "post-" colonial subjectivity. As the beneficiaries of racial privilege, Paul's light-skinned family limns whiteness in *No Telephone to Heaven;*

Christopher inserts evidence of the system from which they benefit into the site of naturalized reproduction. Inserted into the putative originary scene of psychoanalysis, the bottle points outward, toward Paul (who remains oblivious), toward critics and readers, demanding acknowledgment of the intimacies of racialized colonial violence on which the privileged identities of whiteness rely. This scene is what makes "you" "you." It invites painful conversations about trauma, identity, and privilege that require an acknowledgment of intimate, personal, everyday investment in systemic colonialist legacies.

Both Michelle Cliff and Paule Marshall introduce rum critically in their texts as a product that shapes everyday interactions as outcomes of historical patterns stemming from colonialism. Their respective constructions of verisimilitude connect the "micropolitics of everyday life" to the "larger processes that recolonize the culture and identities of people across the globe" (Mohanty 508–9). We do not need rum, necessarily, to get the retributive logic of Christopher's death at the hands of a government that protects classes of people against whom Christopher revenged himself. We do need it, however, to transform the studied ennui of northern observers, drinking to pass the time while Jamaicans self-destruct, into an ethical question about the cost of comfortable northern identities. We do not need it to understand Avey Johnson's amendment, her return to celebrating her African ancestry, as part of the rituals on Carriacou; we do need it to see that her transformation is at a beginning, and she is only partially aware of those she leaves behind. Rum poetics further disseminates this perspective into the realm of professional critical habits to chart boundaries on what can be said and thought. These reflections on the structuring of interpretive limits lead back to Tim Mitchell's question about whether "we even listen" but also "how . . . we listen" to drinking, particularly excessive drinking, depending on who drinks (1). In this light, it is useful to return to the work of Nancy Topping Bazin and Krista Ratcliffe on teaching alcoholism in fiction. Bazin argues against pathologizing alcoholism as a third-world phenomenon, encouraging instead an empathetic recognition of the sources of "pain" that led to alcoholism (132). Ratcliffe likewise identifies alcoholism as a pain point when she discusses how ingrained taboos discourage the exclusion of the topic from class discussion. When taboos and habits about drinking—many of them shared across the regions from which these texts are drawn—govern our critical thinking and our pedagogies, we risk economical readings that align with neocolonial economic impulses. What I have called, broadly, a libations approach establishes commonality and recognizes connection without romanticizing or rhapsodizing.

"Post-" Postcolonial Reading: Sympathy Problems

Diana McCauley's 2012 novel *Huracan* does not rhapsodize or romanticize; it begins with rum and ends with a section entitled "Ferment." Rum is the sociocultural counterpart to the natural phenomenon that gives the novel its title, and the protagonist meditates explicitly on drunkenness as a rational response to systemic economic disadvantage with roots in slavery. McCauley, like Marshall and Cliff, produces a narrative that has internalized rum poetics and, like other twenty-first-century writers whose works appear in this study, McCauley's use of rum poetics takes on a performativity that resonates with the academic; in other words, the novel is informed by the insights postcolonial theory brings to commodity critique. This novel iterates a history of colonialism: the narrator, thirty-year-old Leigh McCauley, returns to Jamaica after a long absence to help out on her family's plantation, now a tourist attraction, and Leigh's experiences (1986–87) layer onto those of her ancestors Zachary (1780s) and John (1880s). In viewing the present as the product of historical fermentation and reflecting on the rationale for alcoholism, *Huracan* usefully brings together several themes that run through this study to address methodological problems associated with white privilege in an age of self-consciousness about white privilege.

"Rum" is the last word of the first sentence of this novel. As Leigh McCauley leaves Jamaica's main airport, she is hailed by a homeless drunk: "'White gal!' the barefoot man shouted, pointing at her with a half empty bottle of white rum. He wore a vest and torn shorts and his eyes glared" (*Huracan* 11). As in *No Telephone,* the rum bottle sticks out, hailing an interlocutor who is a "white gal" in a challenge her national belonging. The epithet "white gal" mischaracterizes her as an outsider: "She was not a tourist. She wanted to explain this to the man. I was born here. I am coming home" (11). The dissemination of meaning across "white," "tourist," and "home" links race to national identity in Jamaica in Leigh's consciousness. The relationship between the anonymous man and the protagonist begins with perceived exclusion through stereotype from Leigh's point of view, prompting, in return, an attempt to position the man in her working knowledge of the island: "The light changed and they drove on. The man remained where he was, leaning against an unrendered concrete wall covered with peeling, bleached-out posters advertising dances and plays. His anger seemed to have passed. He tipped the bottle of white rum to his head and Leigh could see his throat muscles working. How to describe him—poor man, sufferer, black man, rum head, *bhuto,* Jamaican man?" (11).

The concluding list of types, a tentative acknowledgment of her inability to classify him, nevertheless ends with "Jamaican man." While she consciously resists stereotyping him, the range of positions she makes available to him is narrow. The reproduction of this typology in earlier historical sections of the novel makes this man the first version of a consistent stock character—one that never advances beyond type.[20] He represents a type that fails to develop across time, in contrast to Leigh's ability to move (on). The description suggests that this pattern is a product of white textual privilege, as he is "bleached-out" and "unrendered" so that Leigh can continue. In contrast to his flatness as a character, his body is magnified such that Leigh can see "his throat muscles working" to swallow the rum as she is driven away. The discordant combination of his anonymity and his obtrusive physical presence—the "pointing" bottle and "working" throat—suggests that rum's history continues to work the scene, force-feeding Leigh and readers a narrative that requires flattening this man into the background, into the past, into the simplifications of a "poster," so Leigh can center her story.

Leigh exhibits an epistemology of postcolonial knowledge that recognizes the subaltern as a mode of reinforcing the privileging of her knowledge. Ultimately, she places this man in the background as one incapable of understanding her story. Her perspective is metacritical and self-conscious in method but without significant investment in the work of reparation. It is paranoid reading, in Sedgwick's terms, that attempts to avert surprise by prophylactic exculpation. Leigh, for example, opines, "Middle class guilt. So boring and predictable" (*Huracan* 264). This inoculation does not shield her from an undesirable surprise: the rejection of "well-meaning whiteness" (Savory 311) as sufficiently reparative. In the "Ferment" section of the novel, a fully realized version of the anonymous drunk "Jamaican man" refuses to comply with her story. Banjo, a longtime, elderly employee of Leigh's family, trips a stereotype when she finds him "drunk" on rum (*Huracan* 226) on a work morning: "Leigh dredged for anger—this was a work morning and there was no other job for Banjo for miles—but she could not find it. Banjo was older than her father—much older—and he lived alone here on the edge of the forest in the kind of shed the Libbeys might have built to store their lawn mower. No wonder he was drunk" (226).

Although this internal thought process appears compassionate, it continues to enact the priorities of a capitalist market. Leigh cannot "find" anger at employees who do not recognize their good luck in a precarious labor market, but she still thinks "there was no other job for Banjo for miles." The threat of termination remains as a rational response from the plantation owner; she has the privilege even when she chooses not to exercise it. Leigh also sets up maudlin comparisons (the age of her father, the Libbey family's wealth) that telescope his drunkenness to failed interpersonal relations. While these comparisons resonate with the historical and the structural (namely, the location on a plantation), her conclusion—"No wonder he was drunk"—retains the privilege of judgment. In other words, as Leigh analyzes why Banjo is the way he is, she also classifies his behavior as unsurprising and inevitable.

Banjo does surprise Leigh, though, when she attempts reparations incommensurate with the historical and psychological forces in which they are enmeshed. Her effort takes the form of asking Banjo to abandon custom and call her by her first name rather than "Miss." When he demurs, she commands, "Say it." His response turns the work of middle-class liberalism back on her: "'So what you doing here, *Leigh?*' he said and arched his back to ease the strain" (286, italics in the original). Etched in his responses are echoes of the opening scene—a body burdened by the charge of drunkenness, a claim to home challenged. Banjo exhibits no gratitude for her enlightened understanding, refusing an emotional debt that, as Saidiya Hartman has argued, comes with financial strings attached (131). To accept Leigh's olive branch is to accept the operations of the labor market and the rights of workers as she has imposed them. Rather, Banjo's ingratitude repulses the logic by which Leigh arrives at her liberal gesture, a gesture possible only with reference to a system in which laboring Black bodies remain commodified, deemed more or less productive by their willingness to accommodate to neocolonial exploitation. In other words, Banjo proposes an anticommodity saga, one in which a "wondrous system . . . without which you would not, you suddenly realize, be yourself" (Robbins 456) does not self-evidently guarantee the sufficiency of Leigh's inclusive move. Banjo's ungrateful response is a question about the future (why are you here now?) and the past (how did you get here?). As "Miss," perhaps the answer is easy. As "Leigh," less so, as Banjo questions the priority of white agency.

Such concerns circle back to the solipsistic narrator of O'Neill's *Netherland*. As Elaine Savory notes in a review of the novel, *Huracan* explores "the relation of liberal, middle class whites to Jamaica's present social fabric" (308). The notion of "liberal, middle class whites" redounds on the novel's readership just as the first words of the novel, "White gal!," press through the fictional wall to hail a demographic of readers who must account for their powerful interpretations of Caribbean scenes and subjects—except that the "white gal" whose narrative drives this novel is not, according to the one drop rule, white, but the great-great-great-great-great-great-great-grandchild of Madu, an enslaved woman whose owners raped her. This knowledge, available to readers but not to Leigh, opens a fissure from the past to the present, subtly reshaping the initial confrontation between Black man and white woman with a past that is different than the narrator's truth. This is not to propose that Leigh would have a better defense against the man's accusatory naming if she knew, or that she would be able to relate to his situation, or that this information undoes the racial privilege accorded to women who figure as, and benefit from being, "white." Nor does it, by implication, imagine a world where a "white gal" can easily or ethically "be" the other. McCauley's surprising revelation about Leigh's past proposes, however, that race is a powerful historical fiction that obscures Leigh's understanding of her body's history in relation to plantation slavery. While in *Huracan* a joint purpose under the sign of rum does not yet exist, and *Praisesong* and *No Telephone* warn of the difficulties of negotiating this territory, all three novels do suggest the critical energy available in liberating commodities from white-washed protocols of interpretation.

6 Is the Rum Gone?
Imperial Nostalgia

> We invented. . . . We had a scene with the story, the legend in it but then I thought it was so boring I . . . cut the scene, you know. It was sort of a legend of the pirate in the Caribbean. When your pirate has his daughters stolen and he was allowed to get drunk or something like that but then it was . . . I couldn't stand it anymore.
> —Claire Denis

ABOVE, CLAIRE Denis reflects on her decision to cut explanatory scenes that would have provided a backstory for the title of her 2008 film *35 rhums* (*35 Shots of Rum*).[1] Tentative and elliptical, full of qualifications and understatements, her explanation withholds as much as it offers, replicating the affect of the film. She hints at the elements of the plot—a "pirate in the Caribbean" with "daughters stolen" who is "allowed to get drunk"—but the clichés never add up, just as *35 rhums* ends without the thirty-fifth shot drunk. Denis characterizes the "invented" legend as both "boring" and intolerable (she "couldn't stand it"): she refuses the introduction of anodyne pirate lore that might unsettle the film's subtle engagement with slavery, colonialism, and structural debt.[2] Piracy has a mixed role in Caribbean history, as it can be associated with European colonists who benefited from an illicit yet legal slave trade and forms of communal resistance to military and state power, but Denis's distaste has a more immediate source: Disney's blockbuster *Pirates of the Caribbean* trilogy, completed with the release of *At World's End* in 2007.[3] The series catchphrase spawned the popular "Why has the rum gone?" meme, and the trilogy went on to become a quintet.[4] The parodic and metacritical stance of the *Pirates* series compounds the problem, as the films draw on literary and cinematic clichés rather than "factual pirate accounts" (Petersen 64). To risk this intertext could gloss Denis's film as a pirate-themed drinking game. Yo ho ho.

Further, Denis's mixed-race young heroine, Josephine, navigating life choices amid the legacies of French colonialism and just beginning to analyze these forces, faces a formidable competitor in the figure of

Elizabeth Swann, arguably the most powerful reader in *Pirates of the Caribbean*. Her uncritical consumption of highly fictionalized accounts of piracy drives the plot of the first film, *The Curse of the Black Pearl* (2003); meeting her narrative demands also requires an enormous investment of resources. During the film, Swann triumphantly declares, "The entire British Navy is out looking for me." As the representative of white womanhood in this film, *Curse* both weaponizes and blames her for the existence of the British Empire; her protofeminist desire for self-determination prompts a further pincer move in which her agency burdens both imperialists and pirates-as-other.[5] Swann, then, brings together the ways rum flavors the consumption of narratives about the Caribbean—most important because she is the reason that the film has the catchphrase "Why is the rum gone?"[6]

In a well-known scene from *Curse of the Black Pearl*, in which Swann and Captain Jack Sparrow are marooned, she demands that Sparrow perform according to the expectations raised by stories of his derring-do. Sparrow's real story outrages her heroic ideals. Instead of derring-do, Sparrow offers lucky coincidence: small-time rum smugglers happened by to check their stash, and Sparrow hitched a ride. Swann sputters, "So that's it, then? That's the secret grand adventure of the infamous Jack Sparrow? You spent three days lying on a beach, drinking rum?" Sparrow's reply: "Welcome to the Caribbean, love." With a characteristic wink, the film invokes, undermines, and celebrates clichés of Caribbean tourism. Sparrow substitutes contemporary tourism for colonial history, suggesting that the images are equally marketed to deceive. Swann routes her outrage through a moralistic reference to drinking habits, which prepares the scene for her response to Sparrow's question "Why is the rum gone?" She invokes temperance rhetoric to justify using the rum to enhance their signal fire: "Rum is a vile drink that turns even the most respectable men into complete scoundrels." In short, from Swann's perspective, Sparrow has taken an illegal alcoholic time-out when he should have been meeting the imperatives of pirate literature. Sparrow's countering anachronism transforms Swann into an uptight tourist who prefers a Disney ride to the realities of Caribbean history, as Anne Petersen suggests in her reading of the film as a commodification of "a theme park ride" (64). Sparrow's remark also links past economic structures (sugar plantations) to contemporary ones (tourism) through the conduit of a product on which both rely to generate profits: rum.

Embedded in *Curse of the Black Pearl*'s one-liners are some effective methods of cost shifting. After Jack makes this remark, the camera shifts to follow Sparrow rather than Swann. The audience dutifully follows as he marches toward the beach, rum bottles in hand. Swann follows clumsily, slipping in the sand, an unwilling participant in an alternative story line. But Sparrow's intervention returns to the status of time-out when Swann lures him into dancing around a bonfire and singing pirate songs. Swann wrests control of the rum and the narrative, turning all the resources of the island to the fulfillment of her desires. She burns the rum, along with "all the food, the shade," in the signal fire, allowing the navy ships to locate her and restart a narrative she controls. Figuratively, Swann expropriates "all" the natural resources and consumer goods of the Caribbean to support her version of the story. Sparrow's quip when he sees the navy ship—"There'll be no living with her now"—both addresses her privilege and literally references the probable result of his capture (i.e., execution). The truth of his statement is evident from the set-dressing (to which Jack Sparrow occasionally calls attention), which teems with incarcerated, traumatized bodies recalling the punishment of pirates and enslaved people. People starve in jail cells, scarred; skeletal men labor endlessly on cursed ships; and executed bodies blister and twist on the ramparts. The answers to the question "Why is the rum gone?" are less immediate than ideological: the waste of an implicitly masculine world of adventure results from the consumption habits of white women, imperialism's avatars.

On the one hand, Swann is a familiar type. The compliance—also the willful collaboration—of white women in colonialism is well documented in history and well represented in this study in characters both round and flat (from, say, Harriet Amron of *The Chosen Place* to the anonymous woman who closes off the beach in *Land of Love and Drowning*). *Pirates of the Caribbean* makes Swann the rationale for British imperialism, and according to this logic her protofeminism becomes an extra cost extracted from the Caribbean. As the daughter of an aristocrat, Swann is clearly a sign of Anglo-European male dominance: the investment in her appearance, cleanliness, and leisure countersigns masculine imperial power. Yet her enforced obliviousness to what she costs to maintain weighs on the British military, as they are drawn from the real work of empire by her fantasies about pirates. Like Kurtz's Intended, she is the horror, blamed for an ignorance men collude to perpetuate. As a result, Swann's feminist bid for freedom relies on "a problematic alignment of gender-based and ... race-based discrimination" that positions her as a scapegoat for both the patriarchal establishment (her father, the navy) and pirates as multivalent representations of "othered" groups (Marston).

On the other hand, the division of white feminism from identification with other social justice efforts is a deliberate compositional strategy in *Pirates*. A deleted extension of the "Why has the rum gone?" scene proves that Jack Sparrow's separation from the film's background of trauma and violence is notional at best.[7] In response to Swann's question about whether there is "any truth" to the other tales of Sparrow's heroics, Sparrow rolls up his sleeves and opens his shirt to reveal scars that striate his arms and chest. "No truth at all," he remarks. The alignment of Sparrow with routine bodily abuse of sailors, pirates, criminals, and enslaved people moves these deleted scenes from hero worship to historical witness because Sparrow's body testifies to the human cost of the colonial trade in sugar, rum, and slaves. The *Pirates* production team forecloses an alternate response—any response—from Swann: her reaction, the reverse shot, never appears in the film or the deleted scenes. If this scene, although hidden in the film's ancillary materials, could activate "the uncertain line between witness and spectator" (Hartman 4), then the production never allows the ask. Swann's potential to align proto–white feminism with other social justice causes is not represented. Instead, the white-feminist-as-usurper narrative continues through the series, as Swann eventually becomes the Pirate Queen. Moreover, her occlusion also releases *the audience* from any obligation to consider these complex questions of identification, accountability, and responsibility. To object that these deletions are a matter of genre is to ignore a white Anglo-American privilege that pleasures itself through these fantasies.

Swann's position within the *Pirates* iconography supports a masculine fantasy world in which Sparrow's forlorn "Why is the rum gone?" is a gendered ubi sunt that marks the film's multiple, incompletely parodic, engagements with American imperial nostalgia. Disney's revival of the pirate genre rehearses historical patterns in which the Caribbean functions as a proxy site for resolving European conflicts. On one level, Jack Sparrow's search for "freedom" and escape from British tyranny situates him as an iconic American individualist defending himself from colonization, economic exploitation, and domesticity. "Freedom" is rum—a perpetual time-out from rules, customs, and institutions. As Petersen notes, Sparrow "lacks any sort of character arc. . . . his goals and character development remain wholly static throughout the film" (72; see also Steinhoff 126n19); this fixity renders him an exemplar of life, liberty, and the pursuit of happiness tout court. Of course, in Disney's re-creation of the eighteenth-century world, the United States is absent because it does not yet exist, but Jack stands in for the chaotic energies and idealistic principles associated with the new nation to be.[8] As Heiki Steinhoff claims, "The film's critique of globalization is 'safely' directed at the British imperial machinery within the diegetic world" of the film (129). Characters like British Commander Beckett seek control of the Caribbean seas, strategically asserting military strength in the name of "good business" (*At World's End*).[9] Following Steinhoff's argument, pirates—and Sparrow particularly—represent but are historically innocent of United States imperialism; Sparrow functions as a victim of globalization rather than as a perpetrator.[10] Moreover, the deliberate polyvalence of Johnny Depp's costume and mannerisms (effeminate, queer, dark, virile, bohemian) meld markers of oppression into a singular, anarchic "freedom" seeker. "Why has the rum gone?" expresses nostalgia for a world in which it is possible to believe that the founding principles of US democracy are neither selectively applied nor a justification for greed and domination—they are just about guaranteeing "freedom."

Considered as the phrase reverberates into contemporary geopolitics, "Why is the rum gone?" is at once an immediate, practical question about threats to US economic dominance and a nostalgic lament for a masculine fantasy of endless frontiers. In the realpolitik of global capitalism, the rhetoric of freedom often supports efforts to dominate and influence in the name of free trade. A 2012 argument over rum subsidies in the US budget indicates the impact seemingly insignificant actions on the part of the United States can have on fragile Caribbean economies. According to NBC News, "an obscure federal law" dedicates all liquor taxes paid on rum to Puerto Rico and the USVI (McFadden). These dollars subsidize Bacardi Limited and Cruzan Rum, huge players in the US domestic rum market and companies that are part of multinational alcohol producers with dozens of brands to their names. Several subsidy deals had been brokered that, according to Caribbean rum producers, will make the market landscape impossibly uncompetitive for smaller producers. This is an important issue "because rum . . . is one of the few competitive industries for the tourism-dependent region's tiny, vulnerable economies" (McFadden). In this regard, the United States functions more as the East India Company does in the *Pirates* films, smothering—Kraken-like—the efforts of smaller producers.

"Why has the rum gone?" has proved a durable and adaptable part of the meme economy. We might return to Ian Baucom's association of genre with stages of financialization in *Specters of the Atlantic:* successful memes could be seen as the ultimate in speculative fiction, capitalizing on prior assets by attaching to other contexts and literally profiting from the share.[11] In the 2016 presidential campaign, some citizens capitalized on the kangaroo word, *rum,* in Donald Trump's last name to ridicule his candidacy. Campaign signs with the first and last letters cut off *Trump* satirized the candidate by questioning his sobriety; Jack Sparrow made appearances in Facebook posts to amplify the critique. The link of Trump's candidacy with rum and *Pirates* is more than serendipitous wordplay; rather the coincidence points to the imperial nostalgia implicit in Trump's "Make America Great Again!" agenda. The rum- and *Pirates of the Caribbean*–related memes capture something strange about this idea of greatness by linking it to US participation in the slave trade and our excesses of imperial expansionism. Trump defines his vision of American greatness in comparison to the "the turn of the [twentieth] century," a "pretty wild time," and "the late '40s and '50s," when "we [the United States] were not pushed around, we were respected by everybody, we had just won a war, we were pretty much doing what we had to do" (Sanger and Haberman). These are times of imperial and neoimperial expansion, points at which the United States acquired colonies (taking up the "White Man's Burden") and, after World War II, competed with the Soviet Union for influence in the decolonizing world.[12] President Trump's America First narrative is rum. To put this idea another way, it is possible to imagine that returning to the material relations rum historically represents could make America great again—in Trump's terms.

This dystopic future past resonates with our present, as documented in a film like *Big Sugar* (2005), one of many nonfiction and fictional works that contrast the lavish spending of the Florida-based Fanjul brothers with the exploitative conditions on the sugar plantations they own in the Dominican Republic. In figurative terms, Grenadian Jacob Ross repositions long-standing tropes of representing US-Caribbean relations as a copacetic and pleasing cocktail in his 1999 story "Rum an Coke." The horrors of sugar production lamented by abolitionist boycotters in the eighteenth and nineteenth centuries recur in Norma's decision to injure herself "so that she could get the insurance to send her boy off to a high-class school. . . . Inside a canemill, besides!" (413). Her son, now addicted to cocaine (possibly as a result of racism he experienced at school), uses a new combination of "rum-an-coke" to perpetuate systemic violence in social relations built on drug economy (413). The United States does not appear directly in this story, but it is figured in the name of its friendliest ambassador commodity, Coke. In Ross's revision of the trope, US influence has very little to do with life, liberty, and the pursuit of happiness—or the "perfect harmony" promised in Coca-Cola's best-known advertising campaign.

As a balance to these sinister ironies, Ta-Nehisi Coates's brief reference to rum and Coke in *Between the World and Me* (2015) makes available a future transformed by the potential of a Global South. His is not a utopian vision, but Coates renders the spatial hierarchies of Washington, DC, unstable, first by describing Howard University as "Mecca" and thus installing an alternate omphalos at the center of (white) US power two miles to the northeast (40). Second, he describes the collegiate club scene as a time-out that figures communal purpose and cooperation: "On the outside black people controlled nothing, least of all the fate of their bodies, which could be commandeered by the police; which could be erased by the guns, which were so profligate; which could be raped, beaten, jailed. But in the clubs, under the influence of two-for-one rum and Cokes, under the spell of low lights, in thrall of hip-hop music, I felt them to be in total control of every step, every nod, every pivot" (62).

This description invokes the concept of time-out: a temporary escape from political and social realities to leisure ratified by the presence of alcohol.[13] The scene is not a countercultural utopia that yields to systemic racism in return for minimal square footage; it refigures democratic institutions in the "step," "nod," and "pivot" that negotiates the health, safety, and pleasure of the community. Uniting this language with that of spiritual transformation ("influence"; "thrall"; "spell") recalls the ceremonies of the Beg Pardon in Marshall's *Praisesong* and the everyday activism of Anette's BOMB in Yanique's *Land of Love and Drowning*. One could lean this description over into racist primitivism, drawing on tropes designed to constrain African Americans, but dwelling on the affect—what is "felt" as "total control"—imagines a future in which the "two-for-one rum and Cokes" marks a past that could have been different and a future that will be.

By reading closely across texts that operate at various levels of literariness and intersect across specialist and popular discourses, the texture of rum as a signifier that carries meaning and history across oceans and overland emerges. It surfaces not just what was, but what is already and can be. While this study has prioritized the Anglophone Caribbean as a generation point, there are clear corollaries in Hispanophone, Francophone, and Dutch literatures. Further, references to "look-like whiskey ... stuff that almost tastes like rum" in *Netherland* (50) and the transference of rum's narrative to the Pacific island of Hawaii in *Fluke* (99) point toward linkages and transactions that, like those of sugar, may surface in further explorations. *Rum Histories* intersects with the questions of scale engaged by scholarship that traces connections across a broad imperial field, refining and specifying the effects of the colonial durée, but it starts at the bottom of the chain to track the objects and ideas the circulate through commodities. It offers insight into the ways subjects make sense—or make sense by refusing to make sense—of their positionality in large, inertial systems with decisive effects on everyday exchanges and interactions.

In the decades since decolonization began in earnest with Partition, rum appears in literature as a site that captures contradictory potentials and anxieties surrounding the implementation of postcolonial relationships. In the image of rum, such potentials and anxieties simultaneously explain and obscure the construction of putatively postcolonial subjects by legacies of colonial power. *Rum Histories* has sought to advance reading practices that explore the corners of colonized minds by looking at rum in both unsurprising and surprising textual and geographical locations; it seeks, I argue, to examine what we can do with explication informed by the planetary, global, transnational perspectives that have characterized theorizations in modernist and postcolonial studies of the past twenty years. This network of textual relationships attaches ethical concerns to institutional patterns and personal decisions about the parameters for interpreting rum. When I draw on Eve Kosofsky Sedgwick's language of reparative reading, it leads me toward Edouard Glissant's more challenging language of *antillanité* (becoming) and this work as a libation of sorts. This libation, then, acknowledges a commitment to more, to a willingness to speculate about a world in which the salience of rum to interpretive practices is de rigueur rather than idiosyncratic—something I no longer have the privilege to ignore. Strangely, reading rum histories patterns a postcolonial world as emergent, not distant, perceptible, not speculative. Look and see.

Notes

Introduction

1. As Warner Allen remarks in exasperation, "Rum-running, Rum Row, and the like are at least as much concerned with Whisky" (18).

2. These stereotypes collapse on examination. Despite the strong associations with the Caribbean, sugarcane originates from the Middle East, where the first sugar-based alcoholic beverages were fermented. The contemporary stereotype of eighteenth-century pirate culture devolves largely from a nineteenth-century fiction, Stevenson's *Treasure Island* (1883), where "Yo Ho Ho" first appears. *Demon rum* and *rum-running* are both misnomers: in the nineteenth century, *rum* refers to all types of hard alcohol (Sisk 113), and Maingot reports that more Scotch than rum was smuggled during Prohibition, though *Scotch-runner* is a less mellifluous term (245). The fancy cocktails I concede, but even the austere martini has its florid iterations.

3. This is true of many of the sources consulted for this project, where the title included the word *rum*, but the actual topic was alcohol consumption in general. The current, most egregious, case of such behavior comes, in my opinion, from the education field, where an article on the complexity of special programs is titled "Parental Voices on Individualized Education Programs: 'Oh, IEP Meeting Tomorrow? Rum Tonight!'" (Zeitlin and Curcic).

4. Thus, while this study focuses on texts of the English-speaking Caribbean and the Northern sites of the United States, Canada, and England, I do not use the terms *West Indies* and *West Indian* unless I refer solely to former British colonies. The term *Caribbean* is more capacious, allowing for the multiple, layered influences of Europe on some of the islands from which texts originate. This practice has its clumsy moments, as it may give the impression that I mean to collapse a richly varied set of cultures and experiences under one category, but in the sense that many English and American readers do not differentiate among these island polities (see Sheller 7), there is some accuracy in this usage.

There is much to be done with rum in Francophone texts, where the works of Chamoiseau, Condé, and Zobel contrast with Anglophone tropes. Mahler's analysis of sugarcane novels indicates potential in Hispanophone fiction (see page 27), and Battaglia has gestured toward rum's role in Cuban detective fiction.

5. See Doyle, Friedman, and Doyle and Winkiel.

6. In "The Angel of Progress," McClintock asserts that the "post-" in postcolonial masks uneven and partial progress toward actual decolonization. Ngũgĩ, in *Decolonizing the Mind* (1986), analyzes the persistence of colonizing ideologies in the institutions of a "post-" colonial world. Both McClintock and Ngũgĩ argue, in essence, that the prefix *post-* promotes the belief that colonization and imperialism are over, thus preventing clear thinking about current conditions and discouraging social change. At the end of her essay, McClintock calls for "a *proliferation* of historically nuanced theories and strategies . . . which may enable us to engage more effectively in the politics of affiliation" (303), a call that leads forward to the introduction of new terms to describe international interactions after World War II.

7. Mao and Walkowitz 738. Relevant studies include those of Kalliney, Lowe, J. Dillon Brown, Edmondson, Lassner, Stephens, Cudjoe, and Ramchand, as well as J. Dillon Brown and Leah Reade Rosenberg's collection *Beyond Windrush* (2015).

8. Bill Brown's essay, from 2001, has generated volumes of scholarship since it first appeared. At the Modern Language Association Conference in 2017, a panel for which Brown was the respondent considered the contribution this essay has made to the field of literature; Brown himself had recently published *Other Things* (2015). Alternative approaches to thing-ness that have had purchase in the literary world include Harman's object-oriented ontology (2013 and 2012), and Bennett's *Vibrant Matter* (2010), among a host of more specific applications of these ideas to literature and art. Despite the elaborations stemming from the original article, Brown best articulates the pragmatic knowability of things and their essential otherness.

9. Noland's work on the role of the somatic in agency for change resonates with Edwards's use of the term *décalage* to name the articulation point for "a changing core of difference . . . an unidentifiable point that is incessantly touched and fingered and pressed" (14). Like Noland, Edwards sees this point as beyond translation and he promotes its physicality as its potential: "In the body it is *only* difference—the separation between bones or members—that allows movement" (15). Edwards chronicles the untranslatable in interwar black internationalist print cultures to probe for "the uncertain harmony of a new song" (318).

10. The Oxford English Dictionary Online, from which these definitions are taken, lists other definitions of *rum,* including usage as a verb, but these are all obsolete.

11. For more on the role of rum in West Indian culture, consult F. Smith. For popular histories, see Coulombe, Curtis, or I. Williams. In 1944, Eric Williams

began arguments rooting the humanitarian impulse toward abolition in the declining economic importance of the West Indian colonies (*Capitalism and Slavery* 1944; 1966). Historians and anthropologists have investigated the role of rum in coercing and pacifying colonial workforces (enslaved, indentured, or waged): see essays by Ambler and Angrosino in Jankowiak and Bradburd.

For discussions of rum as a subsidiary of the sugar trade, see Sheridan and Dunn. For recent popular accounts, see MacInnis and Abbot.

12. See also Ambler 84. Rorabaugh's account of the early days of the United States suggests a similarly pervasive drinking culture: "Early nineteenth-century America may not have been 'a nation of drunkards,' but Americans were certainly enjoying a spectacular binge" (21). According to Knowlton and Berridge, the Colonial Office expressed concern about alcoholism as a problem for "national efficiency" (440). They sought to keep alcoholics or potential alcoholics from colonial service and to prevent their officers from excessive drinking, which was thought to be a risk in the tropics.

13. See essays by Ambler and Kelley for further discussion of the role of African traders in creating a demand for rum.

14. For example, in Merry's "The Slaves: An Elegy" (1788): "Are Drops of Blood the Horrible Manure/That fills the luscious juice the teeming Cane?" and "Yes, 'tis their anguish mantles in the bowl,/Their sighs excite the Briton's drunken joy" (lines 21–22 and 29–30). Southey, in Sonnet 3 (1797), addresses readers "who at your ease/Sip the blood-sweeten'd beverage" (10–11). Pringle, in the poem "Slavery" from 1823, writes, "OH SLAVERY! Thou art a bitter draught!/And twice accursèd is thy poisoned bowl,/.../The Master, though in luxury's lap he loll,/Feels the foul venom, like a rankling shaft,/Strike through his reins." (1–2, 7–9). The anonymous author of *Jamaica; A Poem* wrote feelingly of the plight of the enslaved: "Their labor ends not with the setting sun:/.../They pick the canes, and tend the loaded teams,/Or in alternate watch, with ceaseless toil,/The rums distil, or smoky sugar boil" (part 2, 44, 46–48). By contrast, Grainger's speaker praises "heart-recruiting rum" as relief for "when, with thirst,/With heat, with labour, and wan care opprest" (book 3, lines 491, 493–94).

15. The *Times* reported that "the abolition was not an economy measure," according to officials, but rather "the rum issue was no longer compatible with the high standards of efficiency required in ships with complex and often delicate machinery" (Gingell 1). Editorialists begged to differ, claiming that the "daily tot" did not affect "the sounder management of the Navy or its overall integration within the defence pattern as a whole" ("Mean-Spirited and Modern" 9).

16. The use of rum both to gain access to labor and then to increase productivity conforms to the general schema Jankowiak and Bradburd propose for the European use of drug-foods (3–29).

17. This transition appears in Dabydeen's novel *The Counting House* (1996), in which the male protagonist Vidia states that he "hated drinking rum, especially

during the day. It slowed down his work so that he made less money" (77). While Vidia despises his work mate Kampta, "wondering what made men allow themselves to be disfigured by rum" (78), Kampta's condition reflects Angresino's conclusion that rum "represented an important cultural surrender to the harsh fact that they could never go home again" (111).

18. Beachey's brief description of the late century rum trade indicates rum's continuing importance and desirability as an export, particularly in Jamaica (73–77). In the nineteenth century, Parliament lowered duties on rum while simultaneously opening the British sugar market, which had previously been monopolized by West Indian sugar. According to F. Smith, parliament may have tried to reduce the negative effects of equalizing sugar duties by improving economic conditions for rum (201). Shepherd, in the introduction to *Slavery without Sugar* (2002), emphasizes the diversification of the trade economies of Caribbean islands, noting lively internal trading relationships as well as varied exports (2–3). While making this argument, Shepherd confirms the dominance of sugar, which in 1832 accounted for 76 percent of income in Jamaica and 97 percent in Barbados (4).

19. This subsidy was not supported by all the London-based sugar trade. West Indian interests supported subsidies, which amounted to approximately 40 percent of the price, but London sugar traders in the reexport business depended on the "ability to import raw sugar at the lowest world prices" (Stahl 37).

20. J. Dillon Brown indicates the dissonance between the way the English perceived their post-war experience, as "a potent combination of external and internal destabilization" (*Migrant Modernism* 21), with the perceptions of newly arrived Caribbean people who still experienced British imperial power as relatively solid.

21. Addressing this disparity from another angle, McBain warns that aggregate statistics for Caribbean islands mask the fact that profits and losses disproportionately affect islands dependent on specific exports. For example, Trinidad and Tobago achieve strong numbers by exporting petroleum to the United States, but this wealth did not spread to include other islands; similarly, declining oil prices in the 1990s affected Trinidad and Tobago more than other islands (18–20). Import dependence remains a problem even as Caribbean countries shift their trading relationships to Central and South American partners (McBain 32). Moreover, the liberalization of markets—the elimination of trade barriers (i.e., subsidies)—withdrew what few protections were available to West Indian islands. As Martínez-Vergne and Knight observe, "Globalization . . . is nothing new to the Caribbean region," where successive waves of international trading, conducted at varying levels of coercion, have "not so far resulted in a market relationship between the various participants that is more equitable and just" (7). The incommensurability between small Caribbean markets and enormous trading partners leaves little doubt about the hegemonic effects of globalization. For example, in 2012 the United States increased subsidies to multinational beverage conglomerates, leading West Indian producers "to urge their governments to complain to the World Trade Organization" (McFadden).

22. France forced the new nation of Haiti into a relationship of debt that continues to this day (Dubois 303–4). Dalleo shows that the US occupation of Haiti from 1915 to 1934 helped West Indian political thinkers understand "political independence as an insufficient solution to imperialist domination" even as the revolution itself inspired anti-colonial politics (20). In a reading of James's revisions to *The Black Jacobins* (1938), Scott points out that, despite the success of the Haitian Revolution, economic imperatives may mean that "the colonial past may never let go" (220).

23. For an account of this historical period, see Neptune.

24. R. F. Smith 19. The rhetorical use of rum in discussions of US-Caribbean relations is discussed in chapter 1.

25. In making this statement, I do not imply that Americans, for example, do not have their own internal narratives of government or corporate corruption and waste, but that a special brand of cognitive dissonance operates to differentiate our actions from those of other nations. We have a right to waste what we have made ourselves (even when that wealth has accrued through the exploitation of other populations and landscapes), but others have no right to waste—again, as defined by the donating power—what is given. This strategic segmentation of the "public" exemplifies the processes Duggan identifies with neoliberalism, which "organizes material and political life *in terms of* race, gender and sexuality as well as economic class and nationality, or ethnicity and religion. But the categories . . . *actively obscure* the connections among these organizing terms" (3, italics in the original).

26. Ambler refutes temperance rhetoric as exaggeration: "Although the specter of a river of cheap booze flooding the West African interior would become a stock image of the temperance campaigns of the late nineteenth century, there is little evidence that much of the liquor sold on the West African coast before that time ever got very far beyond the coast" (78).

27. Temperance was a lightning rod channeling other issues like domestic abuse (Nadelhaft) and religious prejudice combined with anti-immigrant sentiment (Bendroth).

28. Alcoholics Anonymous (AA), founded in the 1930s, expanded exponentially in the postwar period and transformed attitudes toward excessive drinking. Djos reports that AA's founding text, *Alcoholics Anonymous: The Story of How Many Thousands of Men and Women Have Recovered from Alcoholism* (1939), sold over fifty thousand copies by 1961. The millionth copy was presented to President Nixon in 1973, and ten million copies had been sold by 1990. In Britain and North America, AA established major research and policy organs after the war (Rotskoff 69; Plant and Plant 21–22; Williams and Brake).

AA or AA-like chapters were formed at various sites in the Caribbean. In 1957, Beaubrun wrote of the existence of a chapter in Aruba in a piece for the *Caribbean Medical Journal* (142). Lloyd, in a 1976 article on rates of rehabilitation and recidivism among alcoholics, notes that Alcoholics Anonymous is "an organization whose network reaches throughout the islands of Trinidad and Tobago and which figures prominently in all phases of recruiting patients for treatment" (45).

29. Scholars who study normative drinking or drug use are obliged to insert disclaimers exonerating themselves in advance from these charges. Marcus, then-president of the International Center for Alcohol Policies, writes in his introduction to Heath's *Drinking Occasions* (2000), "Time and again, we confronted the question of how to portray normal drinking behavior without condoning—or even appearing to condone—reckless drinking" (xiv). Lenson prefaces his *On Drugs* (1995) by exposing the rhetorics that silence a multifaceted, reasonable discussion of the role of drugs, including alcohol, in US culture (ix–xx). As recently as 2010, Banco has decried the "strangely common (and, in my opinion, scurrilous) assumption that a literary analysis of drugs must necessarily be irresponsibly celebratory" (4) in the introduction to his book *Travel and Drugs in Twentieth-Century Literature* (2010). These disclaimers participate, in an odd way, in the silencing and marginalization of studies of normative drug and alcohol use, since they repeatedly cite their own marginalization.

30. Zeiger makes a similar point in her introduction to *Inventing the Addict* (2008). She finds a "curiously recursive loop at the heart of the common definition of *addiction*. . . . this definition posits a past, before the addiction began its time-destroying repetitions, but the precise moment of this past—of the beginning of the addiction—is always on the horizon, never fully specifiable" (3, italics in the original). Djos exemplifies this conundrum in his definition of alcoholism: "Alcoholism is extremely difficult to define, especially during the early stages of an individual's drinking history, when it may be impossible to distinguish heavy drinkers, problem drinkers (who are typically involved in the first stage of alcoholism), chronic alcoholics, and individuals who are cross-addicted to other chemicals" (1).

31. The "social problem" model has intensified as research stemming from the Human Genome Project claims to identify genes that predispose people to alcoholism and, more recently, a gene that makes people feel "more" inebriated after a few drinks and thus less likely to proceed to addictive drinking. According to the study, "The first few drinks during a night out will leave these individuals feeling more inebriated than their friends" (Radowitz). However, researchers relied on subject reports of "feeling" inebriated, a method which calls into question whether social expectations affect perception of feelings. This study is about representation, not genetics.

32. Statistics bear out this division throughout the cultures of the Atlantic Basin. However, gender differences may not be as pronounced as data indicate due to underreporting. In the 1950s and 1960s, prohibitions on women's social drinking relaxed somewhat, but drinking was still risky for women. Rotskoff reports that women could drink socially, but images from popular culture depict "women as comfortable, even happy, in the presence of alcohol" but not actually drinking (202–5). Since alcoholism is considered a male problem, women alcoholics

are frequently seen as more deviant and pathological than men (who are, by this definition, "normal" alcoholics; see Dann 10; Vaillant 123; Ridlon 34). Further, proscriptions on female drinking led women to hide or disguise alcohol (see also Rorabaugh 12–13).

A World Bank study from 2002 finds that "alcohol abuse and use are linked to men's and women's roles and expectations in society. Men are more likely to drink heavily and excessively than are women, and less likely to abstain from alcohol consumption" (Pyne et al. v). Dann reports that there are substantial costs for women who admit to drinking: "Even though drinking alcohol has been said to form part of Barbadian culture, participation in the activity can also be culturally proscribed. It may be considered by many to represent deviant behavior. Women respondents in particular, even if they do not feel themselves to be thus limited, may view the admission of such actions to a young interviewer as constituting an ego threat or etiquette barrier" (10). According to the data, 73.8 percent of men admitted drinking, while only 42.4 percent of women did (12). A 1989 study of alcohol consumption in Guadeloupe reports similar gender division among men and women (Moutet et al.). In Barbados in 1974, 78 percent of alcoholics admitted for treatment were men (Stoute and Ifill 150).

33. Until the 1970s, most of the research on alcohol abuse focused on white men, and much of the data on different demographic groups remained riddled with stereotype. Watts and Wright, in their introduction to *Black Alcoholism* (1983), claim that Black people drink for the same varied reasons Caucasians do. Early research into racial, gender, and ethnic differences in alcohol use was used to contradict stereotypes of drunkenness associated with minorities. Caetano and his colleagues confirm that studies of drinking habits among US Black populations contradict many of the stereotypes about higher rates of drinking and resultant dysfunction in African American communities: in fact, studies from the mid-1990s show that Black men and women are more likely to abstain than white people. In a foreword to *The American Experience with Alcohol* (1985), Room notes that ethnic differentiations in alcohol use were studied in the 1950s, and that such studies were often used to repudiate racist stereotypes about "Italians, Jews, and the Chinese" (xii). Harper reviewed alcoholism literature in 1983 to find that, of sixteen thousand articles, only seventy-seven specifically mentioned Black people, and just eleven were "primarily" about Black usage (19). Caetano and his colleagues report that the first American survey to focus on the experience of Blacks and Hispanics was conducted in 1984; national surveys of alcohol use had been in place since 1964 (233).

Research into women's drinking habits has also lagged behind studies of men. Ridlon points out that there was a "paucity of studies on female alcoholics" when she began working on the issue in 1970. Vaillant first published the results of a longitudinal study of alcohol use in 1983 without reference to women; the 1995 edition includes a section reviewing available research. Early collections addressing women's experience include Plant's *Women and Alcohol* (1980), Ridlon's *A*

Fallen Angel (1988), and Sandmaier's *The Invisible Alcoholics* (1980). Martin Plant and Moira Plant address shifts in British women's drinking in their 2006 volume *Binge Britain,* but Waterson reports that few studies emphasize women's normative drinking in her *Women and Alcohol in Social Context* (2000). Recent studies of discourse around drinking and gender in social media indicate that not much has changed, even if women believe they are in control of audience perception (Rolando et al. 501).

Black women's drinking is also heavily stereotyped. Sandmaier writes in 1980 that "it is often assumed that black women tend to be either abstainers or hard-drinking, unreachable prostitutes" (144). While she provides no proof for this stereotype, Herd does report that African American women have "conservative drinking norms" ("Racial Differences" 146). Harris-Hastrick indicates that immigrating Caribbean women are likely to match and exceed African American women in their conservative attitudes about drinking (61), but she affirms that Black people of various ethnic and national origins cannot be lumped together under one set of parameters.

34. Pyne et al. report that data on the Caribbean is still relatively scarce. While studies exist for many countries in Central and South America, only Trinidad and Tobago is represented in figures for deaths from cirrhosis (5); Cuba, Haiti, and the Dominican Republic appear in per capita consumption graphs (14–15). Dann, in the introduction to his 1980 report *Patterns of Drinking in Barbados,* notes that his is the first "overall evaluation of the drinking of alcohol in Barbados" (xiii). Some previous work, amounting to what Dann calls "guesstimates" (xiii), has "project[ed] North American statistics on to the Barbadian population" (xiiin2). Surveying the development of psychiatry in Trinidad and Tobago, Maharajh and Parasram note that, as of 1999, "alcoholism and drug addiction" is the "most researched field in this country," citing Beaubrun as the pioneer in raising awareness of the social and health costs of alcoholism (178). Moutet et al. has studied drinking in Guadeloupe and Wittig-Wells has discussed drinking among elderly women in the US Virgin Islands.

35. Writing about Barbados in 1979, Stoute and Ifill state unequivocally, "A woman seen in this area [the bar area of a rum shop] was usually considered to be of ill-repute" (147). Peter J. Wilson, in a 1973 study of the island of Providencia (166–67), and Yawney, in a 1979 study of Trinidad (95–96), confirm that rum shops are masculine domains. Harris-Hastrick confirms a gender division in drinking habits in a 2001 study (61). F. Smith updates this portrait, indicating that women are present as employees and can engage in activities at the margins, but rum shops remain "centers of male activity" (244–45).

36. Djos repeats an idea well-known in the therapeutic community: "alcoholic" is a notoriously slippery term, and its definition often depends on the judge and the context. Djos proposes a definition that depends either on self-reporting, the standard used by Alcoholics Anonymous, that "anyone who says he or she is an alcoholic probably *is* an alcoholic" (1, italics in the original), or external

assessment, that "the addict has demonstrated persistent, self-destructive drinking behavior or has indicated a profound change in personality when under the influence of alcohol" (2).

37. Room surveys research conducted since the publication of MacAndrew and Edgerton's study, concluding that its major arguments remain foundational and largely unchallenged as the "best-recognized conceptual contribution from the ethnographic literature to alcohol studies in general" ("Intoxication" 189).

38. MacAndrew and Edgerton report that "progressive impairment in the exercise of certain of one's sensorimotor capabilities" is constant across cultures. If disinhibition has a physiological component, it "*ought* to be evident in *all* people. In point of fact, however, *it is not*" (36, italics in the original).

39. F. Smith 246. Smith also details significant changes in production location (194–98).

40. Adler has studied deliberate attempts by alcohol marketers in the twentieth century to replace older models of alcohol as gift exchange that increases communal ties with a new model that promotes alcohol choice as an expression of "the atomized individual" (379).

41. See Gilmore 11–13 and Dardis 4.

42. Many individual and book-length studies have seen drinking as a response to social ills like modern commodity capitalism (Crowley), patriarchal oppression (Vice), fear of failure (McCarron), and antisocial, anticapitalist urges (Dollar). The question is not whether critics will admit a positive dimension to drunken comportment, but that they tend to emphasize negative consequences.

43. Both Noland and Roth, by invoking expressive functions that act below and/or above the register of the rationally legible, position semiosis as a process with reparative potential. The space of noise, of the prelinguistic body, is designated as the site of un-meaning—that which cannot be recognized as meant: meaning otherwise is at the core of rum poetics.

44. Examination of other commodities has also proceeded apace, particularly in the area of food culture. Specific instances include Lynn Marie Houston's figuration of Caribbean writing in the context of "making do"; Few and Phillips Lewis on gender and, respectively, chocolate and cocoa; Farnsworth and Wilkie on the sources of Bahamian foodways; De Loughrey's examination of a failed attempt to bring breadfruit from Tahiti to the Caribbean ("Globalizing"); Chan's work on curry; and Kennedy's work on salt in the Turks and Caicos. See Beushausen et al, Loichot, and Sheller for broad examinations of tropical foodways.

45. In popular form, this habit of representation emerges in the television series *Cane* (2007). The show pits Alex Vega, who anticipates revamping his father-in-law's sugar empire to produce ethanol, against Frank Duque, who wants his father to sell out of sugar and focus on the family's assets in rum. Since Jimmy Smits plays Alex Vega, he is probably the good guy. Alex is certainly the modern guy, looking to future industrial uses for sugar, while Frank is focused on past products and juvenile pleasures.

1. Rum's (In)significance

1. Miranda's "new world" suffers from its affiliation with the fetishized foodie culture that has arisen since the novel's publication.

2. MacAndrew and Edgerton devote two chapters to refuting the stereotype that "Indians Can't Hold Their Liquor." Historical records demonstrate that Native Americans learned the rules of drunken behavior from the colonists: "The Indians of this continent took as their exemplars of alcohol's effects on comportment the drunken doings of the very white men who introduced alcohol to them" (136). Like the colonists, Native Americans "set up limits among themselves beyond which the excuse of drunkenness did not hold," but these limits do not translate across ethnic lines: "In cases where their drunken transgressions impinged on the health and welfare of the white man, the matter was taken entirely out of their hands. . . . And it mattered not a whit whether the Indian had been drunk or sober at the time he committed the deed that incurred their wrath" (159).

3. For a recent reframing of archipelagic arguments, see Roberts and Stephens.

4. See Allen 20–23. Allen genders his portrait of healthful, civilized rum-drinking by including a story of his teetotalling aunt, who was outraged when her poor handwriting resulted in the delivery of a dozen bottles of rum to her home (20). For more specific discussions of punch as a British drink, see Cozzi 135–37 and, more generally, Wondrich's *Punch*. Wondrich refers to "the islands of Jamaica and Barbados" as "two of the three main strongholds of British rum-making during the Punch Age" (75), a nomenclature that is historically accurate and, for the present day, telling.

5. We might also look to titles like *Spirits of Defiance*, in which Drowne considers the politics of Prohibition in literary works, and *Spirits of America*, a title chosen by both Nicholas Warner and Burns for chronicles of alcohol in American contexts.

6. Lucozade, now marketed as an energy drink, was sold by pharmacists and produced by Beecham's, an antecedent of pharmaceutical multinational GlaxoSmithKline.

7. This story is recounted in Curtis (203–7) and Coulombe (250–51). Waligora-Davis examines the process of refiguring the calypso as an American "national anthem" (199).

8. In 1994, Cuba permitted the use of dollars as currency; this policy was rescinded in 2004.

9. The master's assessment of his experience recalls the bitterness expressed by prominent World War I poets. He calls airplanes "diabolical machines" near the end of the novel (*Orchid House* 179), and he confesses that he "wishes he had never gone" to war (149).

10. The autobiographical sources Allfrey uses as source material for the novel reflect the importance of white patriarchal lineage and the tragedy of its decline. The addiction of the Master follows autobiographical detail in Allfrey's own life, except that her father, a judge, drank rather than smoked narcotics.

According to Paravisini-Gebert, Allfrey's father "was not the addict depicted in the novel" (23), but he was sometimes drunk in court, frequently drunk in the evenings, and prone to temper when intoxicated. As in *The Orchid House,* the women of the household compensated and controlled for his behavior so that his position—and their own—was not compromised on Dominica.

11. The Young Master bears some resemblance to *Mrs. Dalloway*'s Septimus Smith: their immediate illnesses stem from shell shock, but questions about their psychosexual stability predate the war. Lally claims she knew the Young Master could "bring trouble" (*Orchid House* 4).

12. Paravisini-Gebert, Allfrey's biographer, reports that Christophine is based on real-life events: Allfrey was "incapable of pure invention in fiction" (82). Julia, the Shand family cook, was "a constant source of amusement" (22). Julia "would cook best when she had had a tot or two of rum": "On Saturday nights, when she had been to the Hole in the Wall, as the local rum shop was called, you could hear the clang of the pans as she tossed them around in the kitchen" (22).

13. The resonances of narrator's protest with those of Woolf indicate the limitations of her critique. The narrator explicitly links her resistance rooted in feminist revisions of history and literature when she compares American money to "Virginia Woolf's feet" (Jiles 11). The heroine shares with Woolf an interest in allying with the working classes and racialized others, but she signifies over them to encourage feminist progress, as scholars like Jane Marcus have demonstrated.

14. Jiles refers to the detective fiction genre as "hard-boiled" rather than *noir* (8), but the heroine's determination to replay scenes "you've seen . . . a million times in black and white" (7) renders the usage indistinguishable in this case.

15. Parts of this chapter were previously published in *Perennial Empires: Postcolonial, Transnational, and Literary Perspectives,* edited by Chantal Zabus and Silvia Nagy-Zekmi (Amherst, NY: Cambria, 2011), and reproduced by permission from the publisher.

16. A discussion of this poem appears on page 19 of this study.

17. Mardorossian claims that "the premises of the colonialist discourse do not falter and lose ground when the black subalterns speak but paradoxically when they are silenced and stereotyped" ("Shutting Up" 1072). Noland discusses similar ideas in the concluding chapters of *Agency and Embodiment.*

18. The interaction presented here becomes even more fraught if the suicidal person is interpreted as Black. Benson witnesses the suicide right after walking by the Yoruba Club and wondering why "there was never anyone there when he passed, never any sign of life. What were the secret hours of the Yoruba?" (3). From the outset, the novel foreshadows England support for slavery as a self-inflicted blow to national identity. Slave-trading begins the historical processes that lead, inevitably if slowly, to England as a postcolonial state. The Yoruba Club (1974–85) was part of a vibrant immigrant presence in Liverpool that declined, according to one source, as Thatcherism took hold (Lashua).

19. Kalliney offers several detailed case studies of tense alliances between established English writers and colonial authors seeking to build careers in London. J. Dillon Brown, in *Migrant Modernisms,* also explores the fortuitous and conflicted aspects of these collaborations, which he summarizes in his overview of literary culture in the postwar period (39–41).

20. Unsworth's depiction of the Fictioneers promotes diversity and coalition among the writers of the future, belying the tendency of science fiction think of racism "as one of the social problems the genre leaves behind as a relic of a past that has been transcended" (Kilgore 9) or to consider the genre as "closed to blacks" (Saunders 399). The topic of race in speculative fiction has also been recently examined in Chude-Sokei, Iton, and Jackson and Moody-Freeman.

21. A wealthy businessman named Slater, Benson's wartime commander, is staging a spectacle at his estate to commemorate the Battle of Brunanburh in 937. The site of the battle lies "somewhere between here [his estate] and the river" according to Slater's reckoning, even though the historical support for his contention is slim (*Sugar and Rum* 178). According to Slater, the battle is the first manifestation of English national unity. "Athelstan was the first Saxon King to have effective rule over the whole of England," Slater contends. "The army he was commanding was an English army . . . fighting as one nation to repel the foreign invader" (178–79).

22. Unsworth 1998. This quotation comes from the back of the paperback edition.

2. Frustrated Drunks

1. Such moments of simultaneous possibility/inevitable disappointment form tropes in the literature. As Christophine opines of a different era in *Wide Sargasso Sea,* "No more slavery! She had to laugh! 'These new ones have Letter of the Law. Same thing. They got magistrate. They got fine. . . . New ones worse than old ones—more cunning, that's all'" (26).

2. Pointedly, this combination of dreary repetition and underemployment seems universal rather than intrinsic to Puerto Rico. Kemp considers a friend "breaking his ass in New York" and another "drinking himself to death in Rome" (42).

3. Crichlow, Pittmann, Thieme, and Westall ("Men in the Yard") have all written about male identity in *Miguel Street.* Crichlow concludes that Naipaul has, by the end of the book, proposed an alternative masculine identity that "moves from the man of pure physicality . . . to the refined man of words and knowledge" (298). This argument concurs with Edmondson's contention that many West Indian male authors sought to authorize themselves as writers who are "masters of a literary tradition" modelled on the English Victorian gentleman (9).

4. *The Middle Passage* might be read as an ethnographic counterpart to this text. As is well known, Naipaul claims that Trinidad is "unimportant, uncreative, cynical" (*Middle Passage* 34) and "a society which produced nothing" (35). He later argues that West Indian writers who do not chronicle these features of

Trinidad have "not only failed to diagnose the sickness of [their] society but ha[ve] aggravated it" (66).

5. Naipaul notes that "every film Bogart made" was popular in Trinidad, and although Naipaul refers to a generic "audience," audience comments identify exclusively with the male hero, indicating that this audience is largely male (*Middle Passage* 54). This version of "virility" is exemplified by the callous treatment of women (55), a clear aspect of Bogart's character. The aspirational quality of West Indian masculinity recurs in *Miguel Street*'s "The Coward," in which "a champion of the Royal Air Force" defeats the local bully Big Foot in a boxing match (75). Later, the street learns Big Foot's opponent was an imposter, a move that designates British masculinity a hoax and still inaccessible to the men of Miguel Street. "Bogart" entered the *Oxford English Dictionary* in the 1960s, meaning "to appropriate (a marijuana cigarette) greedily or selfishly. Hence more generally: to take or use most of; to steal."

6. This narrative presents these ideas as internal, but the line of dialogue that follows it indicates that the narrator must have voiced some version of his ideas to Hat.

7. In this chapter, I follow their lead, and the readings emphasize the ways female characters function to bolster or to threaten the plot of male exceptionalism; undoubted issues of white female privilege lie fallow until the next chapter, though in the case of Chenault I address some issues in endnotes.

8. Like that of the woman in "Bogart," what might be called female protests against this confined role are noisy but inarticulate. George's daughter Dolly "pick[s] up a handful of gravel from the yard and [is] making as if to throw it at the sailor" who suggests she would bring more profit to her father as a prostitute, "but she stopped suddenly, and burst into tears" (*Miguel Street* 34–35).

9. Viewed retrospectively, women emerge as central to the economic and social stability of Miguel Street, despite the off-stage and subsidiary structural role Naipaul chooses in this narrative. For example, Popo's wife uses her position to get the narrator access to grass clippings. The narrator reports simply, "Grass was good for the hens," but that remark intimates an unseen network of women like Popo's wife and the narrator's mother, supporting each other to make do economically (20). Naipaul's subtlety in creating female characters merits further scrutiny.

10. The scene draws on early twentieth-century stereotypes of zombification (Dalleo 183).

11. Mirroring Chenault's devaluation is the dehumanization of her partner on the dance floor. Kemp first describes him as a "small, spade-bearded man we had met earlier" (153–54) but he quickly becomes a "brute" (155) and "a crazy thug" (162).

12. There is evidence that Chenault anticipates Kemp's reaction to her reappearance, because he is mystified that her "expression" contains "a shade of sadness and amusement that was almost a smile" (169). She recovers after a night of

rest and a shower, and then she seduces Kemp—actions that could, or could not, be symptomatic of trauma. He may not know the real story, but she knows what story he will choose to tell himself. When he later marvels that she "could look so peaceful and content" (187) after her experiences, the question of what, exactly, those experiences were recurs.

13. Austin Clarke's "Griff!" (1971) demonstrates the violence encoded in alcohol's relationship to masculine success and identification as it plays out in immigrant communities. Clark's eponymous protagonist, a Bajan immigrant to Toronto, seeks to assuage his masculine pride, wounded by economic failure compared to his friends, by manipulating the consumption and distribution of rum and Scotch, beverages he associates—respectively—with Bajan subsistence labor and sophisticated Englishness. When these efforts fail, he compensates by strangling his wife, another form of male property he cannot control. See Nesbitt, "Rum."

14. In positing Puerto Rico as a dysfunctional backwater, Thompson feeds into policy debates of the time. As he wrote to Alfred Kazin, author of a scathing account of the island for *Commentary* (February 1960), "Whenever I think I'm being a little rough on the Puerto Ricans I read the article again and I know I still have leeway" (*Proud Highway* 288). Lévi-Strauss, writing in 1955, captures this effect from a different angle: "It was at Puerto Rico that I first made contact with the United States. . . . It was here, too, but from the rather special angle of the Greater Antilles, that I first perceived certain features of the typical American town; the flimsiness of the buildings, and the desire to create an eye-catching effect, made it look like some world exhibition that had become permanent, except that, in this instance, one might have imagined oneself to be in the Spanish section" (35).

15. Thompson's remarks resonate with a story Naipaul reports in *The Middle Passage* about "a successful American businessman" in Trinidad who characterizes himself as a "second-rater" who shows to advantage in a "third-rate place" (43).

16. Waywell inadvertently invokes rum's status as a belated product of sugar production when he remarks that the novel "contains the seeds and the chewed stalks of the career it anticipates and strives to book-end" (44). The phrasing refers to both the appearance of cane-fields after harvest and the local practice of chewing sugarcane to release cane juice. Although sugarcane can produce seeds, most farmers use slips.

17. Only Waywell successfully both historicizes the novel and assesses the depiction of Puerto Rico as a narrative effect rather than a realistic description.

18. My reading will seem counter to the concluding image in this novel, in which the narrator sees himself as a "dancing dwarf" on the airport tarmac: "I left them all and walked briskly toward the aeroplane, not looking back, looking only at my shadow before me, a dancing dwarf on the tarmac" (222). Although the figure "not looking back" confirms my reading, the idea of becoming a "shadow" or a "dancing dwarf" may foreshadow the experience of diminishment West Indian immigrants experienced when they encountered English racism. This concatenation of dark, deformed figures may proleptically assuage metropolitan readers

uncomfortable with uppity colonials; it may be a sly autobiographical reference, as the young Naipaul had considerable acrobatic skill (French 58). The narrator has mixed feelings; Naipaul had almost none. He wrote to his family of the pleasure he felt in leaving Trinidad: "The process of my emergence really begins with getting on that plane. For the first time in my life I was dead alone—and I enjoyed it" (*Between Father and Son* 104).

19. Policy approaches reflect this progression. The late twentieth-century "war on drugs" musters technology and trained personnel to combat an equally sophisticated regime of laboratories and distribution networks; by contrast, alcohol treatment remains largely low-tech, using psychotherapy and support groups reflecting the melodrama of temperance efforts to squash "demon rum."

20. James's *Beyond a Boundary* (1963) is the typical entry point into the study of cricket and colonialism, followed by numerous studies. *Netherland* has proved a fruitful site for critique; Duvall discusses the homoerotics and cross-racial desires at play; Hill sets the novel in the context of its literary antecedents; Golimowska ponders cricket's therapeutic effects after the 9/11 trauma; McGarrity historicizes the use of cricket by Irish novelists to inform a reading of the novel.

21. Westall severs the overarching import of the parable from its detailed accounting of commodity history, noting Chuck's "brief references to sugar, cocoa and tonka-beans" at another point in the argument ("Cricket and the World-System" 297).

3. Drunken Sluts

1. In a 1985 article that brought *Wide Sargasso Sea* to the center of feminist-postcolonial debates, "Three Women's Texts and a Critique of Imperialism," Spivak argues that "the emergent perspective of feminist criticism reproduces the axioms of imperialism" because it remains blind to its constitution within these axioms (896). Thus, she claims, white feminists gain the status of speaking subject—of human being—by replicating their dehumanization as gendered others on racial (or racialized) others (897). The elision of gender and race as equivalent oppressions is problematic because the categories are often dissociated from the historical context. For example, being a married white Englishwoman in the nineteenth century is not the same as being a female slave, even though the doctrine of coverture eliminated the individual rights of most married women. Perkin, in her study *Women and Marriage in Nineteenth-Century England* (1989), corroborates both of Spivak's points when she notes that men could make their wives "little better than slaves" under the law (8). But, so long as husbands did not brutally enforce their prerogatives, many nineteenth-century women found marriage a release from parental control.

Perkin explains that "in the absence of valid agreements and actions to the contrary," English common law made wives economically and physically subject to their husbands (16, italics omitted). Unless property were settled in trust for them—apparently not the case for Antoinette or Julia—women had no legal control over the assets they brought into the marriage. Husbands were also legal custodians for all children. Although agitation for change in the marriage laws began early in the nineteenth century, wives could not generally own, buy, and sell property in their own names until the Married Women's Property Act passed in 1882.

Although Perkin does not cover marriage law in the West Indies, Antoinette's marriage agreement reflects the conditions she describes in England. Antoinette's Aunt Cora is appalled that Richard Mason is "handing over everything the child [Antoinette] owns to a perfect stranger" (*Wide Sargasso* 114). She claims that Antoinette "should be protected, legally" because "a settlement can be arranged" (114). Aunt Cora knows what is possible "legally" and she accuses Richard of negligence in leaving Antoinette vulnerable to an agreement between "honorable" gentlemen (114).

Spivak's reading, originally published in 1985, unleashed a broad reinterpretation of *Wide Sargasso Sea,* and many critics since then have explored the racial politics of Rhys's novel, usually by comparing Antoinette to Christophine, her Black nurse. Mardorossian summarizes this debate in her chapter on *Wide Sargasso Sea,* balancing Spivak's views with those of Benita Parry (*Reclaiming Difference* 60–64). Other critics exploring these issues include Uraizee, van Neck-Yoder, Drake, Erwin, and L. Wilson. For an overview of the ways the sensitivity of Rhys criticism to postcolonial issues has paralleled the evolution of feminist criticism, see Mardorossian, "Double (De)colonization."

2. The role of drinking in Rhys's prewar work has been discussed by both Nardin and Wedge. Nardin discusses *Voyage in the Dark,* chronicling how Anna Morgan's conflicted position as a Creole feeds her drinking but without particular reference to rum (see above). Wedge explores the benefits and drawbacks of drinking for Rhys herself. Warner's lover Valentine Ackland recounts her struggle with alcoholism in *For Sylvia* (1985). It is possible that Julia Barnard owes something to Ackland's experience; see Nesbitt, "Sharing" 35–36.

3. Written in 1945, the story was not published until 1968 (Hawthorne 102).

4. In *Wide Sargasso Sea,* the husband is never named as Edward Rochester, and the practice of critics referring to this character varies. I am going to call him "the husband" since I claim that that he does not become "Edward Rochester" until the end of the novel.

5. Brontë 323. For the major descriptions of Rochester's mad first wife in *Jane Eyre,* consult vol. 2, chap. 9, 305–8; and vol. 3, chap. 1, 321–27. According to F. Smith, "White women in the Caribbean were more temperate" than their male partners (133).

6. For a brief discussion of rum and temperance melodrama, see I. Williams, 187–99. There is a book to be written on Warner's sardonic use of biblical quotation and imagery.

7. In *Wide Sargasso Sea,* rum likewise positions other characters in roles established by colonialism. For example, Christophine plies Jo-Jo, another native servant, with a glass of rum before he takes Antoinette back to her husband.

Christophine characterizes Jo-Jo as a "leaky calabash" (116) who will inappropriately carry tales of his white mistress's unseemly appearance—"Your eyes red like *soucriant*," he tells Antoinette (116)—but a shot of rum enables him to perform his role as a submissive Black servant blamelessly. Daniel Cosway prepares to recount his version of Antoinette's ancestry by "tak[ing] a good shot of rum" (121). The narrative he offers exploits the husband's deepest psychological suspicions about Creole sexual behavior by claiming Antoinette as his sister, "'not yellow. . . . But [his] sister just the same'" (126).

    8. See also Spivak, "Three Women's Texts," 904.

    9. Dramatizing this process, however, cracks open the smooth surfaces of colonial power. As Mardorossian has claimed in reference to this novel, "The premises of colonialist discourse do not falter and lose ground when the black subalterns speak but paradoxically when they are silenced and stereotyped" ("Shutting Up" 1072).

    10. See Mezei 195–209. Mezei discusses the importance of historical time in the novel, claiming that "as long as Antoinette can remember and order the events of her memories into a temporal or causal sequence . . . then she can hold her life and self together" (197). Mezei later notes that the husband dismisses Antoinette's attempts to hold onto time as a symptom of madness (201), yet another way he dismisses her claim to empathy and ethical treatment.

    11. Huggan furthers this point when he argues that the husband's drawing writes Antoinette into the position of her literary ancestor, Bertha Mason of *Jane Eyre* ("Tale of Two Parrots" 653). See also Mezei 205.

    12. For historical analyses of Christophine's obeah, see Thomas 158–66 and Mardorossian, "Shutting Up" 1077–80. Mardorossian provides a discursive analysis of obeah's presence in *Reclaiming Difference,* a reworking of her earlier essay. Mardorossian adds, "Rochester capitalizes on the love drink he was given (despite its failure at achieving any effect) because he needs to rationalize his overwhelming sexual desire for Antoinette and to displace its source on [*sic*] an external agent. He genuinely believes that only foul play and an intoxicating drug could possibly drive a respectable Victorian gentleman like him to feel love and sexual desire for a woman whose mixed blood (which the 'disturbing letters' have exposed) mark her as belonging to an inferior species" (76–77).

    13. See Schivelbusch 153–63. Schivelbusch summarizes the ruinous effects of gin drinking on working-class social organization and the horrified response of the British authorities. He connects the rise in inebriation to dislocation and alienation as industrialism reshaped English work patterns and locations. See also F. Smith 73–78.

    14. In this regard, it is interesting to return to the climactic scene of *The Rum Diary.* Yeamon, Kemp's alter ego, braces himself to attack his former boss by "sharing a pint of gin" with a girl at the party (197).

    15. For further information on boycotts, see Midgeley 35–40 and I. Williams 199–202.

16. To my knowledge, only Maynard has linked specific historical events—the housing riots of the 1960s—to features of *Wide Sargasso Sea*. Gregg summarizes midcentury debates about Rhys's place in a West Indian "national" literature; Rhys continues to be a figure of controversy, as shown in Kalliney's recent discussion (218–44).

17. See chapter 2, n8.

18. Parsad finds that male violence is prevalent in South Asian households in Guyana to demonstrate dominance, and—as in other geographic locations—the violence can increase when a women gains economic independence (54–55).

19. Wouk's novel begins by describing the acquisition of the island Kinja by the United States "peaceably in 1940, as part of the shuffling of old destroyers and Caribbean real estate that went on between Mr. Roosevelt and Mr. Churchill" (3–4). Yanique's emphasis on World War II as a watershed links, through Wouk, to Naipaul's *Miguel Street* and Kanhai's "Rum Sweet Rum."

20. The Andrews Sisters didn't steal the song—Morey Amsterdam did—but these women were the public face of Lord Invader's loss.

21. Eeona's exceptionalism, history of sexual abuse, and ultimate madness link her to the tragic mulatta. Carby claims that mulatto figures function narratively "as a vehicle for the exploration of the relation between the races and, at the same time, an expression of the relationship between the races" (89). Eeona embodies the anxieties produced internally and interpretively when a character represents both "white privilege and black lack of privilege" (89). Eeona's lover McKenzie is associated with the trickster figure Anancy. McKenzie's house "appeared overnight like a spider's web" (*Land of Love* 161), and he has a "pre-spider history" (177). Wilson Harris has suggested that "the spider syndrome and phantom limb of the gods arising in Negro fable and legend" are creatively productive for West Indian artists (159), but, according to Emily Marshall, Anancy's role as "hoaxer, a cunning deceiver, a master of lies and malice" triggered debates about his suitability as a Jamaican folk hero in the early 2000s (127). Transferring insights from one island to another has limited relevance, but Marshall's conclusion that Anansi figures take advantage of contingencies arising from "a postcolonial country trying to develop to face the challenges of a changing world" fits McKenzie's unapologetic exploitation of Eeona, whom he sees as a figure of privilege against his own dispossession (135).

22. Televised reports about the civil rights movement have already appalled Virgin Islanders because US racism undermines the ideals of democracy sold abroad as a benefit of US intervention. Anette makes this equivalence—and American hypocrisy—clear by comparing her group's actions to those of civil rights activists: "If lunch counters in the State of Georgia were being made to serve Negroes, then it seemed that Virgin Islands beaches would be made to serve Virgin Islanders" (*Land of Love* 324).

23. The Coca-Cola Company registered "Coke" as an additional trademark in 1945 (*125 Years*), and it is perhaps significant that this is the only time the

phrase "rum and Coke"—as opposed to "rum and Coca-Cola" or "rum and cola"—appears in the novel.

4. Libations I

1. In Caribbean usage, the verb *fire* means "to drink (hard liquor)," often rum, often as part of a group drinking session (*Dictionary of Caribbean English Usage* 232). *Philoctete* means "fire" in this sense, but the word's proximity to *advance* allows semiotic drift to other contexts in which these words have different connotations.

2. Research has addressed the interpretation of alcohol use in politics as well as the material role of alcohol in politics. Authorities can use alcohol to dismiss political protesters as an unruly mob and thus "[avoid] a confrontation with the issues and conflicts posed by dissidence" (Gusfield 411). In the context of plantation slavery in the United States, Southern whites claimed that alcohol exacerbated tendencies toward chaotic violence among enslaved people while also fearing that alcohol fomented violent political resistance; the stereotype of the drunken Black "beast" replaces a rational response of Black people to enslavement. Political activity is also sequestered spatially. Bars, taverns, and other leisure establishments have historically been monitored for "working-class political dissidence" (Gusfield 412). In the early American republic, taverns were important sites for the acquisition and diffusion of political knowledge. Some commentators "lamented the impact of consumption of spirits on the capacity of new citizens to read and judge reasonably" (Conroy 42). In the Caribbean context, sociologists Japal and Benoit encourage researchers and professionals to recall alcohol's "sociocultural benefits" (7); they cite the rum shop as a setting for "healthy deliberations . . . where political issues are the main discussion point" as well as for efforts by politicians to curry favor by "providing alcohol for potential voters" (9; see also Herd, "Paradox" 367).

3. Fanon has argued that myths of a precolonial culture block national progress because they encourage neocolonial institutional forms ("Pitfalls" 129).

4. The title is a quotation from *The Tempest*, 1.2.334. The main plot concerns the efforts of a West Indian artist, Teeton, to free himself from the patronage of the Old Dowager, the widow of a Prospero figure. For a learned analysis of the role of *The Tempest* in *Water with Berries*, see Robinson, and for an overview of *The Tempest* in early postcolonial writing, see Nixon.

5. Robinson, who focuses on the Teeton-Dowager plot in his essay, lumps this crime into "assorted misadventures" that have made "two Caribbean artists . . . [go] quite mad" (447). In this perspective, he follows interviews with Lamming, cited in the article, who sees such actions as byproducts of a battle with Prospero (447).

6. Lamming reflects on these stereotypes of Caribbean "manhood" in other works as well. As the Jamaican in *The Emigrants* reports, "The only thing that West Indians in de R. A. F. din't want to prove, de only thing him feel no need to prove is his capability wid a bottle or a blonde" (64–65).

7. In his introduction to *Out of Place*, Baucom summarizes the debates surrounding the definition of "British" and "English" citizenship as immigration from former colonies to England increased after World War II.

8. Both Josephs and Harrison trace these references; Bedward also appears in sections of Cliff's *Free Enterprise*, discussed later in this chapter.

9. See Barnes, Toland-Dix, B. D. Harris, and Harrison.

10. Josephs argues that the limited communion between Barton and O'Malley arises "between two minds marked as mad by the colonial authorities," a position I agree with in principle (51). There is a benefit, however, in distinguishing religious monomania from alcoholism, given the emphasis Wynter places on the role of rum in their conversations.

11. According to F. Smith, alcohol-based hospitality was historically common and extremely important throughout the Caribbean (124). Such class and color distinctions persist into the twentieth century (177).

12. See Johnson's essay on "ghostwriting" as a narrative technique that "depicts epistemological—as well as physical and political—resistance to hegemonic historical narratives that elide her subjects" (119). Dunick argues that Cliff creates "a dialogical cacophony of voices all attempting to insert themselves and their versions of themselves into history" (38), while Potocki uses the concept of cosmopolitanism to consider the potential and limitations of transnational political commitment in this novel (70–74).

13. Garvey claims that the bottle tree symbolizes a diasporic "family tree" (264), while Johnson uses the tree as an image for the polyvocal and multi-genre form of the novel (126).

14. In the history of HIV/AIDS as a disease, the 1980s and early 1990s are a period of panic because there were uncertainties about transmission vectors and limited treatment options for the virus. In 1985, Ryan White, a high school student infected with HIV by a blood transfusion, was barred from attending school; he died in 1990. Magic Johnson retired from professional sports with an HIV diagnosis in 1991; Queen lead singer Freddie Mercury died from HIV complications a few weeks later. In 1993, when *Free Enterprise* was published, there were an estimated 2.5 million cases of AIDS; those testing positive for HIV were forbidden to travel to the United States. *Free Enterprise* also appears coincidentally with many seminal developments in queer theory, including Butler's *Bodies That Matter* (1993), and postcolonial hybridity, such as Young's *Colonial Desire* (1995).

5. Libations 2

1. Kazanjian argues for a speculative mode of interpreting quotidian historical documents; literary scholars will recognize that he argues for the legitimacy of what we call close reading for historical documents historians usually deem out of bounds for linguistic nuance. In this chapter, I argue for the inverse, the value of assessing the "apparent quotidiana" of literary critical work—independent of its

overall influence or perceived importance in our field—as the background against which we develop received readings of works of literature.

2. Both instances resonate with work on queer failure and negative affect, including Ngai's *Ugly Feelings*, Love's *Feeling Backwards,* and Halberstam's *The Queer Art of Failure.*

3. It is not clear whether Sidney manipulates Gerald's desires to advance his career or feels affection for him. Throughout "British Guiana," Sidney has sexual intercourse with women; he sometimes uses drugs to pacify them, which means that he is a serial rapist (78).

4. Although this novel centers on a development project, it is not a novel of development per se. In the conclusion to his well-known study of the modernist bildungsroman, *Unseasonable Youth* (2012), Esty extends his analysis beyond 1945 and indicates that "few self-consciously literary writers produce realist coming-of-age tales that sustain an unproblematic national allegory of progress without some reference to the modernist scrambling of developmental time or some recourse to the acknowledged failures of 'development' as both Western ideology and global policy mantra" (208). Rather than track a youthful protagonist, *The Chosen Place, the Timeless People* centers on the ideological imperatives of development as retarding—or, in fact, requiring—the production of subjects who cannot develop.

5. The nightclub decor echoes the international trade routes and multiple populations that run through the West Indies, for wall decorations run to quotidian items like "jewelry, wallets, keys," but also "a plump Buddha" and "a toy model of a mosque" (references to nineteenth-century importation of coolies from China and India?), "a huge Teddy bear" (an allusion to President Roosevelt's actions in Cuba and Panama?), and a "painted talking drum, silent now" (African cultural remnants?) (*Chosen Place* 82–83). In general, "it could have been the dumping ground of the world. All the discards of the nations, all the things that had become worn out over the centuries and fallen into disuse might have been brought and piled in a great charnel heap here" (82). The decor in Sugar's club condenses attitudes about West Indian colonies as wasted spaces, outmoded for modern industry and significant only for their past. However, the decorations not only offer a timeline of colonization but also assert the centrality of Caribbean islands to European power struggles.

6. Marshall initially characterizes him as a Cumean Sybil, "like a mummy, a gnome" with a "tiny ageless face [that] was a neutral, indeterminate beige (all the colors known to man might have come together and been canceled out in him)" (*Chosen Place* 83–84). Sugar is an ursubject, timeless and, more important, raceless, who proliferates and differentiates into the racialized subjects required for plantation economies. Under his aegis are produced the many clients of the nightclub, including tourists, prostitutes, disappointed scholars, corporate lackeys, gigolos, and "the solid, moneyed men" who might be "foreigners" or "Bourne Island whites" (87). Sugar's fungibility as a subject echoes his association with

pure exchange value: "He can arrange anything," Merle remarks. "Not that you don't have to pay through the nose!" (84). Yet Marshall undermines any attempts to mystify Sugar as a cipher by giving him a nationality—American—which aligns him with the United States' concrete historical position as an economic superpower at midcentury.

7. This moment foreshadows Saul's efforts, in coordination with local men, to alleviate economic ruin for Bournehills. When Kingsley and Company breaks with its usual practice of helping the small farmers transport their cane to a processor—thus threatening the livelihood of Bournehills—Saul works with the Bournehills farmers to organize independent transport. The Bournehills community spends a "hectic two to three weeks . . . transporting the peasant canes to the factory at Brighton" (*Chosen Place* 404).

8. The protagonist Merle does indicate that rum can oppress, when she expresses the sentiment that "the church and the rumshop" are "a damn conspiracy to keep us pacified and in ignorance": "Come the revolution we're going to ban them both" (*Chosen Place* 133). In her 1991 novel *Daughters*, Marshall takes a more skeptical view of rum in politics, which is in line of the development of the theme in *Praisesong*.

9. The imagery linking Avey's voyage to the Middle Passage is common knowledge: "She was alone in the deckhouse. That much she was certain of. Yet she had the impression as her mind flickered on briefly of other bodies lying crowded in with her in the hot, airless dark. A multitude it felt like lay packed around her in the filth and stench of themselves, just as she was. Their moans, rising and falling with each rise and plunge of the schooner, enlarged upon the one filling her head. Their suffering—the depth of it, the weight of it in the cramped space—made hers of no consequence" (*Praisesong* 209). Carriacou itself links Avey's Gullah childhood to Africa because the wharf resembles "a home movie she remembered Marion had made her last trip to Ghana" (187), and Rosalie Parvay's house contains a wardrobe "similar to one in her parents' bedroom" (215).

10. Although Marshall telegraphs color imagery early—the cruise ship is named *Bianca Pride,* for example—Avey's transformation begins as stomach trouble, as she is inexplicably disgusted by a parfait of peaches and whipped cream, the top "covered with chocolate sprinkles" (*Praisesong* 49). The parfait, a figuration of herself as an exception among the largely white passengers, admitted due to her wealth, also signals a history of institutionalized sexual assault on Black women's bodies.

11. In the twenty-first century, these associations have been recuperated by women, and marketed to women, as a feminist resistance to the stigma on female drinking. A random sampling from the Internet: "I'm a woman. I have needs. Pass me the wine"; "I heard there are people who can actually drink a glass of wine, instead of the bottle . . . underachievers"; and "Wine! Because no great story started with someone eating a salad." These slogans partake of a long history of pundits and philosophers opining on the joys and pains of alcohol consumption,

but there is a particular vector of alcohol-snark that trades on the negation of effeminacy and presents alcohol consumption as a feminist act.

12. See *Praisesong* 185, 186, 187, 207, 217, 224, 236, and 243.

13. These references illustrate a general lack of attention to the role of rum in this novel; there are others. Some critics elide the rum shop entirely. For example, Smith does not include it in her plot summary: "She finds herself taking a small journey by foot across the beach, which in turn leads to her acceptance of Lebert Joseph's offer" (720). Christian omits the location of Avey's first meeting with Lebert Joseph, emphasizing his parental, guiding role.

14. In *Abeng*, the rum shop shares the street with "the Tabernacle," a movie theater that shows American films, two gambling options and a brothel (16). Cliff and Marshall both make this point in their work (see note 8 above); neither is unaware of the consequences of alcoholism.

15. Although women did participate in rum-shop culture, moral strictures on women in bars and women as drinkers may have tacitly excluded women due to risks to reputation. In research documenting West Indian rum shops as political and economic networking sites during the seventeenth and eighteenth centuries, Goodall cites factors making it "likely that even more women participated in this public sphere than is recorded," including women proprietors and "men seeking the company of women" (102). While women do enter, own, or visit rum shops in twentieth-century literature (in Walcott's *Omeros*, for example, the owner is a woman), Avey Jackson enters a rum shop by accident—it is possible she would not have gone in had she noticed the sign. Rum shops described in *Netherland, The Chosen Place, the Timeless People, Abeng*, and *No Telephone to Heaven* are dominated by men.

16. The narrator may mean to cast doubt on the absolute difference John D. proposes between one product—rum—condemned for its ideological significance while another—marijuana—is "pure Jamaican gold" (*No Telephone* 21). Warf reports that in the nineteenth century "ganja's use was closely wrapped up with that of rum, so that the two drugs became intertwined in the cycle of work, debt, and poverty that characterized latifundal life on the sugar plantation" (428). Benard gives evidence that the marijuana symbolism prominent among Rastafarians develops out of material conditions stemming from the end of forced labor and, later, "the integration of capitalism in Jamaica" in the twentieth century (91). By contrast, in *No Telephone*, the rebel group "smoked ganja only occasionally" but uses marijuana to finance their rebellion (11).

17. *No Telephone*'s plot is well known: the rebel group to which Clare and Harriet belong attacks a US film production because its romanticized take on the maroon leader Nanny misappropriates Jamaican history for Western/Northern consumption. The Jamaican government, which has allowed the production and contracted to use its military assets in the film, turns a key battle scene into a real battlefield, killing insurgents (including Clare) and Jamaican cast members.

18. This posting has been deleted from the website where it appeared.

19. Danticat explores this transformation in the collection *The Dew Breaker*, where the "urine-colored rum" of "The Funeral Singer" (170) returns in the title story when Duvalier's prisoners perform a "ritual cure" by urinating on a beaten prisoner to "help seal the open wounds on his face and body and keep his bones from feeling as though they were breaking apart" (219).

20. Echoes of the anonymous man occur in the historical sections of the novel as well, confirming rum as a sign of individual and societal failure under the regime of slavery. The gaoler in the nineteenth-century section of the story is "a ragged man with no teeth in his head and a bottle of rum in his hand" (McCauley 256). John's brother Bruce, betrothed to a Black woman, carried a "faint whiff of rum" from coping with the prejudice his actions generate. "Then there were the men of Fortress, nine of them. They lived in an old slave barracks and hired themselves out as working gangs. They were thin, muscular and ragged and they congregated each evening in Prudence's shop and drank rum until they passed out. They smoked a sweetish-smelling weed they called ganja and were alleged to rape the daughters of Fortress" (164).

6. Is the Rum Gone?

1. As film scholar Bíró asks, "Is it important to know [what the title means]? Would it add anything to the depiction of the workers' relationship? Not at all" (40).

2. Self-consciously open-ended, *35 rhums* centers on a father and daughter, Lionel and Josephine, negotiating their shifting relationship as she enters adulthood and elects to marry. They live in a Paris suburb: he is a commuter train operator, she is a college student. Critics have remarked on Denis's refusal to make race a central plot point in the film, thus, as Rosalind Galt claims, constituting "an unremarked and yet total reversal of the white film imaginary" (102). Denis decenters expectations for a racially charged narrative, but she saturates the mise-en-scène with quotidian reminders of French colonialism that remained invisible to most critics (e.g., J. S. Williams 47). A retiring worker receives an African-inspired staff and wall hanging as gifts; a street sign reads "Rue de la Guadeloupe"; a Martiniquan sings a Cuban classic in a local bar; the pianist in the final scene is from Guadeloupe. Denis stages the lacunae between colonialism's everyday presence and its abstractions by including a self-reflexive discussion of Franz Fanon's theories in the film. The bald insertion of political commentary has annoyed critics (see Galt 101) and the body of critical work on the film usually contains references to this scene (see Munro 65 and Royer and Thompson 197). This context repudiates universal themes and sovereign protagonists: Josephine's decision to marry is also about colonialism's legacy. Her fiancé Noe's career takes him on long assignments to nations like Gabon; his parents, to whom he alludes briefly, also earned their living in the French colonies. Although the exact

nature of his work is unspecified, it is clear that Josephine's decision to marry is also a decision to travel the literal and narrative routes paved by colonialism.

3. See essays by Waters and Fradera.

4. There are two additional films in the *Pirates* series, neither of which is particularly relevant here. The fourth, *On Stranger Tides* (2011), departs from the plot arc of the trilogy with a new set of characters and plot. The fifth, *Dead Men Tell No Tales* (2017), returns to the original plot arc, but direct references to rum are very few. Representatives of the British Empire do, however, roam the seas making remarks about capturing the Trident of Poseidon in order to rule the sea; Spanish commanders make similar remarks. Disney is developing two additional *Pirates* films as of this writing.

5. See Marston's reading of Elizabeth Swann (Keira Knightley) as a "stifled female protagonist" whose successful bid for freedom from restrictive gender roles relies on "a problematic alignment of gender-based and . . . race-based discrimination." Readers of Spivak's critique of *Jane Eyre* and *Wide Sargasso Sea* will find analogies in the ways that "the hegemony of white patriarchy is critiqued and yet upheld via a certain compromise, a compromise identifiable through the mobilization of aristocratic white femininity" (Marston).

6. Later films in the series repeat this line in less symbolically charged ways. In a scene from the second film, *Dead Man's Chest,* the question confirms the reputations of pirates as heavy drinkers. Jack Sparrow quips, "Why is the rum always gone?" and, realizing he is drunk, answers his own question: "Oh, that's why." In *At World's End,* the pirates pause dramatically when Will Turner orders the rum sacrificed to defeat the kraken, an allusion to Elizabeth Swann's rescue effort in the first film.

7. The deleted scene containing this footage is called "No Truth at All (Elizabeth Teaches Jack the Song)," which can be found on disc 2 of *Pirates of the Caribbean: Curse of the Black Pearl.*

8. See R. F. Smith, 1–10. According to R. F. Smith, during the eighteenth century, recruits from North American colonies participated in Britain's military efforts to establish and maintain colonies in the Caribbean. By 1821, the United States had established a "West Indies squadron" that cooperated with the Royal Navy to avoid trials in US courts, which often ended in the release of pirates. The United States acquired New Orleans in 1803. Smith excuses such actions as "necessary, normal, and legal" to protect shipping, as well as essential for a nation that "wanted to be taken seriously and have its interests treated with respect by other powers."

9. The *Pirates* series was apparently good for business: the *Daily Mail* reported that rum sales had "surged by 31%" between 2006 and 2007 ("Rum Sales Soar"), the year the third installment of the series appeared.

10. Steinhoff contends that the pirate is "an impersonation of key US-American national myths but conversely also functions to construct a transnational

and subversive image of the pirate community (with anti-globalization undertones)" (128).

11. The tagline resonates more generally with shifting complexities in global maritime trade. A recent working paper about piracy's impact on Chinese shipping choices is titled "Where Has the Rum Gone?" (Sandkamp and Yang). For an intriguing perspective on the meme economy, see Literat and van den Berg.

12. The United States acquired the colonies of the Philippines, Guam, and Puerto Rico in 1898; Cuba and American Samoa in 1899; and the Panama Canal Zone in 1903.

13. Nair warns of sublimating political action as cultural resistance: "While music and dance are not in themselves marginal activities, trying to place them in a peripheral culture of resistance that neglects the systemic over the lived paradoxically limits and overstates the potential of these expressive cultures" ("Expressive Countercultures" 85).

Bibliography

Abbott, Elizabeth. *Sugar: A Bittersweet History.* Penguin, 2008.
Ackland, Valentine. *For Sylvia, an Honest Account.* Norton, 1985.
Adler, Marianna. "From Symbolic Exchange to Commodity Consumption: Anthropological Notes on Drinking as a Symbolic Practice." In Barrows and Room, pp. 376–98.
Allen, H. Warner. *Rum.* Faber, 1934.
Allfrey, Phyllis Shand. *The Orchid House.* Dutton, 1953.
Ambler, Charles. "Alcohol and the Slave Trade in West Africa, 1400–1850." In Jankowiak and Bradburd, pp. 73–87.
Angrosino, Michael V. "Rum and Ganja: Indenture, Drug Foods, Labor Motivation, and the Evolution of the Modern Sugar Industry in Trinidad." In Jankowiak and Bradburd, 101–16.
Appadurai, Arjun. "Introduction." *The Social Life of Things: Commodities in Cultural Perspective,* edited by Arjun Appadurai. Cambridge UP, 1986, pp. 3–63.
Banco, Lindsey Michael. *Travel and Drugs in Twentieth-Century Literature.* Routledge, 2010.
Barnes, Natasha. *Cultural Conundrums: Gender, Race, Nation, and the Making of Caribbean Cultural Politics.* U of Michigan P, 2006.
Barrows, Susanna, and Robin Room, editors. *Drinking: Behavior and Belief in Modern History.* U of California P, 1991.
Battaglia, Diana. "Ajiaco, Rum, and Coffee: Food and Identity in Leonardo Paduro's Detective Fiction." *Blood on the Table: Essays on Food in International Crime Fiction,* edited by Jean Anderson, Carolina Miranda, and Barbara Pezzotti. McFarlane, 2018, pp. 99–112.
Baucom, Ian. *Specters of the Atlantic: Financial Capital, Slavery, and the Philosophy of History.* Duke UP, 2005.
———. *Out of Place: Englishness, Empire, and the Locations of Identity.* Princeton UP, 1999.

Bazin, Nancy Topping. "Alcoholism in Third-World Literature: Buchi Emecheta, Athol Fugard, and Anita Desai." In Lilienfeld and Oxford, pp. 123–32.

Beachey, R. W. *The British West Indies Sugar Industry in the Late 19th Century.* 1957. Greenwood, 1978.

Beaubrun, M. H. "Of Alcohol and Alcoholics." *Caribbean Medical Journal,* vol. 19, nos. 3–4, 1957, pp. 137–42.

Benard, Akeia A. "The Material Roots of Rastafarian Marijuana Symbolism." *History and Anthropology,* vol. 18, no. 1, March 2007, pp. 89–99.

Bendroth, Margaret. "Rum, Romanism, and Evangelism: Protestants and Catholics in Late-Nineteenth-Century Boston." *Church History,* vol. 68, no. 3, 1999, pp. 627–48.

Benediktsson, Mike. Review of *The Rum Diary,* by Hunter S. Thompson. *Library Journal,* 15 Oct. 1998, p. 101.

Benítez-Rojo, Antonio. "Nicolás Guillén and Sugar." *Callaloo* 31, Spring 1987, pp. 329–51.

———. *The Repeating Island: The Caribbean and the Postmodern Perspective.* Duke UP, 1996.

Bennett, Jane. *Vibrant Matter: A Political Ecology of Things.* Duke UP, 2010.

Bennett, Linda A., and Genevieve M. Ames, editors. *The American Experience with Alcohol.* Plenum, 1985.

Beushausen, Wiebke, Anne Brüske, Ana-Sofia Commichau, Patrick Helber, and Sinah Kloß. *Caribbean Food Culture: Culinary Practices and Consumption in the Caribbean and Its Diasporas.* Transcript, 2014.

Big Sugar. Directed by Brian McKenna. Galafilm, 2005.

Bíró, Yvette. "A Subtle Story: *35 Shots of Rum.*" *Film Quarterly,* vol. 63, no. 2, Winter 2009/10, pp. 38–43.

Black, George. *The Good Neighbor: How the United States Wrote the History of Central America and the Caribbean.* Pantheon, 1988.

"Bogart." Oxford English Dictionary Online. https://oed.com.

Brana-Shute, Gary. "Drinking Shops and Social Structure: Some Ideas on Lower-Class West Indian Male Behavior." *Urban Anthropology,* vol. 5, no. 1, 1976, pp. 53–68.

Brontë, Charlotte. *Jane Eyre.* 1847. Oxford UP, 1993.

Brown, Bill. "Thing Theory." *Critical Inquiry,* vol. 28, no. 1, Autumn 2001, pp. 1–16.

Brown, J. Dillon. "Geographies of Migration in the Caribbean Novel." In Gikandi, ed., pp. 120–34.

———. *Migrant Modernism: Post-War London and the West Indian Novel.* U of Virginia P, 2013.

Brown, J. Dillon, and Leah Reade Rosenberg, editors. *Beyond Windrush: Rethinking Postwar Anglophone Caribbean Literature.* U of Mississippi P, 2015.

Brown, Susan. "Paulette Jiles's Transnational Railway Ride: Generic Change and Economic Change in *Sitting in the Club Car Drinking Rum and Karma-Kola*." *American Review of Canadian Studies*, vol. 26, no. 3, Autumn 1996, pp. 391–403.

Brown-Hinds, Paulette. "Dance as Healing Ritual in Paule Marshall's *Praisesong for the Widow*." *Religion & Literature*, vol. 27, no. 1, 1995, pp. 107–17.

Burns, Eric. *The Spirits of America: A Social History of Alcohol*. Temple UP, 2004.

Bystrom, Kerry, and Joseph R. Slaughter, editors. *The Global South Atlantic*. Fordham UP, 2018.

Caetano, Raul, Catherine L. Clark, and Tammy Tam. "Alcohol Consumption Among Racial/Ethnic Minorities: Theory and Research." *Alcohol Research and Health*, vol. 22, no. 4, 1998, pp. 233–38.

Cane. Directed by Christian Duguey and Sanford Bookstaver. ABC Studios, 2007.

Carby, Hazel V. *Reconstructing Womanhood: The Emergence of the Afro-American Woman Novelist*. Oxford UP, 1988.

Cartwright, Keith. "Notes Toward a Voodoo Hermeneutics: Soul Rhythms, Marvelous Transitions, and Passages to the Creole Saints in *Praisesong for the Widow*." *Southern Quarterly*, vol. 41, no. 4, 2003, pp. 127–43.

Chan, Winnie. "Curry on the Divide in Rudyard Kipling's *Kim* and Gurinder Chadha's *Bend It Like Beckham*." *ARIEL*, vol. 36, nos. 3–4, 2005, pp. 1–23.

Christian, Barbara. "Ritualistic Process and the Structure of Paule Marshall's *Praisesong for the Widow*." *Callaloo*, no. 18, 1983, pp. 74–84.

Chude-Sokei, Louis. *The Sound of Culture: Diaspora and Black Technopoetics*. Wesleyan UP, 2015.

Clarke, Austin. "Griff!" *An Anthology of Colonial and Postcolonial Short Fiction*, edited by Dean Baldwin and Patrick J. Quinn. Houghton Mifflin, 2007, pp. 374–89.

Cliff, Michelle. *Abeng*. Plume, 1984.

———. *Free Enterprise*. Dutton, 1993.

———. *No Telephone to Heaven*. Penguin, 1987.

Coates, Ta-Nehisi. *Between the World and Me*. Spiegel & Grau, 2015.

"Cocktail Politics." *Picong*, ca. 1940, pp. 21–22.

Cohen, Rich. "Sugar Love." *National Geographic*, vol. 224, no. 2, August 2013, pp. 78–79, 81–88, 91, 93–94, 96–97.

Conroy, David W. "In the Public Sphere: Efforts to Curb the Consumption of Rum in Connecticut, 1760–1820." *Alcohol: A Social and Cultural History*, edited by Mack P. Holt. Berg, 2006, pp. 41–60.

Coovadia, Imraan. *Authority and Authorship in V. S. Naipaul*. Palgrave MacMillan, 2009.

Coughtry, Jay. *The Notorious Triangle: Rhode Island and the African Slave Trade, 1700–1807*. Temple UP, 1981.

Coulombe, Charles. *Rum: The Epic Story of the Drink That Conquered the World*. Citadel, 2004.
Cowper, William. *Cowper's Poems*. Dent, 1931.
Cozzi, Annette. *The Discourses of Food in Nineteenth-Century British Fiction*. Palgrave Macmillan, 2010.
Crichlow, Veronica. "Playing Man: What Defines 'Man' in Naipaul's *Miguel Street* and *The Mystic Masseur*." *Torre*, vol. 10, nos. 36–37, 2005, pp. 291–99.
Crowley, John W. *The White Logic: Alcoholism and Gender in American Modernist Fiction*. U of Massachusetts P, 1994.
Cudjoe, Selwyn. *Resistance and Caribbean Literature*. Ohio UP, 1980.
Curtis, Wayne. *And a Bottle of Rum: A History of the New World in Ten Cocktails*. Crown, 2006.
da Silva, A. J. Simoes. *The Luxury of Nationalist Despair*. Rodopi, 2000.
Dabydeen, David. *The Counting House*. 1996. Rev. ed., Peepal Tree, 2005.
Dalleo, Raphael. *American Imperialism's Undead: The Occupation of Haiti and the Rise of Caribbean Anticolonialism*. U of Virginia P, 2016.
Dann, Graham. *Patterns of Drinking in Barbados: The Findings of a Sample Survey of Adult Residents*. CEDAR, 1980.
Danticat, Edwidge. *The Dew Breaker*. Vintage, 2004.
Dardis, Tom. *The Thirsty Muse: Alcohol and the American Writer*. Ticknor & Fields, 1989.
Darwin, John. *Britain and Decolonisation*. St. Martin's, 1988.
De Boissière, Jean. "With Me Rum in Me Head." *Picong*, ca. 1940, pp. 18–20.
De Boissière, Ralph. *Rum and Coca-Cola*. 1956. Allison & Busby, 1984.
Deere, Carmen Diana, Peggy Antrobus, Lynn Bolles, Edwin Melendez, Peter Phillips, Marcia Rivera, and Helen Safa. *In the Shadows of the Sun: Caribbean Development Alternatives and U.S. Policy*. PACCA/Westview, 1990.
DeLoughrey, Elizabeth M. "Globalizing the Routes of Breadfruit and Other Bounties." *Journal of Colonialism and Colonial History*, vol. 8, no. 3, 2008, n.p.
———. *Routes and Roots: Navigating Caribbean and Pacific Island Literatures*. U of Hawaii P, 2007.
Dictionary of Caribbean English Usage. Edited by Richard Allsopp. U of West Indies P, 2003.
Djos, Matts G. *Writing Under the Influence: Alcoholism and the Alcoholic Perception from Hemingway to Berryman*. Palgrave Macmillan, 2010.
Dollar, J. Gerard. "Addiction and the 'Other Self' in Three Late Victorian Novels." In Vice et al., pp. 268–74.
Donnell, Alison. "Sexuality and Gender in the Anglophone Caribbean Novel." In Gikandi, pp. 152–66.
Döring, Tobias. *Caribbean-English Passages*. Routledge, 2002.
Doyle, Laura. "Inter-imperiality: An Introduction." *Modern Fiction Studies*, vol. 64, no. 3, 2018, pp. 395–402.

Doyle, Laura, and Laura Winkiel. "Introduction: The Global Horizons of Modernism." *Geomodernisms: Race, Modernism, Modernity*, edited by Laura Doyle and Laura Winkiel. U of Indiana P, 2005, pp. 1–14.

Drake, Sandra. "All that Foolishness/That All Foolishness: Race and Caribbean Culture as Thematics of Liberation in Jean Rhys's *Wide Sargasso Sea*." *Critica*, vol. 2, no. 2, 1990, pp. 97–112.

Dreisinger, Baz. "On a Tropical Rum Trail." *New York Times*, 23 Feb. 2014, pp. 6–7.

Drowne, Kathleen. *Spirits of Defiance: National Prohibition and Jazz Age Literature, 1920–1933*. Ohio State UP, 2005.

Dubois, Laurent. *Avengers of the New World: The Story of the Haitian Revolution*. Harvard UP, 2004.

Duggan, Lisa. *The Twilight of Equality? Neoliberalism, Cultural Politics, and the Attack on Democracy*. Beacon, 2003.

Dunick, Lisa. "The Dialogic of Diaspora: Michelle Cliff's *Free Enterprise*, Glissant, and the History of Slavery in the New World." *CEA Critic*, vol. 72, no. 2, Winter 2010, pp. 37–51.

Dunn, Richard. *Sugar and Slaves*. U of North Carolina P, 1972.

Duvall, John N. "Cricket Field of Dreams: Queer Racial Identifications in Joseph O'Neill's *Netherland*." *Critique*, vol. 55, no. 4, 2014, pp. 341–57.

Edmondson, Belinda. *Making Men: Gender, Literary Authority, and Women's Writing in Caribbean Narrative*. Duke UP, 1999.

Edwards, Brent Hayes. *The Practice of Diaspora: Literature, Translation, and the Rise of Black Internationalism*. Harvard UP, 2003.

Elia, Nada. *Trances, Dances, and Vociferations: Agency and Resistance in Africana Women's Narratives*. Garland, 2001.

Erwin, Lee. "'Like in a Looking-Glass': History and Narrative in *Wide Sargasso Sea*." *Novel*, 1989, pp. 143–58.

Esty, Jed. *Unseasonable Youth: Modernism, Colonialism, and the Fiction of Development*. Oxford UP, 2012.

Fanon, Frantz. *Black Skin, White Masks*. 1952. Translated by Charles Lam Markmann. Grove, 1962.

———. "On National Culture." Fanon, *The Wretched of the Earth*, pp. 165–99.

———. "The Pitfalls of National Consciousness." Fanon, *The Wretched of the Earth*, pp. 119–63.

———. *The Wretched of the Earth*. 1961. Translated by Constance Farrington. Grove, 1963.

Farnsworth, Paul, and Laurie A. Wilkie. "Fish and Grits: Southern, African, and British Influences in Bahamian Foodways." *Southern Anthropological Society Proceedings*, vol. 38, 2008, pp. 34–72.

Few, Martha. "Chocolate, Sex, and Disorderly Women in Late-Seventeenth- and Early-Eighteenth-Century Guatemala." *Ethnohistory*, vol. 52, no. 4, 2005, pp. 673–87.

Fodor's Guide to the Caribbean, Bahamas, and Bermuda, 1960. David McKay, 1960.

Fradera, Josep M. "The Caribbean Between Empires: Colonists, Pirates, and Slaves." *The Caribbean: A History of the Region and Its Peoples,* edited by Stephan Palmié and Francisco A. Scarano. U of Chicago P, 2011, pp. 165–76.

Friedman, Susan Stanford. *Planetary Modernisms: Provocations on Modernity Across Time.* Columbia UP, 2015.

French, Patrick. *The World Is What It Is: The Authorized Biography of V. S. Naipaul.* Knopf, 2008.

Galt, Rosalind. "Claire Denis and the World Cinema of Refusal." *SubStance,* vol. 43, no. 1, 2014, pp. 96–108.

Garvey, Johanna X. K. "Passages to Identity: Re-Membering the Diaspora in Marshall, Phillips, and Cliff." *Black Imagination and the Middle Passage,* edited by Maria Diedrich, Henry Louis Gates Jr., and Carl Pederson. Oxford UP, 1999, pp. 255–71.

Gernalzick, Nadja. "Sugar and the Global South: Substance of New Solidarities." *The Global South and Literature,* edited by Russell West-Pavlov. Cambridge UP, 2018, pp. 108–19.

Gikandi, Simon, editor. *The Novel in Africa and the Caribbean since 1950. Oxford History of the Novel in English,* vol. 11. Oxford UP, 2016.

———. *Writing in Limbo: Modernism and Caribbean Literature.* 1992. Cornell UP, 2018.

Gilmore, Thomas B. *Equivocal Spirits: Alcoholism and Drinking in Twentieth-Century Literature.* U of North Carolina P, 1987.

Gilroy, Paul. *The Black Atlantic: Modernity and Double Consciousness.* Harvard UP, 1993.

Gingell, Basil. "The Navy to Lose its Daily Rum Ration." *Times of London,* 18 Dec. 1969, p. 1.

Glanz, James, and Frances Robles. "How Bungling Has Kept Puerto Ricans Powerless." *New York Times,* 7 May 2018, p. A1(L).

Glissant, Édouard. *Caribbean Discourse: Selected Essays.* Translated by J. Michael Dash. U of Virginia P, 1989.

———. *Poetics of Relation.* Translated by Betsy Wing. U of Michigan P, 1997.

Golimowska, Karolina. "Cricket as Cure: Post-9/11 Urban Trauma and Displacement in Joseph O'Neill's Novel *Netherland.*" *Journal of American Culture,* vol. 36, no. 3, Sept. 2013, pp. 230–39.

Goodall, Jamie. "Tippling Houses, Rum Shops, and Taverns: How Alcohol Fuelled Informal Commercial Networks and Knowledge Exchange in the West Indies." *Journal for Maritime Research,* vol. 18, no. 2, 2016, pp. 97–121.

Gowin, Joshua. "Your Brain on Alcohol." *Psychology Today,* 18 Jun. 2010, www.psychologytoday.com/us/blog/you-illuminated/201006/your-brain-alcohol.

Grainger, James. *The Sugar-Cane: A Poem, In Four Books.* 1764. In Krise, pp. 166–260.

Gregg, Veronica Marie. *Jean Rhys's Historical Imagination: Reading and Writing the Creole*. U of North Carolina P, 1995.
Günther, Renate. "Alcohol and Writing: Patterns of Obsession in the Work of Marguerite Duras." In Vice et al., pp. 200–205.
Gusfield, Joseph. "Benevolent Repression: Popular Culture, Social Structure, and the Control of Drinking." In Barrows and Room, pp. 399–424.
Hall, Stuart. "Old and New Identities." *Culture, Globalization, and the World-System: Contemporary Conditions for the Representation of Identity*, edited by Anthony D. King. U of Minnesota P, 1997, pp. 41–68.
Harman, Graham. *Bells and Whistles*. Zero, 2013.
———. "The Well-Wrought Broken Hammer: Object-Oriented Literary Criticism." *New Literary History*, vol. 43, no. 2, 2012, pp. 183–203.
Harper, Frederick. "Alcohol Use and Alcoholism Among Black Americans: A Review." In Watts and Wright, pp. 19–36.
Harradine, David. "Abject Identities and Fluid Performances: Theorizing the Leaking Body." *Contemporary Theatre Review* 10, 2000, pp. 69–85.
Harris, Brenda Do. "Aspects of Female Empowerment in Sylvia Wynter's *The Hills of Hebron*." *Zora Neale Hurston Forum*, 1996, pp. 30–34.
Harris-Hastrick, Eda F. "Substance Abuse Issues among English-Speaking Caribbean People of African Ancestry." *Ethnocultural Factors in Substance Abuse Treatment*, edited by Shulamith Straussner and Lala Ashenberg. Guilford, 2001, pp. 52–74.
Harris, Wilson. "History, Fable, and Myth in the Caribbean and Guianas." *Selected Essays of Wilson Harris*. Routledge, 1999, pp. 152–66.
Harrison, Sheri-Marie. "'Who Worked This Evil, Brought Distance between Us': The Politics of Sexual Interaction in Sylvia Wynter's *The Hills of Hebron*." *Modern Fiction Studies*, vol. 59, no. 1, 2013, pp. 156–74.
Hartman, Saidiya. *Scenes of Subjection: Terror, Slavery, and Self-Making in Nineteenth-Century America*. Oxford UP, 1997.
Hawthorne, Evelyn. "'Persistence of (Colonial) Memory': Jean Rhys's Carib Texts and Imperial Historiography." *ARIEL*, vol. 32, no. 3, July 2001, pp. 91–112.
Heath, Dwight B. *Drinking Occasions: Comparative Perspectives on Alcohol and Culture*. Brunner/Mazel, 2000.
Herd, Denise. "Ambiguity in Black Drinking Norms: An Ethnohistorical Interpretation." In Bennett and Ames, pp. 149–70.
———. "The Paradox of Temperance: Blacks and the Alcohol Question in Nineteenth-Century America." In Barrows and Room, pp. 354–75.
———. "Racial Differences in Women's Drinking Norms and Drinking Patterns: A National Study." *Journal of Substance Abuse* 9, 1997, pp. 137–49.
Hill, Jeffrey. "Queering the Pitch: Joseph O'Neill's *Netherland* and the Cricket Novel." *Sport in Society*, vol. 15, no. 2, 2012, pp. 181–93.
The Holiday Guide to Caribbean and the Bahamas. Random House, 1973.

Horn, Maja. "A Sweet Sweet Tale of Terror: Rita Indiana Hernández Writes the Dominican Republic into the Global South Atlantic." In Bystrom and Slaughter, pp. 253–73.

Houston, Lynn Marie. "'Making Do': Caribbean Foodways and the Economics of Postcolonial Literary Culture." *MELUS,* vol. 32, no. 4, 2007, pp. 99–113.

Huggan, Graham. "Prizing 'Otherness': A Short History of the Booker." *Studies in the Novel,* vol. 29, no. 3, Fall 1997, pp. 412–33.

———. "A Tale of Two Parrots: Walcott, Rhys, and the Uses of Colonial Mimicry." *Contemporary Literature,* vol. 35, no. 4, 1994, pp. 643–60.

Iton, Richard. *In Search of the Black Fantastic: Politics and Popular Culture in the Post-Civil Rights Era.* Oxford UP, 2008.

Jackson, Sandra, and Julie Moody-Freeman, editors. *The Black Imagination: Science Fiction, Futurism, and the Speculative.* Peter Lang, 2011.

Jaggassar, Javed. "The Churchill-Roosevelt Highway." Highways of Trinidad, 2016. highwaysoftrinidad.wordpress.com/history-of-highways/the-churchill-roosevelt-highway/. Accessed 11 Jan. 2021.

"Jamaica, A Poem, In Three Parts." 1777. In Krise, pp. 326–39.

James, C. L. R. *Beyond a Boundary.* 1963. Duke UP, 1993.

Jameson, Fredric. *The Political Unconscious: Narrative as a Socially Symbolic Act.* Cornell UP, 1982.

Jankowiak, William, and Daniel Bradburd, editors. *Drugs, Labor, and Colonial Expansion.* U of Arizona P, 2003.

Japal, Elizabeth, and Oliver Benoit. "A Sociological Perspective of Alcohol Use in the Caribbean." *International Public Health Journal,* vol. 9, no. 1, 2017, pp. 7–9.

Jiles, Paulette. *Sitting in the Club Car Drinking Rum and Karma-Kola: A Manual of Etiquette for Ladies Crossing Canada by Train.* Polestar/Raincoat, 1986.

Johnson, Erica L. "Ghostwriting Transnational Histories in Michelle Cliff's *Free Enterprise.*" *Meridians,* vol. 9, no. 1, 2009, pp. 114–39.

Josephs, Kelly Baker. *Disturbers of the Peace: Representations of Madness in Anglophone Caribbean Literature.* U of Virginia P, 2013.

Kalliney, Peter. *Commonwealth of Letters: British Literary Culture and the Emergence of Postcolonial Aesthetics.* Oxford UP, 2013.

Kanhai, Rosanne. "Rum Sweet Rum." In Kanhai, pp. 3–17.

Kanhai, Rosanne, editor. *Matikor: The Politics of Identity for Indo-Caribbean Women.* U of the West Indies, 1999.

Kazanjian, David. "Scenes of Speculation." *Social Text* 33, no. 4, Dec. 2015, pp. 77–84.

Keen, Suzanne. *Romances of the Archive in Contemporary British Fiction.* U of Toronto P, 2001.

Kelley, Sean M. "American Rum, African Consumers, and the Transatlantic Slave Trade." *African Economic History,* vol. 46, no. 2, 2018, pp. 1–29.

Kelly, David. "Fear and Loathing in San Juan." Review of *The Rum Diary*, by Hunter S. Thompson. *New York Times Book Review*, 29 Nov. 1998, archive.nytimes.com/www.nytimes.com/books/98/11/29/reviews/981129.29kellyt.html.

Kennedy, Cynthia M. "The Other White Gold: Salt, Slaves, the Turks and Caicos Islands, and British Colonialism." *Historian*, vol. 69, no. 2, 2007, pp. 215–30.

Kilgore, De Witt Douglas. *Astrofuturism: Science, Race, and Visions of Utopia in Space*. U of Pennsylvania P, 2003.

Kincaid, Jamaica. *Lucy*. Farrar, Straus & Giroux, 1990.

Knight, Franklin W., and Teresita Martínez-Vergne, editors. *Contemporary Caribbean Cultures and Societies in a Global Context*. U of North Carolina P, 2005.

Knowlton, Richard, and Virginia Berridge. "Constructive Imperialism and Sobriety: Evidence of Alcoholism among Candidates for the British Colonial Service from 1898–1904." *Drugs: Education, Prevention and Policy*, vol. 15, no. 5, 2008, pp. 439–50.

Krise, Thomas W., editor. *Caribbeana*. U of Chicago P, 1999.

Kutzinski, Vera. *Sugar's Secrets: Race and the Erotics of Cuban Nationalism*. U of Virginia P, 1993.

Lamming, George. *The Emigrants*. 1954. U of Michigan P, 1994.

———. *Water with Berries*. Holt, Rinehart & Winston, 1971.

Langton, Marcia. "Rum, Seduction, and Death: 'Aboriginality' and Alcohol." *Oceania*, vol. 63, no. 3, 1993, pp. 195–206.

Lashua, Brett. "Popular Music Memoryscapes of Liverpool 8." *Media Fields Journal* 3, 2011, mediafieldsjournal.org/popular-music-memories-of-live/2011/7/21/popular-music-memoryscapes-of-liverpool-8.html.

Lassner, Phyllis. *Colonial Strangers: Women Writing the End of the British Empire*. Rutgers UP, 2004.

Lenson, David. *On Drugs*. U of Minnesota P, 1995.

Lévi-Strauss, Claude. *Tristes Tropiques*. 1955. Penguin, 1992.

Lewis, Kathleen Philips. "Women in the Trinidad Cocoa Industry, 1870–1945." *Journal of Caribbean History*, vol. 34, nos. 1–2, 2000, pp. 20–45.

Lilienfeld, Jane, and Jeffrey Oxford. *The Languages of Addiction*. St. Martin's, 1999.

Literat, Ioana, and Sarah van den Berg. "Buy Memes Low, Sell Memes High: Vernacular Criticism and Collective Negotiations of Value on Reddit's MemeEconomy." *Information, Communication and Society*, vol. 22, no. 2, 2019, pp. 232–49.

Lloyd, A. J. "Alcoholism Treatment in Trinidad." *British Journal of Addiction* 71, 1976, pp. 45–50.

Loichot, Valérie. *The Tropics Bite Back: Culinary Coups in Caribbean Literature*. U of Minnesota P, 2013.

López, Alfred. "Introduction: The (Post) Global South." *Global South*, vol. 1, nos. 1–2, 2007, pp. 1–11.

Lovelace, Earl. *When Gods Are Falling*. Regnery, 1966.
MacAndrew, Craig, and Robert B. Edgerton. *Drunken Comportment*. 1969. Pecheron, 2003.
MacInnis, Peter. *Bittersweet*. Allen & Unwin, 2002.
Maharajh, Hari, and Rampersad Parasram. "The Practice of Psychiatry in Trinidad and Tobago." *International Review of Psychiatry* 11, 1973, pp. 173–83.
Mahler, Anne Garland. "Beyond the Color Curtain: The Metonymic Color Politics of the Tricontinental and the (New) Global South." In Bystrom and Slaughter, pp. 99–123.
———. "South-South Organizing in the Global Plantation Zone: Ramón Marrero Aristy, the *novela de la caña*, and the Caribbean Bureau." *Atlantic Studies* 2018, DOI:10.1080/14788810.2018.1489569.
———. "'Todos los negros y todos los blancos y todos tomamos café': Race and the Cuban Revolution in Nicolàs Guillén Landrián's *Coffea arábiga*." *Small Axe*, vol. 19, no. 1, March 2015, pp. 55–75.
Maingot, Anthony P. "Rum, Revolution, and Globalization: Past, Present, and Future of a Caribbean Product." In Wright and Martínez-Vergne, pp. 233–62.
Mao, Douglas, and Rebecca L. Walkowitz. "The New Modernist Studies." *PMLA*, vol. 123, no. 3, May 2008, pp. 737–48.
Marcus, Anthony. "Drinking Politics: Alcohol, Drugs, and the Problem of US Civil Society." In P. Wilson, pp. 255–76.
Marcus, Grant. "Introduction." In Heath, pp. xiii–xv.
Marcus, Jane. *Hearts of Darkness: White Women Write Race*. Rutgers UP, 2004.
Mardorossian, Carine M. *Reclaiming Difference: Caribbean Women Rewrite Postcolonialism*. U of Virginia P, 2005.
———. "Double (De)colonization and the Feminist Criticism of *Wide Sargasso Sea*." *College Literature*, vol. 26, no. 2, 1999, pp. 79–95.
———. "Shutting Up the Subaltern: Silences, Stereotypes, and Double-Entendre in Jean Rhys's *Wide Sargasso Sea*." *Callaloo*, vol. 22, no. 4, 1999, pp. 1071–90.
Marshall, Emily. "'The Anansi Syndrome': A Debate Concerning Anansi's Influence on Jamaican Culture." *World Literature Written in English*, vol. 39, no. 1, 2001, pp. 127–36.
Marshall, Paule. "British Guiana." In *Soul Clap Hands and Sing*. 1961. Howard UP, 1988, 65–127.
———. *Brown Girl, Brownstones*. 1959. Dover, 2009.
———. *The Chosen Place, the Timeless People*. New York: Vintage, 1992.
———. *Praisesong for the Widow*. Plume, 1983.
Marston, Kendra. "English Ladies to Liberators? How *Pirates of the Caribbean* and *Alice in Wonderland* Mobilize Aristocratic White Femininity." *Jump Cut* 54, 2012, www.ejumpcut.org/archive/jc54.2012/MarstonWhWomenRace/index.html.
Martínez-Vergne, Teresita, and Franklin W. Knight. "Introduction." In Knight and Martínez-Vergne, pp. 5–11.

Marx, Karl. *Capital*. 1867. Edited by Friedrich Engels. Great Books of the Western World. Encyclopedia Britannica, 1994.
Maynard, Jessica. "'Too Much Blue, Too Much Purple, Too Much Green': Reading *Wide Sargasso Sea* in the Sixties." *Jean Rhys Review*, vol. 11, no. 2, 2001, pp. 71–90.
McBain, Helen. "Challenges to Caribbean Economies in the Era of Globalization." In Knight and Martínez-Vergne, pp. 17–42.
McCarron, Kevin. "Alcoholism as Metaphor in William Golding's *The Paper Men*." In Vice et al., pp. 275–82.
McCauley, Diana. *Huracan*. Peepal Tree, 2012.
McClintock, Anne. "The Angel of Progress: Pitfalls of the Term 'Post-colonialism.'" *Social Text*, nos. 31–32, 1992, pp. 84–98. Reprinted in *Colonial Discourse and Post-Colonial Theory*, edited by Patrick Williams and Laura Chrisman. Columbia UP, 1994, pp. 291–304.
McFadden, David. "US Rum Binge Giving Caribbean Distillers a Headache." NBC News, 10 Sept. 2012, www.nbcnews.com/business/markets/us-rum-binge-giving-caribbean-distillers-headache-flna990935.
McGarrity, Maria. "The 'Indecent Postures' of Island Cricket: James Joyce's *A Portrait of the Artist as a Young Man* and Joseph O'Neill's *Netherland*." *James Joyce Quarterly*, vol. 52, nos. 3–4, Spring/Summer 2015, pp. 575–92.
McNeil, Elizabeth. "The Gullah Seeker's Journey in *Praisesong for the Widow*." *MELUS*, vol. 34, no. 1, 2009, pp. 185–209.
Mead, Walter Russell. "Rum and Coca-Cola: The United States and the New Cuba." *World Policy Journal*, vol. 12, no. 3, Fall 1995, pp. 29–53.
"Mean-Spirited and Modern." *Times of London*, 18 Dec. 1969, p. 9.
Merry, Robert. "The Slaves: An Elegy." 1788. In Richardson, pp. 101–2.
Mezei, Kathy. "'And It Kept its Secret': Narration, Memory, and Madness in Jean Rhys's *Wide Sargasso Sea*." *Critique*, 1987, pp. 195–209.
Midgeley, Claire. *Women against Slavery: The British Campaigns, 1780–1870*. Routledge, 1992.
Mitchell, Tim. *Intoxicated Identities: Alcohol's Power in Mexican History and Culture*. Taylor & Francis, 2004.
Mintz, Sidney. *Sweetness and Power*. Penguin, 1985.
Mischke, Dennis. "'It's Not Cricket': Financial Time and Postcolonial Temporalities in Joseph O'Neill's *Netherland*." *Finance and Society*, vol. 4, no. 1, 2018, pp. 92–107.
Mohanty, Chandra Talpade. "'Under Western Eyes' Revisited: Feminist Solidarity Through Anticapitalist Struggles." *Signs*, vol. 28, no. 2, Winter 2003, pp. 499–535.
Moore, Brian L., and Michele A. Johnson. "'Drunk and Disorderly': Alcoholism and the Search for 'Morality' in Jamaica, 1865–1920." *Journal of Caribbean History*, vol. 42, no. 2, 2008, pp. 155–86.
Moore, Christopher. *Fluke*. HarperCollins, 2003.

Moore, Richard. "'We Are a Modern Navy': Abolishing the Royal Navy's Rum Ration." *Mariner's Mirror,* vol. 103, no. 1, 2017, pp. 67–79.

Morrison, Toni. *A Mercy.* Knopf, 2008.

Morton, Timothy. *The Poetics of Spice: Romantic Consumerism and the Exotic.* Cambridge UP, 2000.

Moutet, J. P., et al. "Alcohol Consumption in Guadeloupe." *Alcohol and Alcoholism,* vol. 1, no. 24, 1989, pp. 55–61.

Munro, Jenny. "Denis, Caven, Fassbinder: Reading Performance Intertextuality in *35 rhums.*" *Studies in French Cinema,* vol. 13, no. 1, 2012, pp. 61–74.

Nadelhaft, Jerome. "Alcohol and Wife Abuse in Antebellum Male Temperance Literature." *Canadian Review of American Studies,* vol. 25, no. 1, 1995, pp. 15–44.

Naipaul, V. S. *Between Father and Son: Family Letters.* Edited by Gillon Aitken. Knopf, 2000.

———. *The Middle Passage: The Caribbean Revisited.* 1962. Vintage, 1990.

———. *Miguel Street.* 1959. Vintage, 1997.

———. "Without a Dog's Chance." Review of *After Leaving Mr. Mackenzie,* by Jean Rhys. *New York Review of Books,* 18 May 1972, www.nybooks.com/articles/1972/05/18/without-a-dogs-chance/.

Nair, Supriya. *Caliban's Curse.* U of Michigan P, 1996.

———. "Expressive Countercultures and Postmodern Utopia: A Caribbean Context." *Research in African Literatures,* vol. 27, no. 4, 1996, pp. 71–87.

———. "The Novel and Decolonization in the Caribbean." In Gikandi, pp. 55–68.

Nardin, Jane. "'As Soon As I Sober Up I Start Again': Alcohol and the Will in Jean Rhys's Pre-War Novels." *Papers on Language and Literature,* vol. 42, no. 1, 2006, pp. 46–72.

Nash, June. "Consuming Interests: Water, Rum, and Coca-Cola from Ritual Propitiation to Corporate Expropriation in Highland Chiapas." *Cultural Anthropology,* vol. 22, no. 4, 2007, pp. 621–39.

Neptune, Harvey R. *Caliban and the Yankees: Trinidad and the United States Occupation.* U of North Carolina P, 2007.

Nesbitt, Jennifer Poulos. "Rum: A Case Study for Teaching Material Culture in the Anglophone Caribbean Text." *Teaching Anglophone Caribbean Literature,* edited by Supriya Nair. MLA, 2012, 279–91.

———. "Rum Histories: Decolonizing the Narratives of Jean Rhys's *Wide Sargasso Sea* and Sylvia Townsend Warner's *The Flint Anchor.*" *Tulsa Studies in Women's Literature,* vol. 26, no. 2, Fall 2007, pp. 309–30.

———. "'Sharing a Worldliness of Austerity': Sylvia Townsend Warner and Jane Austen." *Journal of the Sylvia Townsend Warner Society,* 2002, pp. 27–38.

Ngũgĩ wa Thiong'o. *Decolonising the Mind.* Heinemann, 1986.

Nicholls, James. *The Politics of Alcohol: A History of the Drink Question in England.* Manchester UP, 2009.

Nicholson, Mervyn. "Gertrude's Poison Cup: Entering the Unknown World." *LIT,* vol. 8, 1997, pp. 1–21.

Nixon, Rob. "Caribbean and African Appropriations of *The Tempest*." *Critical Inquiry*, vol. 13, no. 3, Spring 1987, pp. 557–78.
Noland, Carrie. *Agency and Embodiment: Performing Gestures/Producing Culture*. Harvard UP, 2009.
———. *Voices of Negritude in Modernist Print: Aesthetic Subjectivity, Diaspora, and the Lyric Regime*. Columbia UP, 2014.
Olmstead, Jane. "The Pull to Memory and the Language of Place in Paule Marshall's *The Chosen Place, the Timeless People*." *African American Review*, vol. 31, no. 2, 1997, pp. 249–67.
125 Years of Sharing Happiness: A Short History of Coca-Cola. Coca-Cola, 2011.
O'Neill, Joseph. *Netherland*. Vintage, 2008.
Osborn, Matthew Warner. *Rum Maniacs: Alcoholic Insanity in the Early American Republic*. U of Chicago P, 2014.
Owens, Joyce Pettis. *Toward Wholeness in Paule Marshall's Fiction*. U of Virginia P, 1995.
Paravisini-Gebert, Lizabeth. *Phyllis Shand Allfrey: A Caribbean Life*. Rutgers UP, 1996.
Parsad, Nasmat Shiw. "Marital Violence Within East Indian Households in Guyana: A Cultural Explanation." In Kanhai, pp. 40–61.
Perham, Margery. "The Colonial Dilemma." *Listener*, 14 Jul. 1949, pp. 51–52, 67.
Perkin, Joan. *Women and Marriage in Nineteenth-Century England*. Lyceum, 1989.
Petersen, Anne. "'You Believe in Pirates, Of Course . . .': Disney's Commodification and 'Closure' vs. Johnny Depp's Aesthetic Piracy in *Pirates of the Caribbean*." *Studies in Popular Culture*, vol. 29, no. 2, Apr. 2007, pp. 63–81.
Pirates of the Caribbean: At World's End. Directed by Gore Verbinski. Walt Disney Pictures, 2007.
Pirates of the Caribbean: The Curse of the Black Pearl. Directed by Gore Verbinski. Walt Disney Pictures, 2003.
Pirates of the Caribbean: Dead Man's Chest. Directed by Gore Verbinski. Walt Disney Pictures, 2006.
Pirates of the Caribbean: Dead Men Tell No Tales. Directed by Joachim Rønning and Espen Sandberg. Walt Disney Pictures, 2017.
Pirates of the Caribbean: On Stranger Tides. Directed by Rob Marshall. Walt Disney Pictures, 2011.
Pittmann, Cynthia S. "Silent Talking: Agency and Voice in V. S. Naipaul's *Miguel Street*." *Torre*, vol. 11, nos. 41–42, 2006, pp. 365–76.
Plant, Martin, and Moira Plant. *Binge Britain: Alcohol and the National Response*. Oxford UP, 2006.
Plant, Moira. *Women and Alcohol: Contemporary and Historical Perspectives*. Free Association, 1997.
Plasa, Carl. *Slaves to Sweetness: British and Caribbean Literatures of Sugar*. Liverpool UP, 2009.

Potocki, Beata. "'Apocalypso': Visions of Cosmopolitanism in Michelle Cliff's Fiction." *Global South,* vol. 7, no. 2, Fall 2013, pp. 62–86.

Pringle, Thomas. "Slavery." 1823. In Richardson et al., p. 343.

Pyne, Hnin Hnin, Mariam Claeson, and Maria Correia. *Gender Dimensions of Alcohol Consumption and Alcohol-Related Problems in Latin America and the Caribbean.* World Bank, 2002.

Rabinovitch, Dina, and Anthony Quinn. "The Booker: Two for the Prize of One." *Independent,* 15 Oct. 1992, p. 17.

Radowitz, Jon. "Scientists Discover 'Drunk' Gene." *Independent,* 20 Oct. 2010, www.independent.co.uk/news/science/scientists-discover-drunk-gene-2111583.html.

Raiskin, Judith L. *Snow on the Cane Fields: Women's Writing and Creole Subjectivity.* U of Minnesota P, 1996.

Ramamurthy, Priti. "Why Is Buying a 'Madras' Cotton Shirt a Political Act? A Feminist Commodity Chain Analysis." *Feminist Studies,* vol. 30, no. 3, Fall 2004, pp. 734–69.

Ramchand, Kenneth. *The West Indian Novel and Its Background.* 2nd ed., Faber, 1970.

Ratcliffe, Krista. "A Rhetoric of Classroom Denial: Resisting Resistance to Alcohol Questions While Teaching Louise Erdrich's *Love Medicine.*" In Lilienfeld and Oxford, pp. 105–21.

Rediker, Marcus. Review of *Rum, Sodomy, and the Lash: Piracy, Sexuality, and Masculine Identity,* by Hans Turley. *Journal of Social History,* vol. 35, no. 1, 2001, pp. 213–15.

Reynolds, David, and Debra Rosenthal. *The Serpent in the Cup: Temperance in American Literature.* U of Massachusetts P, 1997.

Rhys, Jean. "Mixing Cocktails." *Tigers Are Better-Looking.* Popular Library, 1976, pp. 187–90.

———. "Temps Perdi." In *The Collected Short Stories.* Norton, 1987, pp. 256–74.

———. *Wide Sargasso Sea.* Norton, 1966.

Richardson, Alan, editor. *Slavery, Abolition, and Emancipation: Writings in the British Romantic Period.* Vol. 4, Pickering & Chatto, 1999.

Ridlon, Florence V. *A Fallen Angel: The Status Insularity of the Female Alcoholic.* Associated UP, 1988.

Robbins, Bruce. "Commodity Histories." *PMLA,* vol. 102, no. 2, 2005, pp. 454–63.

Roberts, Brian Russell, and Michelle Ann Stephens, editors. *Archipelagic American Studies.* Duke UP, 2017.

Robinson, James E. "Caribbean Caliban: Shifting the 'I' of the Storm." *Comparative Drama,* vol. 33, no. 4, 1999–2000, pp. 431–53.

Rogers, Susan. "Embodying Cultural Memory in Paule Marshall's *Praisesong for the Widow.*" *African American Review,* vol. 34, no. 1, 2000, pp. 77–93.

Rogoziński, Jan. *A Brief History of the Caribbean.* Facts on File, 1992.
Rolando, Sara, Gabriella Taddeo, and Franca Beccaria. "New Media and Old Stereotypes: Images and Discourses About Drunk Women and Men on YouTube." *Journal of Gender Studies,* vol. 25, no. 5, 2015, pp. 492–506.
Room, Robin. "Foreword." In Bennett and Ames, pp. xi–xvii.
———. "Intoxication and Bad Behavior: Understanding Cultural Differences in the Link." *Social Science & Medicine,* vol. 53, no. 2, 2001, pp. 189–98.
Rorabaugh, W. J. *The Alcoholic Republic: An American Tradition.* Oxford UP, 1979.
Rose, Charlie. Interview with Hunter S. Thompson. *Charlie Rose,* PBS, 30 Oct. 1998.
Ross, Jacob. "Rum an Coke." *The Peepal Tree Book of Contemporary Caribbean Short Stories,* edited by Jacob Ross and Jeremy Poynting. Peepal Tree, 2018, pp. 402–16.
Roth, Marty. *Drunk the Night Before: An Anatomy of Intoxication.* U of Minnesota P, 2005.
Rotskoff, Lori. *Love on the Rocks: Men, Women, and Alcohol in Post–World War II America.* U of North Carolina P, 2002.
Royer, Michelle, and Miriam Thompson. "Mobility and Exile in Claire Denis's *35 rhums.*" *Open Roads, Closed Borders: The Contemporary French-Language Road Movie,* edited by Michael Gott and Thibaut Schilt. Intellect Books, 2012, pp. 189–201.
"Rum." Oxford English Dictionary Online. https://oed.com.
"Rum Sales Soar Thanks to *Pirates of the Caribbean* Films." *Daily Mail,* 3 Dec. 2007, www.dailymail.co.uk/news/article-499437/Rum-sales-soar-thanks-Pirates-Caribbean-films.html.
Said, Edward. *Orientalism.* Vintage, 1987.
Sandiford, Keith. *The Cultural Politics of Sugar: Caribbean Slavery and Narratives of Colonialism.* Cambridge UP, 2000.
———. "Paule Marshall's *Praisesong for the Widow*: The Reluctant Heiress, or Whose Life Is It Anyway?" *Black American Literature Forum,* vol. 20, no. 4, 1986, pp. 371–92.
———. *Theorizing a Colonial Caribbean-Atlantic Imaginary: Sugar and Obeah.* Routledge, 2011.
Sandkamp, Alexander, and Shuyao Yang. "Where Has the Rum Gone? Firms' Choice of Transport Mode under the Threat of Maritime Piracy." ifo Working Papers 271, Oct. 2018, Leibniz Institute for Economic Research, University of Munich.
Sandmaier, Marian. *The Invisible Alcoholics: Women and Alcohol.* 2nd ed., Human Services Institute, 1992.
Sanger, David E., and Maggie Haberman. "Transcript: Donald Trump Expounds on his Foreign Policy Views." *New York Times,* 26 Mar. 2016, www.nytimes.com/2016/03/27/us/politics/donald-trump-transcript.html.

Saunders, Charles R. "Why Blacks Should Read (and Write) Science Fiction." *Dark Matter: A Century of Speculative Fiction from the African Diaspora*, edited by Sheree R. Thomas. Warner, 2000, pp. 398–404.

Savory, Elaine. "Generations in Jamaica." Review of *Huracan*, by Diana McCauley. *Caribbean Writer*, vol. 27, 2013, pp. 308–11.

Schivelbusch, Wolfgang. *Tastes of Paradise: A Social History of Spices, Stimulants, and Intoxicants*. Vintage, 1993.

Scott, David. *Conscripts of Modernity: The Tragedy of Colonial Enlightenment*. Duke UP, 2004.

Seaman, Donna. Review of *The Rum Diary*, by Hunter S. Thompson. *Booklist*, 15 Sept. 1998, p. 173.

Sedgwick, Eve Kosofsky. "Paranoid Reading and Reparative Reading, or, You're So Paranoid, You Probably Think This Essay Is About You." *Touching Feeling*. Duke UP, 2002, pp. 123–51.

Sethuraman, Ramchandran. "Evidence-cum-Witness: Subaltern History, Violence, and the (De)formation of Nation in Michelle Cliff's *No Telephone to Heaven*." *Modern Fiction Studies*, vol. 43, no. 1, 1997, pp. 249–79.

Sheller, Mimi. *Consuming the Caribbean: From Arawaks to Zombies*. Routledge, 2003.

Shepherd, Verene A. "Introduction." *Slavery without Sugar*, edited by Verene A. Shepherd. U of Florida P, 2002, pp. 1–18.

Sheridan, Richard B. *Sugar and Slavery*. Johns Hopkins UP, 1974.

Sisk, John P. "The Late Demon Rum." Review of *The Life and Times of the Late Demon Rum*, by J. C. Furnas. *Commonweal*, vol. 82, no. 4, 16 Apr. 1965, pp. 113–16.

Smith, Carissa Turner. "Women's Spiritual Geographies of the African Diaspora: Paule Marshall's *Praisesong for the Widow*." *African American Review*, vol. 42, nos. 3–4, 2008, pp. 715–29.

Smith, Frederick. *Caribbean Rum*. UP of Florida, 2005.

Smith, Robert Freeman. *The Caribbean World and the United States: Mixing Rum and Coca-Cola*. Twayne, 1994.

"Social and Cultural Aspects of Drinking." Social Issues Research Centre (SIRC), www.sirc.org/publik/drinking3.html. Accessed 11 Jan. 2021.

Soderlund, Eric. Conclusion. *Mass Media and Foreign Policy: Post-Cold War Crises in the Caribbean*. Praeger, 2003, pp. 155–66.

Southey, Robert. "Sonnet III." 1797. In Richardson, p. 244.

Spivak, Gayatri Chakravorty. "Three Women's Texts and a Critique of Imperialism." *Feminisms*, edited by Robyn R. Warhol and Diane Price Herndl. Rev. ed., Rutgers UP, 1997, pp. 896–912.

Stahl, Kathleen M. *The Metropolitan Organization of British Colonial Trade*. Faber & Faber, 1951.

Steinberg, Sybil S. Review of *The Rum Diary*, by Hunter S. Thompson. *Publishers Weekly*, 21 Sept. 1998, pp. 71–72.

Steinhoff, Heike. "Gender, Sexuality, Nationality, and the Pirate as Mobile Signifier in *Captain Blood, Anne of the Indies, Cutthroat Island,* and *Pirates of the Caribbean.*" *Pirates, Drifters, Fugitives: Figures of Mobility in the US and Beyond,* edited by Heike Paul, Alexandra Ganser, and Katharina Gerund. Universitätsverlag Winter, 2012, pp. 103–35.

Stephens, Michelle Ann. *Black Empire: The Masculine Global Imaginary of Caribbean Intellectuals in the United States, 1914–1962.* Duke UP, 2005.

Stevenson, Robert Louis. *Treasure Island.* 1883. Tor, 1993.

Stoute, Janet, and Kenneth Ifill. "The Rural Rum Shop." *Everyday Life in Barbados: A Sociological Perspective.* Leiden: Smits Drukkers-Uitgevers/Department of Caribbean Studies, Royal Institute of Linguistics and Anthropology, 1979, pp. 145–67.

Strachan, Ian Gregory. *Paradise and Plantation: Tourism and Culture in the Anglophone Caribbean.* U of Virginia P, 2002.

Stuelke, Patricia. "'Times When Greater Disciplines Are Born': The Zora Neale Hurston Revival and the Neoliberal Transformation of the Caribbean." *American Literature,* vol. 86, no. 1, 2014, pp. 117–45.

Sunshine, Catherine A. *The Caribbean: Survival, Struggle and Sovereignty.* EPICA, 1985.

Taussig, Charles William. *Rum, Romance, and Rebellion.* Minton, Balch. 1928.

35 Shots of Rum [*35 rhums*]. 2008. Directed by Claire Denis. Cinema Guild, 2010.

Thieme, John. "Calypso Allusions in *Miguel Street.*" *Kunapipi,* vol. 3, no. 2, 1981, pp. 18–32.

Thomas, Sue. *The Worlding of Jean Rhys.* Greenwood, 1999.

Thompson, Hunter S. *The Proud Highway: Saga of a Desperate Southern Gentleman, 1955–1967.* Edited by Douglas Brinkley. Villard, 1997.

———. *The Rum Diary.* Simon & Schuster, 1998.

Tiffin, Helen. "The Tyranny of History: George Lamming's *Natives of My Person* and *Water with Berries.*" *ARIEL,* vol. 10, no. 4, 1979, pp. 37–52.

Todd, Richard. *Consuming Fictions: The Booker Prize and Fiction in Britain Today.* Bloomsbury, 1996.

Toland-Dix, Shirley. "*The Hills of Hebron:* Sylvia Wynter's Disruption of the Narrative of the Nation." *Small Axe,* no. 25, Feb. 2008, pp. 57–76.

Underhill, Hal. *Jamaica White.* Macmillan, 1968.

Unsworth, Barry. *Sacred Hunger.* 1992. W. W. Norton, 1993.

———. *Sugar and Rum.* 1988. W. W. Norton, 1999.

Uraizee, Joya. "'She Walked Away Without Looking Back': Christophine and the Enigma of History in Jean Rhys's *Wide Sargasso Sea.*" *Clio,* vol. 28, no. 3, 1999, pp. 261–77.

Vaillant, George. *The Natural History of Alcoholism Revisited.* Harvard UP, 1995.

Van Neck-Yoder, Hilda. "Colonial Desires, Silence, and Metonymy: 'All things considered' in *Wide Sargasso Sea.*" *Texas Studies in Literature and Language,* vol. 40, no. 2, 1998, pp. 184–208.

Vice, Sue. "Love Stories: Women Who Drink in Modern and Contemporary Fiction." *A Babel of Bottles*, edited by James Nicholls and Susan J. Owen. Sheffield Academic, 2000, pp. 132–41.

Vice, Sue, Matthew Campbell, and Tim Armstrong, editors. *Beyond the Pleasure Dome: Writing and Addiction from the Romantics*. Sheffield Academic, 1994.

Wagner, Michael J. "Rum, Policy, and the Portuguese: Or, the Maintenance of Elite Supremacy in Post-Emancipation British Guiana." *Canadian Review of Sociology and Anthropology*, vol. 14, no. 4, 1977, pp. 406–16.

Walcott, Derek. *Omeros*. Noonday, 1992.

Waligora-Davis, Nicole. "'Myth of the Continents': American Vulnerabilities and 'Rum and Coca-Cola.'" In Roberts and Stephens, pp. 191–209.

Walters, Wendy. *At Home in Diaspora: Black International Writing*. U of Minnesota P, 2005.

Warf, Barney. "High Points: An Historical Geography of Cannabis." *Geographical Review*, vol. 104, no. 4, Oct. 2014, pp. 414–38.

Warner, Marina. *Indigo; or, Mapping the Waters*. Simon & Schuster, 1992.

Warner, Nicholas O. *Spirits of America: Intoxication in Nineteenth-Century American Literature*. U of Oklahoma P, 1997.

Warner, Sylvia Townsend. *The Flint Anchor*. Viking, 1954.

Waters, Anita M. "*Pirates of the Caribbean*: Which Version Should We Be Listening To?" *Anthropology News*, Oct. 2006, 17–18.

Waterson, Jan. *Women and Alcohol in Social Context: Mother's Ruin Revisited*. Palgrave, 2000.

Watts, Thomas, and Roosevelt Wright, editors. *Alcoholism in Minority Populations*. Thomas, 1989.

Waywell, Nicholas. "Mapping a Prefab Paradise." Review of *The Rum Diary*, by Hunter S. Thompson. *Spectator*, 14 Nov. 1998, pp. 43–44.

Wedge, George. "Alcohol as Symptom: The Life and Works of Jean Rhys." *Dionysos*, vol. 8, no. 1, Winter 1998, pp. 23–33.

West, Joel. "Ideologemes and Resistance Narrative in Michelle Cliff's *No Telephone to Heaven*." lostbeatblank: The Writing and Scholarship of Joel West, 28 Apr. 2014, www.lostbeatblank.com/blog/ideologemes-and-resistance-narrative-in-michelle-cliff-s-no-telephone-to-heaven.

Westall, Claire. "Cricket and the World-System, or Continuity, 'Riskless Risk,' and Cyclicality in Joseph O'Neill's *Netherland*." *Journal of Postcolonial Writing*, vol. 52, no. 3, 2016, pp. 287–300.

———. "Men in the Yard and On the Street: Cricket and Calypso in *Moon on a Rainbow* and *Miguel Street*." *Anthurium*, vol. 3, no. 2, 2005, pp. 1–14.

Wilder, Gary. *Freedom Time: Negritude, Decolonization, and the Future of the World*. Duke UP, 2015.

Williams, Eric. *Capitalism and Slavery*. 1944. U of North Carolina P, 1994.

Williams, Gwylmor Prys, and George Thompson Brake. *Drink in Great Britain, 1900–1979*. Edsall, 1980.

Williams, Ian. *Rum: A Social and Sociable History of the Real Spirit of 1776.* Nation, 2005.
Williams, James S. "Romancing the Father in Claire Denis's *35 Shots of Rum.*" *Film Quarterly,* vol. 63, no. 2, Winter 2009–10, pp. 44–50.
Wilson, Lucy. "'Women Must Have Spunks': Jean Rhys's West Indian Outcasts." *Modern Fiction Studies,* vol. 32, no. 3, 1986, pp. 439–48.
Wilson, Peter J. *Crab Antics: The Social Anthropology of English-Speaking Negro Societies of the Caribbean.* Yale UP, 1973.
Wilson, Thomas. *Drinking Cultures: Alcohol and Identity.* Berg, 2005.
Wittig-Wells, Deborah. "Perceptions of Native United States Virgin Island Residents Regarding Older Women Who Drink Too Much." *Journal of Multicultural Nursing & Health,* vol. 13, no. 1, 2007, pp. 28–36.
Wondrich, David. *Punch: The Delights (and Dangers) of the Flowing Bowl.* Perigee, 2010.
Wouk, Herman. *Don't Stop the Carnival.* Doubleday, 1965.
Wynter, Sylvia. *The Hills of Hebron.* Simon & Schuster, 1962.
Yanique, Tiphanie. *Land of Love and Drowning.* Riverhead, 2014.
Yawney, Carole. "Drinking Patterns and Alcoholism in Trinidad." *Beliefs, Behaviors, and Alcoholic Beverages: A Cross-Cultural Survey,* edited by Mac Marshall. U of Michigan P, 1979, pp. 94–107.
Yolen, Jane. Foreword. In Stevenson, pp. xiii–xv.
Zeiger, Susan. *Inventing the Addict: Drugs, Race, and Sexuality in Nineteenth-Century British and American Literature.* U of Massachusetts P, 2008.
Zeitlin, Virginia M., and Svjetlana Curcic. "Parental Voices on Individualized Education Programs: 'Oh, IEP Meeting Tomorrow? Rum Tonight!'" *Disability and Society,* vol. 29, no. 3, 2014, pp. 373–87.

Index

Page numbers in italics refer to illustrations.

AA (Alcoholics Anonymous), 157n28, 160n36
abolition movement: boycotts of rum and sugar, 7–8, 88, 150; enslaved laborers' body parts and fluids contained in rum and sugar ("blood sugar"), claims of, 22, 24, 116; in Rhys's *Wide Sargasso Sea*, 83, 93; temperance movement in relation to, 12–13, 43; in Warner's *The Flint Anchor*, 88, 93
abstinence, 11
accountability, 5, 127, 148
Ackland, Valentine, alcoholism of, 168n2
Adler, Marianna, 161n40
adventure: association with rum, 41; masculinity and, 147
Africa: Caribbean as avatar for, 132; International Monetary Fund and, 136; Lovelace's *While Gods Are Falling* and, 104; precolonial African past in Marshall's *Praisesong*, 119, 131, 132, 140, 174n9; temperance rhetoric and, 157n26
African Americans: drinking stereotypes and, 159–60n33; in Marshall's *Praisesong*, 127, 130; obesity rates of, 26. *See also* enslavement and enslaved people
African drinking customs, 6, 100, 102
African slave traders, 6–7, 155n13
agency, 22, 23, 154n9, 161n43; class stereotype vs., 105; drinking and, 16–17, 20, 27, 33; of freed enslaved person, 11, 85; questioning white agency, 90, 143, 146; of racialized others, 90, 94–96, 105; renewed agency in Marshall's *Praisesong*, 130–32; of women, 36, 50, 64–65, 70–71, 90, 93–94, 96, 143, 146
Alcoholics Anonymous (AA), 157n28, 160n36
alcoholism: of authors, 20–21, 168n2; classism of, 67; in Cliff's *Abeng*, 134; considered taboo to discuss, 21, 140; defining, 67, 158n30, 160n36; as "disease of the will," 13–14, 16, 66; economic effects of, 12, 160n34; gender and, 15, 67, 158n32, 159n33; geographic location as factor in, 57, 71; in Kanhai's "Rum Sweet Rum," 96; medical or disease model, 13–17, 66–67, 96, 140; in Naipaul's *Miguel Street*, 66–72; in postcolonial literature, 21; research into, 15, 158nn29–31; rum drinking as leading to, 26–27; shame and stigma associated with, 1, 15, 20, 27, 67; as social problem, 12, 14–15, 158n31; teaching alcoholism in fiction, 140; therapy for, 67; in Thompson's *The Rum Diary*, 66–72; as white noise in literature, 20–21, 71. *See also* drinking and drunkenness; stigma of alcoholism
alcoholism research, 2; Black usage and, 159n33; disclaimers by scholars in, 158n29; marginalization of, 158n29; "rum" used in title instead of "alcohol" to attract readers, 2, 153n3
Allen, H. Warner: *Rum*, 41–44, 153n1, 162n4

Allfrey, Phyllis Shand: autobiographical nature of writing of, 162n10, 163n12; *The Orchid House,* 46–49, 79, 102, 162n10
Ambler, Charles, 157n26
Amsterdam, Morey, 45, 170n20
Anancy, 170n21
Andrews Sisters: "Rum and Coca-Cola," 45, 98, 99, 170n20
Anglophone literature: bias of texts, 2; colonial texts compared to contemporary writers, 23; priority given to, 151
Antigua, lack of artists in, 56, 57
Appadurai, Arjun, 19
Archipelagic studies, 3, 40
Atlantic studies, 3
Australia, Aboriginal society in, 14
authors with excessive drinking habits, 20–21, 168n2

Bacardi, 46, 149
Banco, Lindsey Michael, 158n29
Barbados: alcohol consumption in, 12, 159n32, 160nn34–35; immigrant community in Brooklyn, 120; immigrant community in Toronto, 166n13; sexual exploitation and stereotyping in, 38, 120
Barnes, Natasha, 111
Baucom, Ian: *Out of Place,* 172n7; *Specters of the Atlantic,* 4, 29–30, 149
Bazin, Nancy Topping, 21, 140
Beachey, R. W., 156n18
Beaubrun, M. H., 12, 157n28, 160n34
Bedward, Alexander, 109, 172n8
Benítez-Rojo, Antonio, 2, 23, 25, 39, 75
Bennett, Jane, 154n8
Benoit, Oliver, 171n2
Big Sugar (film), 26, 150
binge-drinking, 14–15
Black, George, 10
Black British writing, 33
Black men. *See* gender; men
Blacks (generally). *See* African Americans; race and ethnicity
Black women. *See* women
blood oaths, 24
Bonny, Anne, as female pirate, 116
Booker Prize, 55
Brana-Shute, Gary, 76
Britain: downplaying rum's roots in slavery, 41; gender and drinking norms in, 32; guilt of current English people for slavery's crimes, 52–53; homosexuality, cultural proscription against, 121; literary culture in, 51–52, 54, 164n19; Married Women's Property Act (1882), 168n1; metropolitanism of, 44; national identity, effect of slavery on, 163n18; racism in, 106–7; ritual alcohol use in, 102; whiskey as symbol of Englishness, 123. *See also* abolition movement; colonialism; decolonization; imperialism
British Guiana: domestic violence in, 170n18; rum trade used to suppress Creole population in, 15
"British Guiana" (Marshall), 120–22; compared to Rhys's *Wide Sargasso Sea,* 121; cross-caste relationality in, 121; homosexuality in, 120–22, 135; political action in, 121–22; reclamation of past in, 120–21; serial rape in, 173n3
British navy. *See* Royal Navy
Brontë, Charlotte: *Jane Eyre,* 79, 81–83, 86–87, 168nn4–5, 169n11, 177n5
Brown, Bill, 4–5, 20, 22, 154n8, 161n43
Brown, J. Dillon, 156n20, 164n19
Brown, John, 115
Brown, Susan, 50–51
Brown-Hinds, Paulette, 115
Burn, Andrew, 25
Burns, Eric, 42, 162n5
Bystrom, Kerry, 2

Caetano, Raul, 159n33
calypso, 45–46, 59, 162n7
Cane (television series), 161n45
capitalism, 10, 49–51, 58, 62, 75, 115, 128, 134–36, 143, 149, 161n42, 175n16
Carby, Hazel V., 170n21
Caribbean: alcohol-based hospitality in, 172n11; alcoholism associated with location of, 6, 57, 71; authors who reside in, 33; as avatar for Africa, 132; diversification of trade economies in, 156n18; domestication of landscape in, 25; economic effects of alcoholism on, 12, 160n34; film depictions of, 10–11, 145–50; imaginary of, 18, 28–29, 108, 113, 135; immorality depictions of, 36; interconnection with Pacific Island cultures, 39; neoliberal order in, 132; postwar image of, 10–11; racialized

sexual codes, 121; research into alcohol use and abuse in, 15, 160n34; rum's associations with, 2, 6–8, 13, 17, 27, 43; rum shops as male preserve in, 15, 25, 43–44, 76, 160n35, 175n15; rum's use at social events, 102; use of term, 153n4; US relationship with, 10–11, 13, 41, 46. *See also* colonialism; pirate culture; trade; West Indies; *specific islands*
Caribbean Basin Initiative, 10
Caribbean Community (CARICOM), 3
Caribbean Federation, 9, 122
Caribbean literary studies, 102
Caribbean Medical Journal, 12, 157n28
Carriacou, 126–32, 174n9
Chiapas, binge-drinking rituals of, 14–15
Chosen Place, the Timeless People, The (Marshall), 122–26; carnival time as "time-out," 124–26; commodity chain in, 123, 136, 174n7; compared to Rhys's *Wide Sargasso Sea*, 125; compared to Thompson's *The Rum Diary*, 126; compared to Wynter's *The Hills of Hebron*, 125; development projects of US-based organizations in, 122–23, 173n4; martini drinking in, 126; nightclub decor in, 124, 173n5; rum shop as male domain in, 175n15; rum vs. sugar in, 124–25; sugar associated with neocolonialist perspective in, 123–24; Sugar (nightclub owner) as subject in, 124, 173n6; whiskey vs. rum in, 123; white women in colonialism and, 147; women's drinking strictures in, 123
Christian, Barbara, 131, 175n13
Christmas, Annie, 115
civil rights movement, 99–100, 170n22
Clarke, Austin: "Griff!," 166n13; *The Polished Hoe*, 25, 122
classism: agency vs. class stereotype, 105; of alcoholism, 67; gin and working class, 86, 87–88, 169n13; in Kanhai's "Rum Sweet Rum," 94, 114; middle-class American values, 127, 129; money as interest of working class, 87; morals of working class, 30, 171n2; stereotypes in terms of drinking, 15, 158–59nn32–33; taverns and bars as sites for working-class political organizing, 171n2; in Warner's *The Flint Anchor*, 92; whiskey vs. rum and, 123; white wine and "white" middle-class America, 127

Cliff, Michelle, 33; *Abeng*, 132–34, 175nn14–15; compared to Marshall, 132, 135, 140, 175n14; compared to McCauley, 141; rum in works by, 118, 132. *See also Free Enterprise*; *No Telephone to Heaven*
Coates, Ta-Nehisi: *Between the World and Me*, 151
Coca-Cola, 123, 150, 170n23. *See also* rum and Coca-Cola metaphor
Cohen, Rich: "Sugar Love" (*National Geographic* article), 26
Cold War, 10, 150
colonialism: alcohol distribution as colonizing strategy, 14–15, 154n10, 155n16; alien women's experience in relation to male beneficiaries of, 80; black subalterns' silence and, 163n17; entrenched legacies and endurance of, 4, 23, 27, 105, 107, 113, 134, 137, 152, 157n22; French colonialism in Denis's *35 rhums* (film), 176n2; heteronormativity as function of, 121; historical fiction's consumption as reification of, 55; language of the colonizer, 4; metropole/periphery relationship, 38, 46–47; mimicking Englishness as legacy of, 105, 123; murderous present linked with violence against indigenous people in, 80, 115; in Naipaul's *The Middle Passage*, 44; rum as cipher for colonial past, 4, 11, 26, 43, 125, 140; tea as colonial commodity, 22; unity among Caribs, Africans, and Indians formed by, 104; white women's compliance in, 147. *See also* enslavement and enslaved people; neocolonial power; postcolonialism
commodity role of rum: in American Revolutionary times, 42; in Anglo-Atlantic culture, 17–20; double signification of term "rum," 4–6, 19–20; in empire, 1–2. *See also* trade
communism, 9–10, 27, 58
Conrad, Joseph: *Heart of Darkness*, 71
consumerism: commodity sagas and, 18; consumer identity and ethical issues, 19; in Marshall's *Praisesong*, 127–28; overcharging tourists, 137; in Warner's *The Flint Anchor*, 92–93. *See also* tourism
cosmopolitanism, 29, 32, 38, 75, 94, 172n12

Coughtry, Jay: *The Notorious Triangle*, 6
Coulombe, Charles, 45, 162n7; *The Epic History of the Drink That Conquered the World*, 18
Cowper, William: "Pity for Poor Africans" (poem), 19, 53, 137
Creoles: drinking and sexual behavior of, 81, 168n2, 169n7; in Marshall's *Praisesong*, 132; in Rhys's *Wide Sargasso Sea*, 81, 169n7; suppression in British Guiana through rum trade, 15; white Creoles' escape to United States, 48; white Creoles in relation to metropolis, 23, 47
Crichlow, Veronica, 164n3
Cruzan Rum, 149
Cuba: alcohol consumption in, 160n34; American tourism and, 46, 162n8; Cold War and, 10; Cuban rum and racism, 46; failed state narrative of, 9–10, 46; gender politics and national identity in, 23, 24–25; privilege of Americans in, 136; Teddy Roosevelt and, 124, 173n5; rum in Cuban detective fiction, 154n4; US imperialism and, 178n12
Cudjoe, Selwyn, 105
Curtis, Wayne, 162n7

Dabydeen, David: *The Counting House*, 155n17; "Introduction to *Slave Song*," 39
Dalleo, Raphael, 9, 157n22
Dann, Graham, 12, 159n32, 160n34
Danticat, Edwidge, 176n19
Dardis, Tom, 20–21
Darwin, John, 9
De Boissière, Jean: "With Me Rum in Me Head," 43–44
De Boissière, Ralph: *Rum and Coca-Cola*, 46
debts owed by Third World countries, 49–50, 145, 157n22
décalage, 161n43
decolonization, 3; in Allfrey's *The Orchid House*, 46–47; British efforts at, 42; in Cliff's *No Telephone to Heaven*, 119; in Marshall's *Praisesong*, 119; in Rhys's *Wide Sargasso Sea*, 79, 93; rum associated with sociopolitical conditions, 6, 9, 13; rum capturing colonization's legacies in, 23, 37, 113, 152; separation of colonial era from decolonized era, 32; shared historical context of England and West Indies after, 102; smaller colonies' poverty and, 9; in Warner's *The Flint Anchor*, 79, 93; women's empowerment and, 36. *See also* postcolonialism
Deere, Carmen Diana, 11
DeLoughrey, Elizabeth, 39
demon rum, use of term, 1–2, 17, 39, 43, 89, 153n2, 167n9
Denis, Claire: *35 rhums (35 Shots of Rum)* (film), 145–46, 176n2
detective fiction genre, 49–50, 163n14
disinhibition and drinking, 2, 16–17, 20, 35–41, 129, 133, 161nn37–38. *See also* drunken comportment
Disney. See *Pirates of the Caribbean*
Djos, Matts G., 157n28, 158n30, 160n36
Dominica, 1, 31, 47, 80, 163n10
Dominican Republic: alcohol consumption in, 160n34; American-owned sugar plantations in, 26, 150
Donnell, Allison, 72
Döring, Tobias, 23, 24–25, 27, 44, 122
Dreisinger, Baz: "On a Tropical Rum Trail" (*New York Times* essay), 28, 28–29
drinking and drunkenness: anthropological studies of, 2, 13–16, 35, 155n11; associated with Caribbean, 6, 29, 35, 172n11; cultural importance of, 20, 102, 174n11; "dysfunctional drinking" model, 14, 106; as escape from everyday life, 6, 16; historical implications repressed through, 16–17; power and agency in, 16–17, 20; research on gender and racial differences in, 15, 159n33; taverns and bars as sites of working-class political organizing, 171n2; tourist bars and drinks, 135–36; water as unsafe to drink connected to, 6. *See also* alcoholism; disinhibition and drinking; drunken comportment; gender; stigma of alcoholism; "time-out"
drinking rituals and toasts, 18, 59–66; funeral libations in Cliff's *Abeng*, 132–33; oath drinks based on African cultural traditions, 6, 102; pirate toast in Cliff's *Free Enterprise*, 115; refusal in Wynter's *The Hills of Hebron*, 112;

transformative ritual in Marshall's *Praisesong*, 118
Drowne, Kathleen, 162n5
drugs: addiction, 47, 158n30; sexual exploitation and, 36, 173n3; social problem model limitations, 158n29; superseding rum, 4, 26, 72–74, 135–36, 150; war on drugs, 136, 167n19. *See also* marijuana
drunken comportment: definition of, 16–17; in literary study, 20–22, 106; modeled by Englishmen, 42; in Naipaul's *Miguel Street*, 61, 69; Native Americans and, 162n2; positive vs. negative consequences of, 161n42; in Thompson's *The Rum Diary*, 62–64. *See also* disinhibition and drinking
Dubois, Laurent, 9
Duggan, Lisa, 157n25
Dunick, Lisa, 172n12
Duras, Marguerite, 21

East India Company, 149
Edmondson, Belinda, 36, 164n3
Edwards, Brent Hayes, 154n9, 161n43
ekphrasis, 93
Elia, Nada, 138
Eliot, T. S.: "Preludes," 129
Engels, Friedrich, 19
England. *See* Britain
enslavement and enslaved people: alcohol use among enslaved people, 102, 171n2; Black women as doubly oppressed by production and reproduction, 139; in Cliff's *Free Enterprise*, 115–16; colonial era texts' views of, 25; commodities produced by, acknowledgment of, 2, 19; comparison to Holocaust, 53; dangers of rum/sugar production, 22, 29, 116; disinhibition of rum consumption and, 35; excessive rum drinking as generational effects of, 132, 134; guilt of current English people for slavery's crimes, 52–53; legacy in alcohol use, 39, 133; logbook of slave ship, 29–30; in Naipaul's *The Middle Passage*, 44; obesity rates of African Americans linked to, 26; persistence in postemanicpation sugar production, 15, 26, 150; postcolonial England and, 163n18; postcolonial existence premised on, 38, 52, 129–30; rum associations with Caribbean plantation slavery, 1, 5, 6–8, 13, 24, 36, 43; sexual violence and, 25, 35–36; sugar as economic base of, 23, 25–26; trading rum for human beings, 6–7, 19, 30, 43; transition to freedom, 11
Erdrich, Louise: *Love Medicine*, 21
eroticism: postcolonialism and, 55; racist stereotypes of, 65; violence and, 2, 35–41, 98–99. *See also* homoeroticism; pornography
Esty, Jed, 173n4
ethical issues, 5, 18–19, 22, 140, 144, 152
Europe: Caribbean colonies of, 153n4; Caribbean involvement in power struggles of, 173n5; drinking patterns of, 6, 64; patriarchy of, 98, 134. *See also* colonialism; imperialism; trade
exoticism: nature of rum and, 2; obeah potion and, 86; postcolonialism and, 55

failure: drinking to compensate for, 57, 120–21; fear of, 161n42
Fanjul brothers, 150
Fanon, Frantz, 22, 171n3, 176n2; *Black Skin, White Masks*, 105; "On National Culture," 103–5
feminism, 5, 49–52, 147–48, 163n13, 167n1, 174n11
film industry, 10, 55, 119, 136–37, 145, 175n17
Flint Anchor, The (Warner), 32, 79, 88–93; civilizing mission in, 90; compared to Rhys's *Wide Sargasso Sea*, 92; Darwell's alcoholism in, 91–92; female consumption in, 89, 92; gender and racial oppression under British imperialism, 80–81; Julia Barnard's rejection of white female privilege, 92; Mary as imperial consumer in, 92–93; mocking rejoinders of rum, 88–93; morality vs. economics in, 88–89; patriarchal power in, 92; temperance rhetoric in, 81, 92; women's moral inferiority in, 89
Fluke (Moore), 39–40, 136, 151
Fodor's Guide to the Caribbean, Bahamas, and Bermuda (1960), 17
folk culture, 101, 170n21
food culture, 37, 161n44, 162n1
Foucault, Michel, 119
Francophone texts, 151, 154n4

Free Enterprise (Cliff), 114–17; bottle tree imagery in, 115, 172n13; Caribs and Arawaks in, 116; critical analysis of, 115; fictional rewriting of national histories, 114, 115, 172n12; free market capitalism in both slave trade and enterprises of freedom in, 115; HIV/AIDS crisis and, 115–16, 172n14; pirate operation of Captain Parsons, 115; queerness and Captain Parsons in, 115–16, 121; rum in, 118, 132; sexual and racial oppression in, 116; silencing of queer trauma in, 117; tavern scene and libations in, 117
French, Patrick, 74
Friedman, Susan Stanford: *Planetary Modernisms*, 30–31
future, the: anxiety and panic produced by postcolonial future, 1, 4, 5; confronting cost of imagined postcolonial subjectivity, 139–40; difficulty of finding alternative routes for postcolonial future, 113, 122; hope for future of grassroots political community, 114–15; lost potential for, 114; nostalgia for imperial future, 46; postcolonial future's existence in the present because of colonial past, 54; speculation about what the future can look like, 33, 119, 122; sugar uses in, 161n45; transformed by Global South's potential, 151; Trump's imperialism and, 150

Galt, Rosalind, 176n2
Garvey, Johanna X. K., 172n13
gender: Cuba, gender politics in, 24; drinking norms and, 15, 21, 32, 79, 158n32; pirates, women as, 116–17; research into drinking and, 15, 159n33; rum and alcoholic beverages coded through, 25; rum shops as masculine domains, 15, 25, 43–44, 76, 160n35, 175n15; transgender woman as "battyman," 134–35. *See also* feminism; men; patriarchy; sexism; women
Gernalzick, Nadja, 23, 26
Gikandi, Simon, 113
Gilmore, Thomas, 20–21
Gilroy, Paul, 2
gin: as drink of the working class, 86, 87–88, 169n13; as unhealthy, 41, 44
Gladstone, William, 53

Glissant, Edouard, 21, 152; *Poetics of Relation*, 5
globalization, 3, 32, 38, 156n21; immigrants from Puerto Rico to New York and, 60; Marshall's *Praisesong* and, 119; O'Neill's *Netherland* and, 74–75; in *Pirates of the Caribbean* (film), 149; reach of rum and, 1, 8, 18, 19, 39; sugar and, 26; transnational resistance to, 50–51
Global South, 2–4, 23, 26, 32, 81, 93, 97, 151
Goodall, Jamie, 175n15
Grainger, James, 155n14
Gregg, Veronica Marie, 170n16
Grenada, 10, 130–31
Guadeloupe: references in *35 rhums*, 176n2; study of alcohol consumption in, 159n32, 160n34
Guillén, Nicolás, 25, 122
Günther, Renate, 21

Haiti: alcohol consumption in, 160n34; endurance of colonial past, 157n22; executive privilege of Americans in, 136; exploitation of Haitian cane-cutters in Dominican Republic, 26; French debt owed by, 157n22; Nixon trip to, 11; revolt and independence, 9, 47, 48, 110; US occupation of, 157n22
Hall, Stuart, 22–23
Harman, Graham, 154n8
Harper, Frederick, 159n33
Harradine, David, 116
Harris, Wilson, 170n21
Harris-Hastrick, Eda F., 160n33, 160n35
Harrison, Sheri-Marie, 163, 172n8
Hartman, Saidiya, 11, 143, 148
Hawaii, 31, 39–40
hedonism, 10, 30, 71, 99, 128
hepatitis as disease from alcoholism, 96
Herd, Denise, 12–13, 160n33
heritage tourism, 37
Hernández, Rita Indiana, 23; *Sugar/Azúcar* project, 26
Hill-Norton, Lord, 42
Hills of Hebron, The (Wynter), 109–14; anticolonial ravings in, 111–12; Barton establishing separatist religious group, 103, 109, 110, 112; compared to Lamming's *Water with Berries*, 109; compared to Lovelace's *While Gods Are*

Falling, 109; compared to Marshall's *The Chosen Place, the Timeless People*, 125; compared to Rhys's *Wide Sargasso Sea*, 109; critical analysis of, 109; failure to establish political empathy marked by libations in, 103, 112; intoxication on rum causing misrecognition of oppression in, 111; Jamaica as setting of, 33; lost potential and lost hope in, 114; O'Malley as alcoholic Irish asylum director and therapist in, 103, 109–13; references to rum in O'Malley-Barton scenes, 103, 110–11, 113
Hispanics, 159n33. *See also* race and ethnicity
Hispaniola, sugar production in, 26
Hispanophone literature, 23, 151, 154n4
HIV/AIDS, 115–16, 172n14
Hogarth, William: *Gin Lane*, 44, 87
Holiday magazine 1973 guide to Caribbean, 17
Holocaust, 53
homoeroticism, 116, 167n20
homosexuality: English cultural proscription against, 121; in Marshall's "British Guiana," 120–22, 135; masculine ambition in context of drinking and, 32, 60, 76; queer failure and negative affect, 173n2; queer rum history in Cliff's *Free Enterprise*, 115–16; queer theory, development of, 172n14
Horn, Maja, 23, 26
Howard University, 151
Huggan, Graham, 55, 169n11
Human Genome Project, 158n31
Huracan (McCauley), 141–44; critical analysis of, 143–44; Jamaica as setting of, 141–44; rationale for alcoholism in, 141, 176n20; reader's knowledge of narrator's truth that is not known by narrator, 144; rejection of well-meaning whiteness in, 142–43; rum poetics in, applying postcolonial theory, 141; stereotypes in, 141–43; white privilege in, 141–42
Hurricane Maria (2017), 11

Ifill, Kenneth, 12, 160n35
immigrants: anti-immigrant sentiment, 157n27; Bajan community of Brooklyn, 120; Baucom on definition of "British" citizenship, 172n7; Caribbean women's views on drinking, 160n33; English experience of, in Lamming's *Water with Berries*, 107; Naipaul's depiction of immigration as welcome escape from Caribbean misery, 72–73, 74; O'Neill's *Netherland* and, 74–78; Portuguese immigrants in British Guiana, 15; from Puerto Rico to New York, 60; return to West Indies after sojourn in England, 44; Yoruba Club in Liverpool, 163n18
imperialism: code of behavior between metropolitan governments and subordinate entities, 11, 46–47; control of white women's drinking to retain, 79; European power struggles over Caribbean islands, 173n5; imperialist narrativization of history, 80; legacies shaping mundane interpersonal interactions, 136; "Make America Great Again!" agenda and, 150; nostalgia for imperial future, 46; obeah potion as product of, 86; in *Pirates of the Caribbean* (film), 146–47; in Rhys's *Wide Sargasso Sea*, 97; rum as engine of, 41–44, 83, 135–36; in Thompson's *The Rum Diary*, 63; of United States, 150, 177n8, 178n12. *See also* colonialism
Independent review of Unsworth's *Sacred Hunger*, 55
Indians, American. *See* Native Americans
Indians, Asian. *See* South Asians
individuality: consumers as separate from systems that govern consumer goods, 18, 161n42; of excessive drinking vs. its larger social effects, 14–15, 161n40; personalization of historical responsibility, 53; prioritizing consumer identity over ethical issues of labor, production, and distribution, 19

Jamaica: Anancy's role as "hoaxer" in folktales of, 170n21; capitalism in, 175n16; Caribbean federation and, 9; in Cliff's novels, 134–38; Jamaican rum and racism, 46; Lovelace's *While Gods Are Falling* on poverty and racism in, 114; novels set in, 31, 33, 36–38, 141–44; rum's role in economy of, 156n18; as stronghold of British rum-making during the "Punch Age," 162n4; temperance campaigns in, 13
James, C. L. R., 157n22, 167n20

Japal, Elizabeth, 171n2
Jiles, Paulette, 163n14; *Sitting in the Club Car Drinking Rum and Karma-Kola*, 49–51, 53
John Brown's raid, 115
Johnson, Erica L., 172nn12–13
Johnson, Magic, 172n14
Johnson, Michele A., 13
Josephs, Kelly Baker, 110, 172n8, 172n10

Kalliney, Peter, 164n19, 170n16
Kanhai, Rosanne, "Rum Sweet Rum," 94–97; crossing borders of class/caste and cosmopolitan standards, 94, 114; domestic violence linked to drinking rum in, 95–96; Naipaul's *Miguel Street* relationship to, 94; rum as liberating substance used in Indian cocktail to murder abusive husband in, 96–97; rum as link between past and present exploitation in, 95; separation of agricultural past from postwar future in, 95; Trinidad as setting of, 94–95; women as main earners in, 95
Kazanjian, David, 31, 119, 131, 172n1
Kazin, Alfred, 166n14
Keen, Suzanne, 53
Kelly, David, 73
Kincaid, Jamaica: *Lucy*, 55–56, 57
Knight, Franklin W., 156n21
Kutzinski, Vera, 23, 24–25, 36

Lamming, George, 33, 109; *The Emigrants*, 171n6; on stereotypes of Caribbean "manhood," 171n6. See also *Water with Berries*
Land of Love and Drowning (Yanique), 97–100; compared to Rhys's *Wide Sargasso Sea*, 97–98; Eeona's abuse in, 98–99, 170n21; history as magic and telling of a story in, 98, 100; Kanhai's "Rum Sweet Rum" relationship to, 170n19; political protest against white woman's usurpation of public property in, 99–100; Prohibition's effect on family business in, 97–98; rum and Coca-Cola metaphor in, 97–100; rum promoting community and uprisings against exploitation in, 100; sexual abuse as expression of patriarchy in, 98; US exploitation as continued male dominance in, 97–99, 114, 151; US Virgin Islands as setting of, 97; white women in colonialism and, 147; Wouk's *Don't Stop the Carnival* linked to, 97, 170n19
Langton, Marcia, 14
Lenson, David, 158n29
Lévi-Strauss, Claude, 166n14
libations: funeral libations in Cliff's *Abeng*, 132–33; as ignored subject of analysis in the text, 101–2, 118; political action and, 101–17; purpose of sharing of alcohol, 101–2, 118, 119, 121, 124–25, 129; reparative models in literary criticism and, 118–44; rum as opiate for the masses, 132. See also drinking rituals and toasts; political action; reparative reading
literary criticism: invisibility of drunken comportment in, 20–22; invisibility of rum in, 119; reparative models in, 118–44; rum as critical aporia in, 33. See also reparative reading; rum poetics
Lloyd, A. J., 157n28
Lord Invader's "Rum and Coca-Cola" calypso, 45–46, 59, 170n20
L'Ouverture, Toussaint, 110
Lovelace, Earl, 33, 109. See also *While Gods Are Falling*

MacAndrew, Craig, and Robert B. Edgerton: *Drunken Comportment*, 16–17, 105, 137, 161nn37–38, 162n2
Maharajh, Hari, and Parasram Rampersad, 160n34
Mahler, Anne Garland, 23, 154n4; "South-South Organizing," 26–27
Maingot, Anthony, 18–19, 153n2
Marcus, Anthony, 17, 158n29
Marcus, Grant, 158n29
Marcus, Jane, 52, 163n13
Mardorossian, Carine, 163n17, 168n1, 169n12; "Shutting Up the Subaltern," 86, 169n9
marijuana, 36, 135–36, 175n16
Maroons, 109
Marshall, Paule, 33; *Brown Girl, Brownstones*, 120; compared to Cliff, 118, 132, 140, 175n14; compared to McCauley, 141; rum's appearance in works by, 118, 120, 127, 129, 131, 174n8. See also "British Guiana"; *The Chosen*

Place, the Timeless People; Praisesong for the Widow
Martínez-Vergne, Teresita, 156n21
Marx, Karl, and Marxism, 19, 39
masculinity. *See* men
Maynard, Jessica, 170n16
McBain, Helen, 156n21
McCauley, Diana, 33; compared to Marshall and Cliff, 141. See also *Huracan*
McClintock, Anne, 154n6
McKenna, Brian: *Big Sugar* (documentary), 26, 150
McNeil, Elizabeth, 131
Mead, Walter Russell, 10, 46
Mehta, Gita: *Karma-Cola*, 51
men, 57–78; alcoholism as emasculating factor, 67; Black male sexuality, 106; colonial fantasy of, 71; drinking as homosocial bonding, 15, 32, 60, 101; English models of masculinity, 110, 121; finance as realm of white men, 84; male literary entitlement, 58; masculine identity and (post)colonial literary ambition, 57–78; masculinity and rum-shop culture, 15, 25, 43–44, 76, 128, 135, 160n35, 175n15; mediation of masculine privilege through colonial power, 60; postcolonial literary marketplace divesting masculinity, 52; social decline of white male rule in colonies, 47; tragic alcoholism of male artists, trope of, 57; transgender woman excluded by code of masculinity, 134–35; underemployment of, 59–60, 164n2; violence encoded in alcohol's relationship to male success and identification, 166n13; women as emasculating factor in Naipaul's *Miguel Street*, 59, 65. *See also* homosexuality
Mercury, Freddie, 172n14
Merry, Robert, 155n14
Mezei, Kathy, 169n10
Middle Passage, 107, 127, 174n9
Miguel Street (Naipaul), 32, 57–74; Bogart's alignment with American domination and masculinity, 61, 165n5; compared to Thompson's *The Rum Diary*, 58, 68, 72, 74; critical analysis of, 164n3; drunken comportment in, 61, 69; English racism experienced by West Indian immigrants, foreshadowing of, 72, 166n18; failed masculine role development, 61–62, 66, 120–21, 165n5; homosocial drinking among the men, 60, 62; infusion of American money in WWII in, 58, 59; Kanhai's "Rum Sweet Rum" relationship to, 94, 170n19; male privilege's intersection with racism, 72; marginalization of women characters in, 64–65, 94; men seeking work in other countries, 59, 60; narrator's replication of colonialist attitudes, 59; narrator's scholarship to study pharmacy in England, 72–73, 74; narrator's victory over drinking, 68; as origin story for genius from Caribbean to emerge as international figure, 58, 72–73; rules of alcoholic sociability, importance of adhering to, 61; rum as part of the past, something to be left behind, 57, 72; as semi-autobiographical work, 57, 74; stigma of alcoholism in, 66–72; "time-out" of men in, 74; Trinidad as setting of, 58–59, 74; underemployment of men in, 59; women as main earners in, 59, 165n9
Mintz, Sidney: *Sweetness and Power: The Place of Sugar in Modern History*, 22–23
Mischke, Dennis, 75
Mitchell, Tim, 140
modernity and modernism: bypassing West Indies, 173n5; failures of development in, 173n4; pitted against tradition, 42; postcolonial theory and, 30–31
Mohanty, Chandra Talpade, 93, 140
money: anthropomorphization of, 50; infusion of American money in Trinidad during WWII, 58, 59; as interest of working class, 87
Moore, Brian, 13
Moore, Christopher. See *Fluke*
morality: alcoholism as "disease of the will" and, 13–14, 16, 66; colonizers using alcohol to manipulate indigenous and/or colonized subjects, 14–15; judgment on people emerging from colonization, 11; judgment on sources of alcoholic dysfunction, 16; shame and moral stigma associated with alcoholism, 12, 14–15, 67
Morrison, Toni: *A Mercy*, 38–39, 49, 79
Morton, Timothy, 23–25, 27
Moutet, J. P., et al., 160n34

mulatta, 24–25, 170n21
Muscovado poetics, 25

Nadelhaft, James, 39
Naipaul, V. S., 33; Black British writing and, 33; compared to Thompson, 57–58; critique of other West Indian authors, 164n4; on leaving Trinidad for England, 74, 167n18; *The Middle Passage: The Caribbean Revisited*, 44, 56, 61, 164n4, 166n15. See also *Miguel Street*
Nair, Supriya, 10, 74, 108, 132, 178n13
Nardin, Jane, 168n2
Nash, June, 14–15
nationalism: Cuban, 23; rum and progressive national imaginary, 41–46; West Indies nationalism, 2
Native Americans: comportment of drunkenness and, 162n2; stereotype of drunk Indian, 39, 162n2
Navigation Acts (Britain), 42
"*negotium,*" 23, 25, 44
neocolonial power: in Marshall's *The Chosen Place, the Timeless People*, 123–24; neocolonial reification of colonial economic models and sugar/rum, 103–4, 124; nondrinking characters invested in, 120; Puerto Rico's neocolonial economic regime, 59; taboos restricting academic discussion of alcoholism facilitating alignment with, 21, 140
Netherland (O'Neill), 74–78, 114, 143; cricket as opportunity for male bonding, 75, 167n20; critical analysis of, 75, 151, 167n20; drinking as homosocial pleasure in, 77; globalization and migration networks in, 74–75; Ramkissoon's parable in, 75–77, 167n21; rum shop as male domain in, 175n15; white male privilege in, 76–77
New England, 31, 38
New Jewel Party (Grenada), 10
New York: African Americans in, 130; O'Neill's *Netherland* set in, 75; in *Praisesong*, 127; in *The Rum Diary*, 60, 62, 164n2
Ngũgĩ wa Thiong'o, 3; *Decolonizing the Mind*, 154n6
Nicholls, James: *The Politics of Alcohol*, 16–17
Nicholson, Mervyn, 20

Nixon, Richard, 11, 157n28
Noland, Carrie, 3–4, 154n9; *Agency and Embodiment*, 22, 161n43, 163n17
No Telephone to Heaven (Cliff), 132–41; *Abeng* foreshadowing, 133; broken rum bottle as weapon of violence in, 118, 138, 141; critical analysis of, 138–40, 144; critique of bar culture in, 135; excessive rum drinking as generational effects of enslavement in, 132; film industry portrayal in, 136–37, 175n17; Freudian psychoanalytic patterns in, 138–39; Jamaica as setting of, 134–38; Jamaican government killing its own citizens in, 137, 175n17; marijuana sales used to finance rebel group in, 136, 175n16; rum shop as male domain in, 175n15; rum's signifying passive consumption in scholarly reading, 137–38; transgender woman excluded by code of masculinity in, 134–35; violence associated with rum in, 118–19

obeah, 23–24, 82–83, 86, 98, 133, 169n12
obesity: negative views of sugar and, 27; rates of African Americans, 26
Olmstead, Jane, 131
Ondaatje, Michael: *The English Patient*, 55
O'Neill, Joseph. See *Netherland* (O'Neill)
oppression: of Carib woman, 80; in everyday life, 19; intoxication on rum causing misrecognition of, 111; Johnny Depp's characterization of Jack Sparrow and, 149; legacy of accumulated history of, 39; sexual oppression as inseparable from racial oppression, 116, 167n1. *See also* colonialism; enslavement and enslaved people; gender; race and ethnicity; whiteness and white privilege
Osborn, Matthew: *Rum Maniacs*, 43
"other," the, 32; alterity of rum, 5; female "others" as naturalized drinkers, 79; fiction of race when "white" can easily be "other," 144; obeah potion and, 87; postcolonial knowledge recognizing, 142; recognition of, 17, 21, 147
Owens, Joyce Pettis, 131

Pacific Island cultures, 39
Paravisini-Gebert, Lizabeth, 163n10, 163n12
Parry, Benita, 168n1

Parsad, Nasmat Shiw, 170n18
paternalism, 25, 88, 139
patriarchy: assumptions of novels of 1950s, 72; in Cliff's novels, 134; diversion of patrimonial inheritance to support female agency, 96; drinking as response to, 89, 161n42; Jamaican gender roles and, 134; in *Pirates of the Caribbean* (film), 147, 177n5; sexual abuse as expression of, 98; white patriarchal lineage, importance of, 47, 162n10; women's drinking as challenge to, 79, 81–82
Perham, Margery, 9
Perkin, Joan, 167n1
Petersen, Anne, 146, 148
Picong (magazine) articles on rum and Trinidadian culture, 43–44
pirate culture, 40–41, 145, 153n2; as American national myths, 177n10; reputation of pirates as heavy drinkers, 146–47, 177n6; Robin Hood–like pirate operation freeing Africans from slave ships, 115; women pirates, 116–17
Pirates of the Caribbean film series, 33, 145–50, 177nn4–5; *At World's End*, 145, 149, 177n6; *The Curse of the Black Pearl*, 33, 40, 146–48, 177n7; *Dead Man's Chest*, 177n6; *Dead Men Tell No Tales*, 177n4; *On Stranger Tides*, 177n4; rum sales' rise associated with film releases, 177n9
Plant, Martin, and Moira Plant, 160n33
Plant, Moira, 159–60n33
plantations: alcohol use to mark celebrations, transactions and pledges of plantocracy, 102; American-owned plantations, exploitation of Haitian cane-cutters on, 26; multinational corporate structure as recreation of plantation slavery, 62. *See also* enslavement and enslaved people
Plasa, Carl, 23, 24–25, 27
Pleasant, Mary Ellen, 115
political action, 32–33, 101–17; in Allfrey's *The Orchid House*, 47–48; as drunken chaos, 32, 101, 102, 171n2; Fanon's ideas of, 104–5; in Jiles's *Sitting in the Club Car Drinking Rum and Karma-Kola*, 49–50; in Marshall's "British Guiana," 121–22; reification of colonial hegemony and, 103–5, 118; research on alcohol use in and its material role in, 171n2; rum shops as political networking sites, 175n15. See also *Free Enterprise*; *Hills of Hebron, The*; *While Gods Are Falling*
pornography, 36, 63, 70, 97, 98
Portuguese immigrants in British Guiana, 15
postcolonial future. *See* future, the
postcolonialism, 2, 4, 30; Bazin's discussion of alcoholism in, 21; colonialist rhetoric for, 44; exoticism and eroticism of, 55; in *Sitting in the Club Car Drinking Rum and Karma-Kola*, 51–52; McCauley's insights from postcolonial theory, 141; obsolescence of term, 3; relationship between postcolonial and psychoanalytic discourses, need to analyze, 139; results of postcolonial "hangover," 33–34; white male fantasies, 74–78
Potocki, Beata, 172n12
Powell, Enoch: "Rivers of Blood," 108
Praisesong for the Widow (Marshall), 126–32; Avey consuming rum instead of communing through it, 120, 127; Avey's experience at rum shop in, 127–28, 131, 175n13, 175n15; Carriacou as setting of, 126–32, 174n9; ceremonial music and use of drums in, 129–31; Coates and, 151; color imagery in, 127, 174n10; critical analysis of, 120, 131–32, 144, 175n13; discursive regularity in, 131; fantasies in, 127, 130; metaphors of digestion and indigestion in, 127, 132, 174n10; multicultural influences in, 132; postcolonial existence premised on enslavement and enslaved people, 129–30; precolonial African past in, 119, 131, 132, 140; recycled present, Avey's desire to remain separate from, 129–30; renewed agency of Avey, 130–32; rum and coconut water served in, 128; transformative ritual with rum in, 118–19, 122, 129, 174n8
Pringle, Thomas, 155n14
Prohibition, 13–14, 97–98, 153n2, 162n5
Puerto Rico, 7, 72, 74; Hurricane Maria devastation (2017), 11; neocolonialism in, 59; New Deal and, 10; rum taxes paid to, 149; Thompson's *The Rum Diary* set in, 58–60, 69, 73, 166n14, 166n17; US acquisition of, 178n12
Pyne, Hnin Hnin et al., 160n34

race and ethnicity: alcohol use associated with racism and "problem deflation," 21; alignment of gender-based and race-based discrimination in *Pirates of the Caribbean* film, 147, 177n5; asymmetrical relationship between white doctor and Black patient, 111; binary of whiteness/race, 23; Black British discrimination, 106–7; Black women's drinking, 160n33; civil rights movement, 99–100; cross-caste relationality in Marshall's "British Guiana," 121; drinking of Black characters in Allfrey's *The Orchid House*, 48; feminist capitalization upon suffering of racialized others to advance its cause, 50; fiction of race when "white" can easily be "other," 144; Jamaican national identity and race, 141; research on alcohol consumption in, 15, 159n33; rum drinking by Blacks vs. whites in Allfrey's *The Orchid House*, 46–47; rum types and, 46; science fiction, viewing racism as relic of the past, 164n20; speculative fiction and race, 164n20; taboos and, 21, 66, 70. *See also* Creoles; mulatta; stereotypes

Raiskin, Judith: *Snow on the Cane Fields*, 83

Ramamurthy, Priti, 20

Rastafarianism, 39, 136, 175n16

Ratcliffe, Krista, 21, 140

Read/Reade, Mary, as female pirate, 117

Reagan, Ronald, 10, 128

realism, 2, 117, 131, 140, 173n4

reclamation of past: in Marshall's "British Guiana," 120–21; in Marshall's *Brown Girl, Brownstones*, 120; in Marshall's *Praisesong*, 129. *See also* postcolonialism

Rediker, Marcus, 35, 40

reparations for slavery, 5, 143

reparative reading, 6, 32, 49, 56, 60, 80, 93, 118–19, 152

resistance: alcohol (rum) consumption and, 20, 105, 107, 125; anticolonial, 5, 9, 23, 24, 101–2, 111, 126, 135, 139; cultural, 178n13; to globalization, 50–51; to local government, 102–3; to sexual and economic oppression rooted in rum and Coca-Cola, 98; to slavery, 23–24; to stories of the "alien," 51. *See also* political action

Revere, Paul, 42

Revolutionary War, US, 42

Reynolds, David S., and Debra J. Rosenthal: *The Serpent in the Cup: Temperance in American Literature*, 12

Rhode Island, 6–7

Rhys, Jean, 1; as controversial figure in West Indian "national" literature, 170n16; critical discussion of drinking prewar work of, 168n2; "Mixing Cocktails," 1; "Temps Perdi," 80; *Voyage in the Dark*, 80, 107, 168n2. *See also Wide Sargasso Sea*

Ridlon, Florence V., 159n33

Robbins, Bruce, 18, 114, 143

Robinson, James E., 171nn4–5

Rogoziński, Jan, 9

Room, Robin, 159n33, 161n37

Roosevelt, Franklin, 10

Roosevelt, Teddy, 124, 173n5

Rorabaugh, W. J.: *The Alcoholic Republic: An American Tradition*, 42–43, 155n12

Rose, Charlie, 73

Rosenthal, Debra J., and David S. Reynolds: *The Serpent in the Cup: Temperance in American Literature*, 12

Ross, Jacob: "Rum an Coke," 150

Roth, Marty, 20, 21–22

Rotskoff, Lori, 158n32

Royal Navy: daily rum ration of, 8, 41–42, 155n15; in *Free Enterprise*, 115; in *Pirates of the Caribbean* film series, 146, 147; US Navy cooperation with, 177n8

"Rum and Coca-Cola": calypso, 59; song, 45, 98, 170n20

rum and Coca-Cola metaphor, 41, 45–46, 51, 97–100, 150–51, 171n23

Rum Diary, The (Thompson), 32, 57–74; carnival on St. Thomas as time-out, 64, 70; compared to Marshall's *The Chosen Place, the Timeless People*, 126; compared to Naipaul's *Miguel Street*, 58, 68, 72, 74; compared to Rhys's *Wide Sargasso Sea*, 66; compared to Wouk's *Don't Stop the Carnival*, 97; critical analysis of, 73; failed masculine role development, 66, 72; fetishized sexuality of female character (Chenault), 65–66, 69–70, 165n12; gin as rum's undoing

Index 211

and, 169n14; Kemp's return to US comforts, 60, 69; marginalization of women characters in, 65, 165n7; multinational corporate structure as recreation of plantation slavery, 62; as origin story for genius from Caribbean to emerge as international figure, 58, 72–73; published out of order among Thompson's novels, 58, 73; Puerto Rico as setting of, 58–60, 69, 73, 166n14; racism and journalistic principle of Kemp in, 59–60; reviews of, 73; rum as part of the past, something to be left behind in, 57, 72–73; rum drinking as coping response for white men in, 62; as semi-autobiographical work, 57, 67; stigma of alcoholism in, 66–72; taboos of white women and Black people intermixing, 66, 70; theft of rum in, 63–64; underemployment of men in, 59–60, 164n2; vocabularies of possession and sharing to describe male drunken comportment in, 62–64; white male expatriates as underprivileged group in, 59, 62–63, 69; white male privilege in, 63, 65, 70, 72
rum poetics, 4–5; Anglo-Americans as uncritical consumers of, 92, 113, 146; "apparent quotidiana" of literary critical work and, 172n1; binaries involved in, 23; commodification of rum in Anglo-Atlantic culture, 1, 17–20; cross-cultural poetics, 21, 113; as different mode of reading identity, 138; disruption introduced by, 49, 51; dual meaning of rum (noun "rum" vs. adjective "rum"), 4–6, 19–20, 49; economical readings, 28–30, 31, 33, 131, 139; libations marking persistent facts from the past that require reckoning, 119; literary criticism expanded by, 140; McCauley's use of, 141; opportunities for reparation and relationality, 27, 32, 56, 80; overreading of, 30–31; priorities of scholars of sugar and, 27; in reading of Marshall's *Praisesong*, 131–32; speculative nature of, 31
rum-running and rum trade: of America after its independence, 43; broad use of term "rum," 153n2; in *Pirates of the Caribbean* film series, 146; profitability in relation to slaveholding, 38; scope of rum trade, 38–39

rum-shop culture. See men; *Praisesong for the Widow*
Rushdie, Salman: *Midnight's Children*, 55

Said, Edward, 109
Sandiford, Keith, 23, 25, 27, 44, 131; *The Cultural Politics of Sugar*, 23–24; *Theorizing a Colonial Caribbean-Atlantic Imaginary: Sugar and Obeah*, 24
Sandmaier, Marian, 160n33
Savory, Elaine, 143–44
Schivelbusch, Wolfgang, 169n13
science fiction, 52, 54, 164n20
Scott, David, 27, 38, 157n22
Seaman, Donna, 73
Sedgwick, Eve Kosofsky, 5, 60, 63, 142, 152
self-medication with alcohol/rum, 47–48, 57
Sethuraman, Ramchandran: "Evidence-Cum-Witness," 138–40
sexism, 21, 25, 49, 58
sexual abuse. See violence
sexuality: Black male sexuality, 106; castration anxiety, 138–39; Creoles, drinking and sexual behavior of, 15, 81, 168n2, 169n7; in Marshall's *The Chosen Place, the Timeless People*, 123; resistance to sexual oppression rooted in rum and Coca-Cola, 98; sexual norms, 121; stereotypes of Black women's sexual promiscuity, 65, 120–22; in Thompson's *The Rum Diary*, 65–66, 69–70, 165n12. See also homosexuality
Shakespeare, William: *The Tempest*, 37, 106, 171nn4–5
shame: associated with alcoholism and drinking, 1, 15, 20, 27, 67; associated with rum, 9, 49; of colonization, 104
Sheller, Mimi, 17–18, 25, 58
Shepherd, Verene A., 156n18
significance/insignificance of rum, 35–56; Allfrey's *The Orchid House*, 46–49; disinhibition and eroticized violence, 2, 35–41; postcolonial access to literary world, 49–56
Slaughter, Joseph R., 2
slavery and slaves. See enslavement and enslaved people
Smith, Carissa Turner, 175n13

Smith, Frederick: *Caribbean Rum*, 6, 8, 12, 87, 156n18, 160n35, 161n39, 168n5, 172n11
Smith, Robert Freeman, 10, 177n8; *The Caribbean World and the United States: Mixing Rum and Coca-Cola*, 46
Social Issues Research Centre, 14
social justice, 49–50, 113, 148
social media: drinking and gender, 160n33; memes, 149–50
South Asians: planters using rum to manipulate Indian workers, 8; rum produced by enslaved workers from, 43
Southey, Robert, 24, 155n14
spider. *See* Anancy
Spivak, Gayatri, 50, 80, 93, 167n1, 177n5
Stahl, Kathleen M.: *The Metropolitan Organization of British Colonial Trade*, 8
Steinhoff, Heiki, 148–49, 177n10
Stephens, Michelle, 36
stereotypes: of Black women's drinking, 160n33; of Black women's sexual promiscuity, 65, 120–22; of drunken people of color in Allfrey's *The Orchid House*, 48; of gender, race, class, and ethnicity in terms of drinking, 15, 158–59nn32–33; in McCauley's *Huracan*, 141–43; of peasantry in Lovelace's *While Gods Are Falling*, 105; racist stereotype and exploitation of Black labor, 87; racist stereotype of drunken Black "beast," 12, 171n2; racist stereotype of eroticism, 2, 65; of West Indian drinking patterns, 6, 153n2; of white women's relationship with Black men, 70; of working-class alcohol use, 30
Stevenson, Robert Louis: "Dead Men's Chest," 40; *Treasure Island*, 40, 153n2
stigma of alcoholism, 1, 12, 15, 27; of female drinking, 21, 174n11; literary reluctance to discuss, 20; in Naipaul's *Miguel Street*, 66–72; in public policy and academic discussions, 14–15; in Thompson's *The Rum Diary*, 66–72
Stoute, Janet, 12, 160n35
Stuelke, Patricia, 128, 131–32
sugar: abolitionist boycott of, 7–8, 88, 150; British government ending West Indian monopoly of, 156n18; British government subsidizing West Indian imports of, 8, 156n19; gendering of, 25; literary criticism's analysis of, 119; literature on, 2, 5, 22–27, 33; as lucrative crop, 8, 37, 156n18; in Marshall's *The Chosen Place, the Timeless People*, 123–24; Middle Eastern origins of sugarcane, 153n2; modernized conditions of production, 25–26; mulatta and, 24–25; rum in context of, 4, 24, 27, 29, 124–25, 138, 155n11, 166n16; sugarcane imagery linked to Black women's sexual availability, 120–22
sugarcane novel (*novela de la caña*), 23, 26, 154n4
sugarcane poetics, 25, 27, 44, 122
suicide, 53, 163n18

taboos. *See* race and ethnicity
Taussig, Charles William: *Rum, Romance, and Revolution*, 41–44
taverns and bars as sites of working-class political organizing, 171n2
temperance movement: abolition movement in relation to, 12–13, 43; in Allfrey's *The Orchid House*, 48; in Caribbean, 13; other issues attached to, 157n27; rhetoric of, 39, 90, 146, 157n26; in Warner's *The Flint Anchor*, 81, 89–90; war on drugs reflecting, 167n19
Thatcherism, 49, 52, 163n18
Thiong'o, Ngũgĩ wa. *See* Ngũgĩ wa Thiong'o
Thomas, Sue: *The Worlding of Jean Rhys*, 86
Thompson, Hunter S., 57; comparison with Naipaul, 57–58; drug-fueled narratives of, 72–73; *Fear and Loathing in Las Vegas*, 73; *Hell's Angels*, 73; New Journalism associated with, 73. *See also Rum Diary, The*
Tiffin, Helen, 107
"time-out": associated with drinking, 16–17, 49, 151; Caribbean people and lands as out of time and, 35; carnival time as, 64, 70, 124–26; history as time-out, 18; in Lovelace's *While Gods Are Falling*, 105; in Marshall's *The Chosen Place, the Timeless People*, 123; Native Americans, when time-out applicable to, 162n2; pirates and, 40, 146–48; spousal abuse and, 39; in Thompson's *The Rum*

Diary and Naipaul's *Miguel Street*, 64; in Underhill's *Jamaica White*, 36, 38; in Wouk's *Don't Stop the Carnival*, 97; in Yanique's *Land of Love and Drowning*, 97
tourism, 28, 28–29, 37, 46, 62, 119, 128, 135, 141, 146
trade: of colonial times, 2, 148; disparity among Caribbean islands, 156n21; free trade and rum subsidies, 149; microeconomics tracking macroeconomic system in, 134; of molasses, 6; rum subsidies, 8, 149, 156n19; sugar trade and consumption, 123–24. *See also* enslavement and enslaved people; globalization; rum-running and rum trade
Trinidad: AA organization in, 158n28; alcoholism as social problem for, 12, 160n34; Caribbean federation and, 9; infusion of American money in World War II, 58, 59; Kanhai's "Rum Sweet Rum" and, 94–95; Lovelace's *While Gods Are Falling* on poverty and racism in, 114; Naipaul's *Miguel Street* and, 58–59, 74; Naipaul's *The Middle Passage* and, 164n4; as petroleum exporter, 156n21; postcolonial politics and consumer behavior in response to rum conditions in, 115; rum shops as masculine domains in, 43–44, 160n35
Trump, Donald, 150
Turley, Hans: *Rum, Sodomy, and the Lash*, 35, 40
Twiss, Frank, 42

Underhill, Hal: *Jamaica White*, 36, 63, 70
United States: Carriacou's relationship with, 130; colonists introducing alcohol to Native Americans, 162n2; development projects of US-based organizations in Caribbean, 122–23, 173n4; as dominant power in Caribbean, 10–11, 13, 41, 46; executive privilege of Americans, 136; gender and drinking norms in, 32; imperialism of, 150, 177n8, 178n12; need to confront ethical questions in Caribbean views, 140; right to waste by Americans vs. by non-Americans, 157n25; rum and Coca-Cola metaphor for relations between Caribbean Islands and US, 41, 45–46; rum in nation-building narrative, 41, 42–43; rum subsidies to Puerto Rico and USVI, 149
Unsworth, Barry: *Sacred Hunger*, 55, 57; semi-autobiographical nature of *Sugar and Rum*, 55; *Sugar and Rum*, 49, 51–55, 135, 164n20
US Virgin Islands: civil rights movement and, 170n22; rum taxes paid to, 149; study of alcohol consumption in, 160n34; Yanique's *Land of Love and Drowning* set in, 97–100

Vaillant, George, 159n33
verisimilitude. *See* realism
violence: in alcohol's relationship to male success and identification, 166n13; broken rum bottle as weapon of, 118, 138, 141; domestic, 39, 95–96, 157n27, 170n18; excessive drinking leading to, 68, 132, 134, 138; Jamaican government killing its own citizens, 137, 175n17; murderous present linked with violence against indigenous people in colonial period, 80, 115; pirates and, 40; prevalence in reporting and writing on Caribbean, 10, 17; sexual, 25, 35–36, 38–39, 63, 98–99, 103, 106, 109, 118, 138, 170n21, 173n3, 174n10

Wagner, Michael, 15
Walcott, Derek: *Omeros*, 101, 175n15
Waligora-Davis, Nicole, 45, 162n7
Wall, Cheryl, 130
Walters, Wendy, 138
Warf, Barney, 175n16
Warner, Marina: *Indigo; or, Mapping the Waters*, 37–38
Warner, Nicholas O., 162n5
Warner, Sylvia Townsend, 168n6. See also *Flint Anchor, The*
war on drugs, 136, 167n19
waste: in Cliff's *Abeng*, 134; expelling rum as urine construed as anticolonial antilibation form of, 139, 176n19; of masculine world of adventure related to white women/imperialism, 147; right to waste by Americans vs. by non-Americans, 157n25; rum as waste of sugarcane processing, 4, 134; West Indian colonies as wasted places, 173n5
Waterson, Jan, 160n33

Water with Berries (Lamming), 102–3, 106–9; compared to Wynter's *The Hills of Hebron*, 109; critical analysis of, 107; lost potential and lost hope in, 114; revolution planned in fictional homeland of San Cristobel in, 102; sexual violence spurred by drinking rum in, 103, 106; Shakespeare's *The Tempest* and, 106, 171nn4–5; slavery invoked by language in, 112; souvenir-sized bottle of rum in, 106, 108

Watts, Thomas, 159n33

Waywell, Nicholas, 73, 166nn16–17

Wedge, George, 168n2

West, Joel, 138–39

Westall, Claire, 75–76, 164n3, 167n21

West India Committee, 8–9

West Indies: British control of economy in, 8–9; British proposal of federated government, 9; as dysfunctional states, 13; literature modeled on English Victorian tradition, 164n3; monopoly of sugar market, end of, 156n18; moral responsibility of white males to enlighten West Indians, 90; nationalism of, 2; use of term, 153n4; US investment in, 10; US West Indies squadron cooperating with British Navy in, 177n8; wasted spaces, colonial view of islands as, 173n5; white female subject protesting at expense of Black West Indian women in novels, 79. *See also* Caribbean; colonialism; *specific islands*

While Gods Are Falling (Lovelace), 102–6; colonialism forming unity among Caribs, Africans, and Indians in, 104; compared to Wynter's *The Hills of Hebron*, 109; critique of neocolonial reification of colonial economic models and meanings of rum, 103–4; disengagement of peasantry from politics in, 102–3; Fanon's ideas of political action in, 104–5; hope for future of grassroots political community in, 114–15; perpetual time-out in cycle of work and hard drinking in, 105; politicization of peasantry in, 105; racism of colonialism recurring in political party's cronyism in, 103–4; rum as metaphor for intoxicating effects of political hierarchies in, 103, 113

whiskey vs. rum and classism, 122–23

White, Ryan, 172n14

whiteness and white privilege: binary of whiteness/race, 23; blindness of, 5, 21, 51, 60, 83, 167n1; British whites as passive observers of colonial conditions, 113; Christianity designed to maintain white dominance, 110; drinking "white" rum signifying racial privilege, 111; in North/South binary, 21; in postcolonial literary marketplace, 52–53; postcolonial white male fantasies, 74–78; publishability of a text determined by white readers, 4; racist expectations of white audience, 4, 108; rejection of well-meaning whiteness, 142–43; research on alcohol abuse focused on white men, 159n33; sexual abuse of enslaved women and, 36; white female privilege in Marshall's *The Chosen Place, the Timeless People*, 126; white female privilege in McCauley's *Huracan*, 141–42, 144; white female privilege in Rhys's *Wide Sargasso Sea*, 81, 83; white female privilege in Thompson's *The Rum Diary*, 165n7; white female privilege in Warner's *The Flint Anchor*, 81; white-feminist-as-usurper narrative in *Pirates of the Caribbean* (film), 147–48, 177n5; white male privilege in O'Neill's *Netherland*, 76–77; white male privilege in Rhys's *Wide Sargasso Sea*, 82; white male privilege in Thompson's *The Rum Diary*, 63, 65, 70, 72; white women's drinking as degrading, 79

Wide Sargasso Sea (Rhys), 32, 79–88, 164n1; colonial roles of characters in, 168n7; compared to Allfrey's *The Orchid House*, 46; compared to Marshall's "British Guiana," 121; compared to Marshall's *The Chosen Place, the Timeless People*, 125; compared to Thompson's *The Rum Diary*, 66; compared to Warner's *The Flint Anchor*, 92; compared to Wynter's *The Hills of Hebron*, 109; compared to Yanique's *Land of Love and Drowning*, 97–98; Creole drinking and sexual behavior in, 81, 169n7; critical analysis of, 167n1; decolonization in, 79, 93; gender and racial oppression under British imperialism, 79, 80, 85, 167n1; gin as rum's

undoing in, 88; gin's association with degradation of working class in, 87, 169n13; history and holding onto time in, 85, 169n10; male economic dominance over women in, 81–84, 86–87; "natural" male behavior, assumptions about, 121; obeah love potion, use of, 82–83, 86, 98, 169n12; racial politics in terms of postcolonial issues in, 168n1; relationship between geography and history in Eurocentric world in, 80, 170n16; relationship to Brontë's *Jane Eyre,* 79, 81–83, 87, 168nn4–5, 169n11, 177n5; rum as energizer to white male privilege in, 82; rum's danger to Antoinette in, 81–88
Wilder, Gary, 2
Williams, Eric, 1, 42; *Capitalism and Slavery,* 1, 2, 38–39, 154n11
Williams, Ian, 7; *Rum: A Social and Sociable History of the Real Spirit of 1776,* 42
Wilson, Peter J., 160n35
Wilson, Thomas, 20
Wittig-Wells, Deborah, 160n34
women, 79–100; agency constraints on, 36, 64–65, 71, 94, 96; Black enslaved women as doubly oppressed, 139; Black women's drinking, 160n33; Black women's history of institutionalized sexual assault, 174n10; Black women with white values, 105; as consumables, 25; coverture, doctrine of, 167n1; drinking strictures on, 15, 64, 79, 123, 158n32, 174n11; empowerment in relation to decolonization, 36; English common law on wives' submission to their husbands, 167n1; feminism, 49–52, 163n13, 167n1; as main earners, 59, 95, 165n9, 170n18; Married Women's Property Act (1882), 168n1; as "other" by race as naturalized drinkers, 79; research into women's drinking, 15, 159n33; in rum shops, 175n15; sexual violence and enslavement, 25; simultaneously victimized and complicit, 113; sugarcane imagery linked to Black women's sexual availability, 120–22; taboos and, 21, 66, 70; white womanhood associated with Elizabeth Swann in *Pirates of the Caribbean* film series, 146, 177n5; women writers' excessive drinking, 21. *See also* gender; patriarchy; sexism; violence: domestic; violence: sexual; whiteness and white privilege: white female privilege
Wondrich, David, 162n4
Woolf, Virginia, 163n13; *Mrs. Dalloway,* 163n11
World Bank study on alcohol use, 12, 159n32
World War I, 46–47, 162n9
World War II, 58
Wouk, Herman: *Don't Stop the Carnival,* 97, 170n19
Wright, Roosevelt, 159n33
writer's block, 51–52
Wynter, Sylvia, 33, 109, 118. *See also Hills of Hebron, The*

Yanique, Tiphanie. See *Land of Love and Drowning*
Yoruba Club, 163n18

Zeiger, Susan, 158n30
zombies, 18, 96, 108, 165n10

RECENT BOOKS IN THE SERIES
New World Studies

Imperial Educación: Race and Republican Motherhood in the Nineteenth-Century Americas
Thomas Genova

Fellow Travelers: How Road Stories Shaped the Idea of the Americas
John Ochoa

The Quebec Connection: A Poetics of Solidarity in Global Francophone Literatures
Julie-Françoise Tolliver

Comrade Sister: Caribbean Feminist Revisions of the Grenada Revolution
Laurie R. Lambert

Cultural Entanglements: Langston Hughes and the Rise of African and Caribbean Literature
Shane Graham

Water Graves: The Art of the Unritual in the Greater Caribbean
Valérie Loichot

The Sacred Act of Reading: Spirituality, Performance, and Power in Afro-Diasporic Literature
Anne Margaret Castro

Caribbean Jewish Crossings: Literary History and Creative Practice
Sarah Phillips Casteel and Heidi Kaufman, editors

Mapping Hispaniola: Third Space in Dominican and Haitian Literature
Megan Jeanette Myers

Mourning El Dorado: Literature and Extractivism in the Contemporary American Tropics
Charlotte Rogers

Edwidge Danticat: The Haitian Diasporic Imaginary
Nadège T. Clitandre

Idle Talk, Deadly Talk: The Uses of Gossip in Caribbean Literature
Ana Rodríguez Navas

Crossing the Line: Early Creole Novels and Anglophone Caribbean Culture in the Age of Emancipation
Candace Ward

Staging Creolization: Women's Theater and Performance from the French Caribbean
Emily Sahakian

American Imperialism's Undead: The Occupation of Haiti and the Rise of Caribbean Anticolonialism
Raphael Dalleo

A Cultural History of Underdevelopment: Latin America in the U.S. Imagination
John Patrick Leary

The Spectre of Races: Latin American Anthropology and Literature between the Wars
Anke Birkenmaier

Performance and Personhood in Caribbean Literature: From Alexis to the Digital Age
Jeannine Murray-Román

Tropical Apocalypse: Haiti and the Caribbean End Times
Martin Munro

Market Aesthetics: The Purchase of the Past in Caribbean Diasporic Fiction
Elena Machado Sáez

Eric Williams and the Anticolonial Tradition: The Making of a Diasporan Intellectual
Maurice St. Pierre

The Pan American Imagination: Contested Visions of the Hemisphere in Twentieth-Century Literature
Stephen M. Park

Journeys of the Slave Narrative in the Early Americas
Nicole N. Aljoe and Ian Finseth, editors

Locating the Destitute: Space and Identity in Caribbean Fiction
Stanka Radović

Bodies and Bones: Feminist Rehearsal and Imagining Caribbean Belonging
Tanya L. Shields

Sounding the Break: African American and Caribbean Routes of World Literature
Jason Frydman

The Haitian Revolution in the Literary Imagination: Radical Horizons, Conservative Constraints
Philip Kaisary